"Is your life filled but unfulfilled? Then let *The Payoff Principle* show you how to uncover—and practice—what truly matters to you."

—Richard Leider, best-selling author of *The Power of Purpose,*
Repacking Your Bags, and *Life Reimagined*

"Everyone wants success, but few achieve it because they lack one or more of the three secrets Dr. Zimmerman reveals in this amazing book. It is a step-by-step guide to finally defining what you want and why, how to get it, and ultimately enjoying the reward. Don't just read it—study it and take action now!"

—Art Sobczak, author of *Smart Calling: Eliminate*
the Fear, Failure, and Rejection from Cold Calling

"Insightful and relevant! Dr. Zimmerman's work is consistently practical and enlightening, and *The Payoff Principle* is no exception. Here he offers a fresh, clear framework to transform your life!"

—David Horsager, best-selling author of *The Trust Edge*

"Life is tough. Work is challenging. Relationships are demanding. And it takes an extraordinary amount of clarity, energy, and skill to make it all come together in a positive and productive way. And that's exactly what *The Payoff Principle* does, in a most captivating and compelling fashion."

—Lisa Ford, coauthor of *Exceptional Customer Service:*
Exceed Customer Expectations to Build Loyalty and Boost Profits

"Read *The Payoff Principle* and then read it again. Keep it within arm's reach and refer to it often. It will become a lighthouse of wisdom, insights, strategies, and ideas that will help you do more and get more of what you have been dreaming about. It is practical and proven to work, and it contains timeless treasures for your heart, mind, and soul."

—Mark LeBlanc, author of *Growing Your Business*

"As a business leader, I know that everyone has the potential to achieve more than he or she ever thought possible—or to use Alan's words, to be a producer who brings about amazing results. In *The Payoff Principle*, you'll learn exactly how to make that happen in your life and work."

—Allan Forbis, director of the State of Missouri Center for Management and Professional Development

"Dr. Alan Zimmerman consistently shows his clients that they hold the power to change their lives, strengthen important relationships, build careers, and achieve more than they ever thought possible. In *The Payoff Principle*, he'll give you the step-by-step tools you need to get the results you want."

—Sandra C. Williams, director of Dealer Training and Development at S.P. Richards Company

"The Payoff Principle really hits home. While reading, your mind will immediately conjure up images and help you think of ways you can do things differently for the first time! Applying the three secrets will send you on the path to something wonderful!"

—Steven R. Desautel, vice president of sales and marketing at Dental Health Products, Inc.

"There's no need to go through life hoping things will change for the better. When Dr. Alan Zimmerman wrote *The Payoff Principle*, he gave everyone who wants to achieve their full potential a clear, tried-and-true pathway to greater fulfillment and more happiness in both life and work. Read this book and take charge of your future."

—Bill Lee, author of *30 Ways Managers Shoot Themselves in the Foot*

"If you're willing to take responsibility for your life, if you're ready to quit blaming others for your troubles, if you want to experience greater success than ever before, read *The Payoff Principle*. I know that Dr. Zimmerman's content and approach has changed the lives of hundreds of thousands of people, and will change yours as well."

—Marjorie Brody, CEO of Brody Professional Development and author of *Speaking Your Way to the Top*

"In the mad rush to succeed in life, few people bother to look inside themselves for the three secrets discovered by Dr. Zimmerman, but they can make all the difference."

—Al Ries, coauthor of *War in the Boardroom*

"I've valued Alan's friendship and his counsel for over twenty-five years. He, his research, and his guidance are solid. When you align your Purpose and Passion with a Process that works, everything in your life is so much better. And that's exactly what *The Payoff Principle* will do for you."

—Jeff Thull, CEO of Prime Resource Group and
author of *Mastering the Complex Sale*

"With *The Payoff Principle*, you have everything you need to be your best and make your dreams come true. Dr. Zimmerman lays out, in methodical and yet compelling fashion, the secrets you need to flourish. They might seem deceptively simple, but in combination with his action plan, they are incredibly effective."

—Jeff Davidson, author of *Breathing Space* and *Dial It Down, Live It Up*

"The world is filled with a lot of good books these days, and no one has time to read them all. But I would place *The Payoff Principle* in the category of great books. Its message is so powerful that you cannot afford to skip it. Dr. Zimmerman has pulled it all together in this book and gives us the true compass for success."

—Brian J. Schmall, national account director at Bemis North America

"There is a reason that Dr. Alan Zimmerman has been so successful as an author, consultant, and professional speaker: he helps his clients unleash the extraordinary in themselves, their people, and their organizations. In *The Payoff Principle*, he'll do the same for you."

—Robert Parsons, executive coach and
organizational development consultant

THE

Payoff
Principle

Discover the 3 Secrets for
Getting What You Want
Out of Life and Work

THE
Payoff
Principle

DR. ALAN R. ZIMMERMAN

GREENLEAF
BOOK GROUP PRESS

Published by Greenleaf Book Group Press
Austin, Texas
www.gbgpress.com

Distributed by Greenleaf Book Group

For ordering information or special discounts for bulk purchases, please contact Greenleaf Book Group at PO Box 91869, Austin, TX 78709, 512.891.6100.

Design and composition by Greenleaf Book Group
Cover design by Greenleaf Book Group

Cataloging-in-Publication data
Zimmerman, Alan R.
   The payoff principle : discover the 3 secrets for getting what you want out of life and work / Dr. Alan R. Zimmerman.—First edition.
     pages : illustrations ; cm
   Issued also as an ebook.
   Includes bibliographical references.
   1. Success—Psychological aspects. 2. Happiness. 3. Self-actualization (Psychology) 4. Motivation (Psychology) 5. Job satisfaction. I. Title.

BF637.S8 Z556 2015
158.1   2014947396
ISBN: 978-1-62634-173-9

Part of the Tree Neutral® program, which offsets the number of trees consumed in the production and printing of this book by taking proactive steps, such as planting trees in direct proportion to the number of trees used: www.treeneutral.com

TreeNeutral®

Printed in the United States of America on acid-free paper

14 15 16 17 18 19   10 9 8 7 6 5 4 3 2 1

First Edition

To my wife, Chris, who has always loved me, believed in me, and brought out my best. Her faith, intellect, courage, and strength have made my life and work so much more fun, exciting, and meaningful.

Contents

PART II: PASSION

PART IV: PAYOFF

Foreword

"I want to be happy. I want to be successful." Ask people what they want from life and you are likely to hear these words, or a version thereof. Inquire further, and you'll find that most people will have at least an idea of what reaching those goals would take.

But in order to achieve a greater degree of happiness and success, three elements must be present, and most people, unfortunately, overlook one or more of these key elements.

In *The Payoff Principle*, you'll learn what these three elements are, and more important, how you can apply them to your life to increase your level of happiness and maximize your opportunities for success.

The Payoff Principle is not just another ordinary self-help or get-rich-quick book. Most books of this genre, while well intentioned, only touch on one, maybe two of the three key elements of success. I believe that *The Payoff Principle* is the first book to combine all three elements into a system that all but guarantees you greater happiness and success, if you apply its lessons to your life.

I was introduced to Dr. Alan Zimmerman many years ago through his newsletter, *The Tuesday Tip*. I was struck by Alan's capacity to motivate people through his unique ability to break down success principles into plain language, illustrated by his many captivating anecdotes and observations on life.

But more than anything else, what kept me coming back again and again to Alan's writing was the pervasive optimism that has become his hallmark. Alan believes there are seeds of greatness inside every individual, and he has dedicated his life mission to helping all those who follow his teachings to achieve their personal best. Alan's optimism is simply contagious, and if you're like me, you'll be glued to *The Payoff Principle* once you start reading.

As a successful professional bodybuilder, *Inc.* 500 entrepreneur, and CEO of Labrada Nutrition, I have relied on the time-proven principles espoused in Alan's book to make goals, work on them passionately, and reach them. During my adult life, I've been on a journey of self-discovery into what constitutes real success.

Years ago when I won the IFBB Mr. Universe title, I thought I had finally become a champion. Like many, I thought being a champion was just about winning. Not quite. A champion is not something you become by winning a major bodybuilding title, professional athletic event, or achieving business accolades. A champion is something you become through a process involving self-improvement, sacrifice, service, and yes, the attainment of goals normally out of reach of all except those willing to pay the price.

My dictionary contains three definitions for the word "champion." The first is "one who wins first place or first prize in a competition." Perhaps, in the broadest, most secular sense of the word, this is an accurate definition. But to limit the meaning of "champion" to these strict confines is to gut it of its essence. I disagree with this definition. To me this is the definition of a "winner." Yes, to be a champion, you must achieve something of value. But the world is full of men and women who have achieved fame and fortune and yet are bankrupt as human beings.

The second definition of champion is "one that is clearly superior or has the attributes of a winner." I like this definition better. This one emphasizes the attributes of a winner.

The third definition is "an ardent defender or supporter of a cause or another person." In my view, a champion is that unusual human being who is an embodiment of these last two definitions.

So why all the talk about what defines a champion? Because in *The Payoff Principle*, Alan's goal is to bring out the champion in *you*.

Alan makes the case that three things are necessary to be personally happy and professionally successful, and those three things are embodied in this formula:

Purpose + Passion + Process = Payoff.

Purpose is all about the direction in which you're going. Where do you hope to go with your life, your career, and your relationships?

Passion is all about the energy. How will you muster the energy to keep on keeping on— in the good times and the bad? How will you keep yourself motivated to move in the right direction?

Process is all about the skills. What skills do you have to learn—and then use—to make sure you get the **payoffs** you want in your professional life and your personal life?

The words and the concepts of purpose, passion, and process have been around for a long time. And you could easily dismiss them as common sense, but bringing them together in one book and one formula is not common practice. *The Payoff Principle* pulls purpose, passion, and process together, and presents them in a step-by-step plan that will help you master all three elements, so your payoffs will be extraordinary.

I wish I could say that I practiced all three principles at every point of my life, but that would be a falsehood. No, these are things I have learned over time, through my experiences. They require work and they are a process, not an end in themselves. Becoming a champion is a lifelong path, not a destination.

As we've seen, being a winner does not make you a champion. There are many winners who are not champions, and many champions who have not experienced public victories. Here's to all the future champions of the world and especially all those who toil quietly in their search for excellence—here's to your success.

—Lee Labrada, IFBB Mr. Universe and CEO of
Labrada Nutrition

CHAPTER 1

What Do You Really, Really, REALLY Want?

The Most Important Question You'll Ask Yourself

Do you know what you really, Really, REALLY want? This is the single most important question you could ever ask yourself, because your answer will affect every aspect of your work and your life—now and forever. Unfortunately, if you're like a lot of people, you haven't even bothered to ask the question. And, as a result, you may be working too hard, living too fast, and feeling like there's got to be more to work and life than what you've been experiencing.

> You can be so much more than you already are, and you can have so much more than you already have. But you're never going to get it if you don't know what you really, Really, REALLY want.

You're right. There is more. You can be so much more than you already are, and you can have so much more than you already have. But you're never going to get it if you don't know what you really, Really, REALLY want.

The problem is, very few of us were ever taught to ask ourselves that question, and fewer yet ever spent any time looking for the answer to the question.

Instead, we were taught platitudes that supposedly applied to everyone. We were taught, for example, to "climb the company ladder." And if we did that, everything would be okay. We would be immune from the tough times that other people had to endure.

Well, that turned out to be a lie. Dr. Jan Halper dispelled that myth in her research. After speaking with 4,126 men and following the careers of forty-three executives, Halper concluded that many men never took the time to figure out what they really wanted; and if they did, they often ignored those thoughts and feelings. Instead, they sacrificed their personal lives and personal values for their careers and companies.

The result? As Halper writes, "By sacrificing their values for status, placing more importance on appearances than happiness, and spending more time in empty or false relationships, these men found themselves saying, 'I feel empty. I'm an impostor!'"[1]

Whether you're a man or a woman, or even a youngster, does that sound anything like you? You think there's got to be more, but you're not quite sure what you really want. And even if you did know, you're not sure how to get it. Let me assure you this book is for you.

I've surveyed thousands of people over the years, asking them what they want out of a job, a relationship, or even life itself. The number one answer is always the same: *"I just want to be happy."* You probably fit into that category as well. You'd like to be happy; indeed, you'd like to have more happiness.

That's great. There's nothing wrong with wanting to be happy. In fact, you *should* want to be happy. The Bible talks repeatedly about the importance of having a joyful heart, and the Declaration of Independence even says we have "certain unalienable Rights . . . Life, Liberty and the pursuit of Happiness." And this book will show you how to be happier than ever.

Of course, the meaning of "happiness" may be unclear to you. You know you want it, but you're not 100 percent sure what it entails. No problem. We'll dig a little deeper into the definition later, because if you can't define it, chances are you won't achieve it.

And the second most common response to my survey is "I want to be successful." That's also great. It's not only the American dream; it's the dream of all people. And this book will show you how to be more successful than ever.

Unfortunately, some of the press and politicians have demonized being successful as though it is selfish or unfair. They seem to equate being successful with the inappropriate, undeserved accumulation of wealth. Of course, that is wrong, but that is also a very twisted and inaccurate definition of success. Real, honest, genuine success is all about becoming a person who achieves more of his or her dreams.

To get there—to experience more happiness and greater success—you've got to start by knowing what you really, Really, REALLY want. But your answers may be a bit vague at this point. And vague answers get vague results.

I don't want you to be like the millions of people who in their twenties, thirties, and forties—and even into their seventies and eighties— say, "I don't know what I want to do when I grow up." I don't want you to be like those people who simply grow older, until one day they realize they blew it. Their life is just about over, and there are no do-overs and there are no second chances for all the years they wasted.

> I don't want you to be like those people who simply grow older, until one day they realize they blew it.

To get more clarity on what you really, Really, REALLY want, ask yourself three additional questions.

Are You Enjoying What You Do?

The trouble is, many people don't enjoy what they do or where they are in their life. The famous comedian George Burns, however, thoroughly enjoyed what he was doing on and off the stage. Perhaps that's why he lived to be so old. When he was ninety-nine and the city of Los Angeles was renaming two streets in honor of him and his wife, Gracie Allen, he was asked how he felt. Burns answered, "It's good to be here. At my age it's nice to be anywhere."[2]

As psychiatrist Elisabeth Kübler-Ross observed in her work with the dying,

> There are dreams of love, life, and adventure in all of us. But we are also sadly filled with reasons why we shouldn't try. These reasons seem to protect us, but in truth they imprison us. They hold life at a distance. Life will be over sooner than we think. If we have bikes to ride and people to love, now is the time.[3]

Did you catch her comment? That *most people don't even* try *to get a life they enjoy* because they are filled with reasons why they shouldn't try. And the most insidious reason of all is that they don't know what they really, Really, REALLY want.

Of course that sounds absolutely ridiculous. Why wouldn't a person know what he or she wants? Or why wouldn't you know?

Confusion from the media is one reason. You are exposed to thousands of commercials every day, and every one of them has the same underlying message that you can't be happy without their product or service. Some of it rubs off on you. And after a while, your wants and needs fall together into one amorphous blob, until you come to the point of not even being sure what your priorities are. And it's pretty hard to enjoy what you're doing if you don't even know what you really, Really, REALLY want to do.

Misunderstood significance is another reason. You may think you're somewhat ordinary, with a regular job and a somewhat dysfunctional family. You may think you've never done anything significant and never will. So how could you possibly enjoy what you're doing?

But you can. You really can enjoy what you're doing no matter what your job is. And no one understood that better than Wilbert Williams. In fact, if you're ever in Chicago, look up his street, Wilbert Williams Way.

As you may know, the city of Chicago can be confusing to navigate because so many streets have two names. On one block you may see a street sign bearing the original designation, but several blocks down, the street sign has changed to a celebrity's name—such as a famous religious leader, an artist, or a business tycoon. It's a way of paying homage to the people who have positively influenced that area or the city in some way.

Some folks might be puzzled when they see the honorary street sign for Wilbert Williams Way erected downtown on a corner of the Magnificent Mile. Wilbert Williams doesn't ring a bell with the greater population of Chicago. But for the hundreds of Chicago residents who were greeted each working day by Wilbert Williams, the sign makes perfect sense.

Mr. Williams served as the doorman at the Women's Athletic Club for forty years, but he was so much more than a doorman. He made everyone who passed by and everyone who entered the building feel ten feet tall. He remembered their names, greeted them with warmth, and treated them with respect. So much so that his reputation for kindness and caring spread throughout the area, growing year by year, traits that prompted one woman to give her Cadillac to Williams! He was a simple, humble man who became bigger than life. He became a legend.

When Williams retired after forty years at his post, the fuss made over his retirement decision caught him by surprise—because he didn't think the way he did his job was anything out of the ordinary. He just enjoyed what he was doing.

But those familiar with Williams know better. They think of him as an icon or a city treasure. As police officer Paul O'Donnell puts it, "I've worked this area for fifteen years, and he's the best down here. In all these years, I've never heard him speak a harsh word about anyone. He's a gentleman; what more can you say?"[4]

What, indeed. It was just Williams's way. He enjoyed what he was doing.

What about you? Are you enjoying what you do? If your answer is "no" or "I'm not sure," then ask yourself two questions. One, what would you do if you knew you could not fail? And two, what would you do if no one would say "no"? Your answers will clarify what you really,

Really, REALLY want. And your answers will move you toward those things you enjoy doing.

Then ask yourself the next question.

Are You Happy with Where You're Going?

Whether you planned it or not, you're going somewhere, whether you like it or not. The question is, "Are you happy with where you're going?"

If you're happy, congratulations! But if you're not happy with where you're going, or you've never even taken the time to think about where you're going, it's time to stop and think.

Think about this for a moment. If you make no changes in your life, your job, your relationships, your financial planning, health-care regimen, or anything else, where are you most likely going to be five, ten, or fifteen years from now? Will your marriage be stronger if you simply take it for granted? Will your bank account be bigger in the future if you make no changes in your use of money today? Will your health be better if you keep on eating and exercising the way you have been?

> If you're not happy with where you're going, take time to discover what you really want right now.

When you think about questions such as these, you will be able to answer the bigger question I've just posed, "Are you happy with where you're going?" Again, if you're not happy with where you're going, take time to discover what you really want right now. Take ten minutes a day for ten days to just plain think about it. For some of you, that may be a rare activity, but you will get some answers.

There will be a lot more about this later in the book, but the best way to be happy with where you're going is to get off autopilot, merely drifting through your life and your work, and get on with the work of creating the future you want.

As Michael Gerber, author of *The E-Myth Revisited* (New York: HarperCollins, 2004), has observed, "The difference between great people and everyone else is that great people create their lives actively, while everyone else is created by their lives, passively waiting to see where life takes them next. The difference between the two is the difference between living fully and just existing."[5]

If you're not happy with where you're going, change it. It's your responsibility. It's not your company's, your boss's, your spouse's, your parents', or the government's responsibility to make your life better.

Even Eleanor Roosevelt, First Lady and UN ambassador, believed this. She said, "One's philosophy is not best expressed in words; it is expressed in the choices one makes. In the long run, we shape our lives and we shape ourselves. The process never ends until we die. And, the choices we make are ultimately our own responsibility."[6]

There are two ways to face the future: one way is with apprehension and the other is with anticipation. To face the future with anticipation, to make sure you will be happy with where you're going, you must create your future.

Finally, ask yourself this question.

Are You Satisfied with What You're Becoming?

When I share this third question with an audience, I know it changes lives. One audience member wrote to me about his experience. He said his life revolved around the stock market. He said he finally realized that he was sick and tired of grabbing the *Wall Street Journal* first thing every morning and organizing his whole life around the financial reports he read. He didn't like what he was becoming. He was too involved with his investments. Indeed, it had become his entire life.

He wrote, "You're going to think I'm off my rocker. I just liquidated my investments. I'm starting a new life. And I'm free."

I'm not saying what he did was right or wrong. I'm not saying you should liquidate your investments. But I am saying you had better take a good hard look at yourself to see if you're satisfied with what you're becoming. Do you like and respect yourself more today than you did one, two, or three years ago?

Are you *becoming* the kind of person you want to be?

Are you *growing* into the kind of person you admire? If you're not sure about your answers, then ask yourself these additional probing questions.

Are You Satisfied with the Direction of Your Growth?

Are you continuing to read books, attend seminars, meet with mentors, listen to educational and motivational recordings, and engage in activities that will help you become a better person? Despite what you've heard, ignorance is not bliss. Ignorance leads to poverty, illness, poor jobs, and broken relationships.

Are You Satisfied with the Rate of Your Growth?

You may be growing too slowly, if at all. You may feel like you continue to get stuck in the same old nonproductive behaviors and nothing ever seems to get better.

> Are you becoming the kind of person you want to be? Are you growing into the kind of person you admire?

Just don't confuse the rate of your growth with the rate of your life. You may be working furiously to get ahead. You may feel like you're working harder than ever but never seem caught up. You may be getting ulcers or finding it harder to sleep at night. There's a huge difference between activity and accomplishment.

Are You Satisfied with the Target of Your Growth?

If all your ambition and hard work is focused on getting more power, more money, more fame, more attention, and bigger cars, houses, titles, and stuff, chances are you won't end up being satisfied with who you become. Ancient history affirms that. King Solomon, who was reputed to be one of the richest men of all time, wrote in Ecclesiastes 2:11: "Then

I considered all that my hands had done and the toil I had expended in doing it, and behold, all was vanity."[7] It meant nothing. He didn't like himself anymore. And modern psychology continues to affirm it. Professors Lan Nguyen Chaplin and Deborah Roedder John discovered that materialism actually creates low self-esteem or less satisfaction with yourself.[8]

In study after study, it has become abundantly clear that the people who are the most satisfied with what they are becoming are those who spend significant amounts of time helping other people.

As novelist Elizabeth Berg sees it, "There is incredible value in being of service to others. I think if many of the people in therapy offices were dragged out to put their finger in a dike, or take up their place in a working line, they would be relieved of terrible burdens."[9] In other words, they would feel so much better about themselves.

To get a clearer handle on whether you're satisfied with what you're becoming, try this exercise. Make a list of ten people you deeply admire—people you'd like to be more like in some way. Your list may include people you know or may include famous people you've never met from politics, religion, books, and movies. Write down every one of their characteristics that you admire and respect. And then ask yourself how you stack up against those characteristics. Are you becoming more or less like them?

Whether you like your answer to that question, you will have taken another step in defining what you really, Really, REALLY want. And that's good. Once you figure that out, this book will help you get more of what you want, because this book is all about making things happen.

Becoming a Person Who Makes Things Happen

Some people say there are three kinds of people in the world: those who wait for things to happen, those who make things happen, and those who wonder what happened. And only one of those has a career worth pursuing or a life worth living—the one who *makes* things happen.

You can and you will become a person who makes things happen as you learn the concepts and apply the skills in the pages ahead. That's good news. The even better news is that you don't have to spend your entire life trying to make things happen. It's not a matter of how long you use these skills but how well you use them.

Charles Richards, engineer, Yale professor, and designer of the Colt single-action army revolver, so aptly warned, "Don't be fooled by the calendar. There are only as many days in the year as you make use of. One man gets only a week's value out of a year while another man gets a full year's value out of a week."[10]

To make things happen, to get the "payoffs" you want at work and in life, you must start with knowing what you really, Really, REALLY want.

My Journey to the Payoff

Beyond the title of this book, you might have noticed I just used the word **payoff** for the first time. Maybe you were wondering when I would get to that word and what it's all about.

> You don't have to spend your entire life trying to make things happen. It's not a matter of how long you use these skills but how well you use them.

In its simplest form, a payoff refers to such things as a result or an outcome. But those words are overused in the business world and trivialized everywhere else, and they don't necessarily refer to positive, productive, or profitable results or outcomes. Personally, I've always wanted positive payoffs in my life—just like you, I suspect. The only problem was I had no idea what that meant or how to get them because, as I mentioned earlier, I had never figured out what I really, Really, REALLY wanted.

I had to learn the slow, hard way. In elementary school, I knew I wanted to be happy and successful in some kind of way. But what does a kid know about those concepts? To me, that boiled down to being popular. And I thought the way to achieve that was to look good. TV commercials made it quite clear that good looks were critical. So I dressed as well as I could, even though some of my clothes came from garage sales. And I was fat. My parents never embarrassed me, but I knew my mother had to buy me the "chubby" or "husky-sized" pants for school. So my "appearance" strategy didn't work. It didn't make me popular.

Then I tried a "social" strategy. I started a number of clubs—from clubs collecting baseball cards to hidden treasure clubs—and invited other kids to join me in those clubs. That made me popular for a little while because most kids want to belong to something. The problem was, I had no idea how to run those clubs. I just appointed myself the leader but acted more like a dictator, telling people what they had to do until everyone eventually quit my clubs. That wasn't the payoff I was looking for.

Time for another strategy—a "perfect kid" strategy. I figured if I did everything the teacher wanted me to do, if I could become the teacher's pet, I would at least be popular with that one person. I might even gain some badly needed self-esteem. Again, that worked for a while, until I decided that being the perfect kid included telling on other kids when they weren't perfect. But instead of earning respect, I was given the "Tattle Tail Award," and the teacher literally strapped a big tail around my waist that I had to wear at school. Instead of this strategy simply failing, it actually backfired and lowered my popularity and self-esteem even more.

To my credit, I wasn't a quitter. I moved on to a "money" strategy. To my way of thinking, if I could make lots of money, even though I was just a kid, people would have to notice and like me. So I began selling greeting cards door-to-door in the second grade, six hours a day, five days a week, for the entire three months of my summer vacation, all the way through sixth grade. By the time I was in eighth grade I owned and operated a small international import company. I gave up my summer vacation, playtime with friends, and all the things associated with the hazy, lazy days of summer that kids are supposed to experience. On the one hand I was successful, because I was undoubtedly the richest kid in the neighborhood with the biggest savings account. But on the other hand, my money strategy failed to give me the self-esteem and acceptance I craved because I had no time for friends and as a result they had no interest in me.

During my high school and college years, I landed on the "excellence" strategy. To my way of thinking, if I studied all the time, if I achieved the highest possible grades, if I became number one in my class, I would have to feel better about myself. I would win the attention (and hopefully respect) of my classmates. Wrong! I rose to the top of my class, but that separated me even further from my classmates. Some kids made fun of me, calling me the "class nerd," while others resented me for breaking the grading curve. It was one more strategy that did not deliver the happiness I sought. And the academic success had a somewhat bitter taste.

In all these situations, my intentions were good. I wanted to be liked. I wanted to be popular. I wanted to find that ever-elusive happiness and success, but none of my approaches worked very well. So I just kept on doing what I was always doing—try, try, try and work, work, work—even though it didn't bring the payoffs I wanted.

Sound like anybody you know? Perhaps you, yourself?

When I was about to graduate from college, my undergraduate adviser, Dr. Sally Webb, told me, "Alan, you have a gift. You're so smart, so capable, that you should teach." That was the furthest thing from my mind; I had never given teaching a moment's thought. I always figured I would go into the ministry, partly because I thought that was a "calling" in my life and partly because that's what everyone expected of me.

But still, not knowing what I really, Really, REALLY wanted, with Dr. Webb's assistance, I secured a part-time teaching position at the University of Minnesota when I was twenty-one. It gave me time to think as I pursued my master's and doctoral degrees.

I got a great education. But, more important, I had a radical *transformation*. Three forces collided in my life simultaneously: First, the *revelation* that everybody wants the same two things—happiness and success—whether or not they know how to get it. Second, the *indica-tion* that some of the things I was learning—some of the ever-changing business buzzwords or the hottest trends in flavor-of-the-month training and development—had very little lasting value. And third, the *inspiration* from several motivational books from several different authors I was reading, in particular, a comment by Zig Ziglar who said, "You can have everything you want in life if you just help enough other people get what they want."[11] (Later in my career I would have the privilege of being in the same professional association and Speaker Hall of Fame as Mr. Ziglar.)

Those three forces helped me discover what I really, Really, REALLY wanted—to be extraordinarily happy, certainly, and highly successful, of course—but I would achieve those things by helping other people attain the happiness and success they were seeking. And with that I took a very different approach in my upcoming roles as a university professor, author, consultant, and professional speaker. I decided I would no longer waste my students' time or my audience members' time by teaching them anything that would not make them happier or more successful. Life was too important and too short to do anything else.

The results were immediate and astounding. I altered the Interpersonal Communication course I was teaching to focus on one thing: the communication skills that would give my students the happiness and success payoffs they were seeking, on or off the job. I crammed this ten-week, thirty-hour class into a five-day, fifty-hour class. We started at 2:00 p.m. on Wednesday and finished at midnight on Sunday. And the students had to be there, in class, the entire time (Wednesday, Thursday, Friday, Saturday, and Sunday), or fail. Each student had to commit to full attendance and active participation.

Of course, the university administrators thought I was crazy. Who would ever come to a class at those ridiculous hours or consent to such a stringent requirement? After some weeks of dialogue and persuasive wrangling, the administrators allowed me to experiment with my approach.

As I said, the results were immediate and astounding. Within three minutes of registration opening, my Interpersonal Communication classes were filled, with a waiting list that would take three years to accommodate. My classes became the very first ones on campus to fill, every quarter, every year.

The results were thrilling, to say the least. In addition to the packed, sold-out classes and the big waiting lists, students began to spread the word. They were saying things like "This was the best class I've ever had," "Your course transformed my work and my relationships," and "This was a life-changing experience." And, despite the fact that more than two decades have passed since I taught those classes at the university, hardly a week goes by without some former student writing, calling, or emailing to say how the class and my focus on payoffs continue to impact their lives.

The little revolution we started in the classroom went way beyond the classroom. People in the community began to hear about what I was teaching in this relatively new field of "people skills" and how I was teaching it. Invitations flooded in from local service clubs, church groups, professional associations, and small businesses. They wanted me to speak to their people. After that, two universities honored me with the Outstanding Faculty Award. And that was followed by invitations to speak to dozens, and eventually hundreds, of organizations around the country.

I'm not sharing this because of some need to brag. I don't have a big ego that needs to be fed. Those things have never driven or motivated me. I'm sharing this because I want you to have the life-changing experience my students and audiences talk about.

My focus on the happiness and success payoffs was working well for my students and my business clients. There was only one problem. I felt something was missing. There had to be something more than just knowing what I or anybody else really, Really, REALLY wanted. And there was. There was *The Payoff Principle* and its three elements. I just didn't know what that principle was or what the three elements were . . . yet. I had to go through a learning process, and so will you in the course of reading this book.

CHAPTER 2

The Payoff Principle
and the Producer

It's a Great Time to Achieve All Your Dreams

Now that you've given more serious thought to what you really, Really, REALLY want, it's time to talk about how you go about getting that. You've got a clearer definition of happiness and a healthier definition of success.

The problem is—and it's a *huge* problem—most people work very hard to get those things but accomplish very little. And God bless them. They try and try and try, even though their efforts don't work, and there is very little evidence that their efforts will ever pay off.

This raises the obvious question, "Why aren't they getting what they want?" Or to get more personal, "Why aren't you getting what you want?" You can't blame it totally on your circumstances.

Birt Duncan knew that. As a cast-off African-American in the South, Birt was bumped from foster home to foster home. He fell asleep in school from a lack of proper nutrition. But he also went on to earn a PhD in psychology from Princeton and an MD from the University of California. He always taught people: "You cannot control the color of your skin, but you can determine the color of your thinking! What color is your thinking? Red or green? Think green. Think go!"[1]

We're living in great times with a world of opportunity. And no, I'm not glossing over the fact that our individual and collective worlds are filled with challenges and inequities. It always has been and always will be. That's life.

Nevertheless, this is still a great time. Over any five-year period, you can have, see, do, or become just about anything you desire. You can visit exotic locations, further your education, start your own business, improve your physical fitness, build your relationships, move to Tahiti, throw the gutless traitors out of Washington, and a million other things.

Of course, there are skeptics out there who say these aren't great times. "Just look at the news. Look at what they're saying on the Internet." I shouldn't have to say this, but don't believe everything you hear on the news or read on the Internet. Do your homework. Do some in-depth research.

> These are still great times for you to be who you want to be, get what you desire, and have what means the most to you.

Unfortunately, that's easier said than done. It's hard to know the whole truth, the positive truth, when members of the media make their living selecting the most negative stories they can find and then emphasizing them. In fact, if you only read the papers, watched the television news, or followed the Internet, it would be easy to conclude that the world is teetering on the edge of disaster. It would be hard to believe these are great times for you to achieve all your dreams.

Yes, there's lots of hurt, pain, and trouble in this world. But these are still great times for you to be who you want to be, get what you desire, and have what means the most to you. So what's the problem?

Dumb Strategies May Be Getting in Your Way

You may not be getting everything you want out of your life, work, and relationships for a very simple reason—dumb strategies.

Dr. Philip Humbert, author of "Nothing Will Change Until You Do!", writes, "My blunt answer is this: many of us are using really dumb strategies. We have goals or desires or dreams, but we are pursuing them with strategies that have almost no chance of success. And yet, too often, we keep on doing the same things in the same ways, year after year. That's probably not very smart."[2]

As I mentioned in the previous chapter, it was a lesson I learned the hard and slow way. It took me years to unlearn some of my dumb strategies and adopt some better strategies and get better payoffs. Now I'm writing this book so you can learn the quick and easy way. But remember, I said it still felt like something was missing.

So I delved into a thirty-year research project, reading every happiness and success book I could get my hands on—hundreds of them. I listened to every motivational and educational recording I could find on the so-called soft skills. I studied communication, leadership, motivation, attitude, change, excellence, teamwork, human capital, self-esteem, emotional intelligence, productivity, relationship building, conflict resolution, the behavior of champions, and a host of similar topics that had a bearing on this always-wanted but hard-to-find happiness and success. I filled twelve bookcases with books, eight file cabinets with notes, and then a few computer hard drives with information.

For a while my studies focused on attitude. I thought attitude or **passion** was the key to everything I wanted. Didn't the book titles tell me "attitude is everything" and "a positive attitude always works"? So I became an expert on attitudes, and I learned to display a very positive attitude most of the time. Indeed, I believe in a positive attitude, and I give numerous seminars on how to get and keep a positive attitude.

But I began to wonder if attitude or passion was really everything. Most of us know someone who is a little ray of sunshine, who is always upbeat and positive, but when it comes to getting the job done, done right, and done on time, that person often falls below the mark. I certainly came across enough of those people in my consulting practice.

So then I focused my studies on **purpose**. That must be the key, I thought. At least the reading public seemed to think so. Books on "the power of purpose" and having a "purpose-driven life" were among the best sellers in history. Millions and millions of copies sold in more than sixty languages across the world. Even Proverbs 29:18 says, "Where there is no vision [purpose], the people perish."[3]

Again, reality hit me in the face. I knew people, just like you do, who have a purpose, but they're not going anywhere. They're not all that happy or successful.

For example, you probably know someone who has an admirable purpose—such as feeding his family or defending her country—but you also hear them say things like "Another day, another dollar," or "I've just got four more years, three months, and two days and I'm out of here." In a sense, they've retired but they haven't told the Personnel Department yet.

Passion and purpose seemed to be pieces of the transformation I was hoping to learn and hoping to teach others, but I knew there was still something missing. My clients were telling me, "We don't care about some fancy academic model or esoteric theory. We just want to know how to do our jobs or live our lives more effectively. Give us the skills we need." So I turned my focus to the **process**, or the tools that would give my clients the payoffs they wanted. Finally, I thought, that must be the key to happiness and success on and off the job.

Alas, I discovered, as I had realized before, that process was *a* key but not *the* key to total transformation. Experience and observation told me that. I kept meeting people who knew how to do their jobs and do them very well. They had mastered the process. They had the skills. But those same people seemed to lack a vision of a bigger and brighter future. They'd resist change and say: "We've always done it this way," "We've never done that kind of thing before," "It's good enough," and "Why bother to change it? It's still working."

In and of themselves, my three areas of study (purpose, passion, and process) were all good things. I could even argue that all three of them were vitally important things. But it finally hit me. The chances of a person achieving all his dreams, or the chances of a person getting all the happiness and success she wanted, by focusing on just one of those three areas were pretty slim.

And then I remembered the story of the blind men touching an elephant and describing what the animal was like. One man focused on the elephant's trunk and said an elephant is like a big hose. Another man touched only the elephant's ear and reported that the animal was like a large fan. Still another man focused on one of the elephant's legs and said the animal was like a tree trunk.

Each of them was right, but each of them was also wrong. By focusing on a part of the elephant instead of the entire creature, none of them got a complete or accurate picture of the elephant.

That's exactly how I felt about the research I was uncovering. The information was correct and even helpful, in a narrow kind of way. But very little or any of the "happiness and success"

> *The chances of a person achieving all his dreams, or the chances of a person getting all the happiness and success she wanted, by focusing on just one of those three areas were pretty slim.*

research gave the big picture. None of it (at least the material I came across) put it all together. And that was exactly what I was looking for—the same thing I believe most people are looking for.

Then it came to me: *The Payoff Principle.* I don't know if it came as the logical conclusion of thirty years of study, from intuition, dumb luck, intellectual insight, or spiritual direction. I tend to think it was the latter. But who knows? Maybe it was a combination of all five. But I had one of those sudden Aha! moments where I said, "That's it. *The Payoff Principle* is what brings it all together."

To enjoy all the happiness you've ever wanted, to achieve all the success you've ever desired, you can't focus on one aspect of the subject, like the blind men with the elephant. You've got to have a formula that encompasses all the aspects of purpose, passion, and process, and you've got to have a simple, foolproof formula you can easily remember and apply to all aspects of your life and work. That's exactly what *The Payoff Principle* does.

So what is it and how does it work?

The Payoff Principle

The Payoff Principle says, "When you find **purpose** in what you do, exhibit **passion** for the outcome, and master the **process** to make it happen, you produce the **payoffs** you want, need, and deserve." In effect, you become a **producer**.

To me, that's not only great news, it's also powerful! I don't know what payoffs you want to see in your life and work. It may be a higher position in the corporation, a bigger paycheck, a healthier body, a better relationship, a stronger self-esteem, a more exciting career, a clearer connection to your Higher Power, a reasonable sense of work-life balance, or a host of other things. But I do know this: when you understand and implement *The Payoff Principle*, you can have those things. After working with thousands of people in hundreds of organizations, I can tell you *this works*.

> When you implement The Payoff Principle, nothing can stop you. But if you don't have purpose, passion, and process, nothing can help you.

In fact, when you implement *The Payoff Principle*, *nothing can stop you*. But if you don't have purpose, passion, and process, *nothing can help you* except finding the purpose, passion, and process that will give you the payoffs you want. In my mind, when you put it all together, it resembles Figure 2.1.

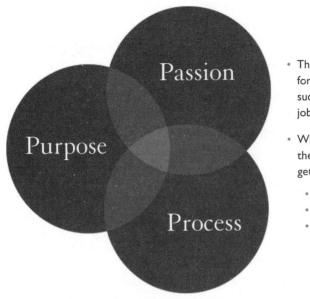

- Three ingredients for happiness and success ... on the job and off

- When you master these three, you get payoffs that are
  - Personal,
  - Professional, and
  - Permanent.

Figure 2.1. The Payoff Principle Illustrated

The Payoff Principle and the Producer

Notice what happens in people's lives and in the world when people truly grasp and follow *The Payoff Principle*. Nelson Mandela, the leader of South Africa, "got it." He said, "A good head and a good heart are always a formidable combination." He adhered, consciously or unconsciously, to *The Payoff Principle* and was an amazingly effective producer as a result.

Lee Labrada, one of the world's most well-known and celebrated bodybuilding legends, gets it. He holds twenty-two professional bodybuilding titles, including the International Federation of Bodybuilding and Fitness title of Mr. Universe. He is one of the few pro bodybuilders in history to consistently have placed in the top four at the Mr. Olympia competition (the Super Bowl of bodybuilding) for seven consecutive years.

But that's only the beginning. Driven by *The Payoff Principle*, Labrada went on to found Labrada Nutrition and create his own line of award-winning sports nutrition and supplement products. He became just as successful in the business world as he was in the fitness world, leading his organization to become one of the fastest-growing privately held companies in the US—earning *Inc.* 500 status—in only six years.

When I interviewed Labrada, I asked what it meant to be a "champion," which, of course, is a key word in his world of bodybuilding and competition. Labrada answered, "*A champion is somebody you become through a process of self-improvement, sacrifice, service, and yes, the attainment of goals normally out of reach of all except those willing to pay the price.*"

Great definition. I would also call him a **producer**, *a person who makes things happen*. A producer creates, designs, shapes, forms, and manages the direction and the outcomes of his or her life and work. Producers are in charge. They know what they really, Really, REALLY want, and they experience the greatest happiness and success.

To quote *The Payoff Principle*, a producer finds purpose in what he or she does, exhibits passion for the outcome, and masters the process to make it happen. As a result, a producer gets the payoffs he or she wants, needs, and deserves. Throughout this book, I'll show you how you get all three of those elements working for you. It will be fun, and you will be transformed.

I'm presuming, of course, that you want to be a producer—that you want to make better things happen in your life, work, relationships, and everywhere else. Right?

That being the case, you need to know what characterizes a producer, and I'll outline the key characteristics in just a moment. However, as I discuss the characteristics, do more than say to yourself, "That's interesting." Interesting never accomplished anything in this world. Instead, apply each characteristic to yourself. Ask yourself what percentage of time you're utilizing that characteristic in your behavior: 100 percent of the time? 50 percent of the time? 20 percent of the time? You'll see where you can pat yourself on the back and where you still have some work to do. This is a good place to start the transformation process you're going to experience.

Characteristic #1: Producers Are Motivated

Sir Edmund Hillary, the first person to climb Mount Everest, exemplified this. When asked about his amazing accomplishment, he replied, "You don't have to be a fantastic hero to do certain things. You can be just an ordinary chap, sufficiently motivated to reach challenging goals."[4]

What percentage of time are you sufficiently motivated? Later in the book, I'll give you a number of strategies you can use to keep yourself motivated. Here are a few to get you started.

Put Positive Fuel into Your Mind

You change your life when you change your fuel. If you feed on negative thoughts, whether self-imposed or inflicted by others, you'll face more difficulties than you need to. But if you feed on positive input, you start a fire that burns through most of your difficulties. You must actively, consciously put positive fuel into your mind.

As a counselor, Carla Erickson learned this concept when she put herself on a steady diet of positive subliminal programming from an audio series I produced called *Mind over Matter*. She listened to this subliminal material every day for eight years and reported, "Before I listened to your recordings, I struggled with a lifetime of difficulty. I lacked self-confidence, and I didn't follow through on things. Then I listened to your subliminal recordings. They have given me a confidence and outlook on life that I have *never* experienced before. I listen to them regularly and even hear the music in my head when I am not listening to the CDs. Thank you so very much, Dr. Zimmerman. Your method works!! Even my family and friends have noticed major changes in me for the better."

In a sense, Erickson learned that what's happening *out* there isn't as important as what's happening *in*side you. It's a key step in the process of becoming a producer—make sure you put in the positive fuel you need to get the payoffs you want.

Refuse to Quit when Setbacks Arrive

Producers stay sufficiently motivated because they refuse to quit when challenges or setbacks arrive. As Mary Kay Ash, founder of Mary Kay Cosmetics and named the "Most Outstanding Woman in Business in the Twentieth Century" by Lifetime Television, proclaimed, "One of the secrets of success is to refuse to let temporary setbacks defeat us."[5]

Debbi Fields, the founder of Mrs. Fields Cookies, was labeled an "empty-headed housewife" when she shared her business philosophy. She said, "I've never felt like I was in the cookie business. I've always been in a feel-good business. My job is to sell joy. My job is to sell happiness. My job is to sell an experience."[6] She fought bankers, family members, friends, vendors, and suppliers who tried to run and ruin her life and her business, but she became an amazing producer because she refused to quit when the setbacks came.

The same thing could be said about the Schnitzers. When a brick shattered their five-year-old son Isaac Schnitzer's bedroom window, the intended target had been a menorah for the Jewish Hanukkah celebration. The FBI told the Schnitzers to keep a low profile because members of a neo-Nazi hate group had attacked minorities in Billings, Montana, before this.

Instead of following their advice, the Schnitzers decided to stand up and speak out. And their neighbors joined them—then, likewise, the local association of churches and the Coalition for Human Rights. A number of pastors led a campaign to distribute and display pictures of menorahs.

Then the churches, schools, and hundreds of people joined the campaign. The neo-Nazis threw more bricks through more windows and even shot a few bullets. But the good people of Billings wouldn't be intimidated. As one Native American shopkeeper said, "I figured if we all put up menorahs there wouldn't be enough bricks to smash them all."

On the eighth and last night of Hanukkah, the Schnitzer family took a drive through town. They saw menorahs on houses, stores, billboards, and some nestled among elaborate Christian displays. Little Isaac was amazed and said, "I didn't know so many people were Jewish." His mother replied, "They're not all Jewish. But they're our friends." And the attacks stopped.[7]

Characteristic #2: Producers Take Responsibility

David Adkins, better known as the comedian/actor Sinbad, says, "My mother and father taught me everything: integrity, honesty, being responsible. My father told me you can't be great at anything unless you accept responsibility."[8]

Dr. Charles Garfield, a professor at the University of California's medical school and head of the Peak Performance Center, agrees. He says, "You have the power to change your habits of mind and acquire certain skills. And if you choose to do so, you can improve your performance, your productivity and the quality of your whole life."[9]

Did you catch the key word in Garfield's comment? It's "choose." It's all about taking responsibility. And the undeniable truth is that producers take responsibility for their lives. They don't blame fate for their failures or luck for their successes.

> The undeniable truth is that producers take responsibility for their lives. They don't blame fate for their failures or luck for their successes.

So I challenge you to make it personal. What percentage of time do you take full responsibility for what happens in your life? And what percentage of time do you blame other people or circumstances for what happens in your life?

Adopt an "It's Up to Me" Attitude

Producers know they are the only ones responsible for their success. And you need to embrace the idea of "it's up to me." No one is responsible for your success, not your boss, your company, your husband, your wife, your parents, or anybody else, only you are. Oh sure, those other people can help, support, and encourage you, but none of them can make you successful. You are responsible for your own success. A producer accepts that responsibility.

I'm sure you've heard the oft-quoted phrase, "If it is to be, it's up to me." That might sound cute or might even sound like a chant you've heard from a rah-rah motivational speaker. But it's not some light, fluffy statement that you can afford to dismiss.

People who dismiss this "it's up to me" attitude end up in trouble. It's why the vast majority of Americans reaching retirement age lack the financial resources to take care of their basic needs . . . without some form of government help. They never fully understood the fact . . . that it was up to them, not the government or their company, to secure their future.

This is why so many people never seem to move ahead in their lives, their careers, or their relationships. They don't buy or read educational books, and they don't invest their own time and money into motivational recordings, written materials, or seminars. They do very little to continue their growth and development . . . and thereby increase their value to their companies and the people in their lives. And they wonder why they aren't better off today than they were last year. It's because they don't have an "it's up to me" attitude that pushes them toward continual education.

However, some immigrant groups, not all, have truly bought into this "it's up to me" attitude. Perhaps that's why a person who immigrates to the United States is four times more likely to become a millionaire than is a person who's born here. Is it because the immigrant is four times luckier than a native-born American? No. Is it because the immigrant is four times smarter? No. Is it because the immigrant works four times harder? No. It's because the immigrant is four times more likely to spot opportunities than problems. He knows if it is to be, it is up to me.

Refute an Attitude of Entitlement

On January 20, 1961, President John F. Kennedy spoke the immortal words, "Ask not what your country can do for you; ask what you can do for your country." These words from Kennedy's inaugural address are filled with enormous wisdom. If only we had listened, we would have more productive organizations and healthier families instead of all the selfish greed and dysfunction we see today.

Most social scientists would agree that we're in the midst of a culture change that is the very opposite of what Kennedy described. Indeed, Kennedy would be shocked if he saw how an attitude of entitlement has swept over so many people. He would see scores of people who no longer ask what they can do for others; they simply demand others give them what they want.

People who live with an entitlement attitude behave somewhat like lobsters. When a lobster is left high and dry among the rocks, he doesn't have the instinct or exert the energy to work his way back into the sea. He waits for the sea to come to him. If it doesn't come, he just sits there and dies, although the slightest effort would get him back into the ocean, which is perhaps a yard away. As author Dr. Orison Swett Marden (1848–1924) wrote, "The world is full of human lobsters: Men stranded on the rocks of indecision and procrastination, who instead of putting forth their own energies, are waiting for some grand billow of good fortune to set them afloat."[10]

Characteristic #3: Producers Are Disciplined

Many years ago, my mentor asked me, "Alan, do you like pleasing habits or pleasing results?" As I pondered the question and squirmed in my chair like a worm at the end of a hook, I knew some of my life and work was off base. I was "saying" that I was interested in pleasing *results*—like a close relationship with my kids. But I was more focused on the easy things, the pleasing *habits,* like buying the kids a bunch of stuff, rather than spending quality time with them.

A few moments later, I answered my mentor, "Deep down I prefer pleasing results." From that moment on, my life changed. I began to do the things that needed to be done, whether or not I felt like it. I learned the value and significance of being disciplined.

I learned what Canadian naval officer and Senator Douglas Everett meant when he said, "There are some people who live in a dream world, and there are some people who face reality . . . and then there are some who turn one into another."[11]

How disciplined are you? What percentage of your life do you live by your disciplined commitments? And what percentage of your life do you live by your ever-changing feelings?

Find Your Direction

To be a producer, your discipline starts with having direction. If you don't know where you're going, you can be busy, very busy. You may have lots of activity in your life, but you won't have much in the way of accomplishment. That's why novelist Ernest Hemingway said, "Never mistake motion for action."[12] And that's why I tell my audiences, as I told you before, "Don't confuse activity with accomplishment."

Without direction, you can't possibly be disciplined. You'll end up like Alice in Lewis Carroll's *Alice's Adventures in Wonderland* (London: MacMillan, 1865) who asks the Cheshire cat:

> "Would you tell me, please, which way I ought to go from here?"

"That depends a good deal on where you want to get to," said the Cat.

"I don't care much where—" said Alice.

"Then it doesn't matter which way you go," said the Cat.

Get Started

Beyond direction, your discipline is reinforced by the simple act of starting. As humorist Mark Twain said so very well, "Good intentions are like crying babies in church. They should be carried out immediately."[13]

Of course, the non-producers will often say they don't feel like getting started. They don't feel like making a move. They don't have any desire, or it's too hard to make that first step. Well you're not going to like this, but your feelings are irrelevant at this point. If you wait until you feel like starting, you may never start. Producers force themselves to take that first step knowing the feelings will come later. In fact, one of the main reasons a producer *is* a producer is because he does what most people don't feel like doing. He does the things that need to be done, not just the things he likes to do.

> Your feelings are irrelevant at this point. If you wait until you feel like starting, you may never start.

If you struggle with starting, try the five-minute action step. It works for me. If there's something I don't want to do, I force myself to spend five minutes on the task. No matter how big or how unpleasant the task may be, I can always give it five minutes. Of course, more often than not, I keep working on the task even though the five minutes are up. People who can't get started don't go anywhere.

You remember the principle in physics that says a body in motion tends to stay in motion? If you know where you want to go and if you will do something to get started, you're becoming a disciplined producer.

Do a Little Bit More

Finally, your discipline kicks into high gear when you do a little bit more. As author A. Lou Vickery states, "Four short words sum up what has lifted most successful individuals above the crowd: a little bit more. They did all that was expected of them and a little bit more."[14]

In a sense, the producer exhibits discipline because she is willing to make short-term sacrifices to meet long-term goals. As nineteenth-century history professor Charles Kendall Adams (1835–1902) put it, "No one ever attains very eminent success by simply doing what is required of him; it is the amount and excellence of what is over and above the required that determines the greatness of ultimate distinction."[15]

A producer knows that if she wants to double her paycheck, she will have to do a little bit more to triple her value. When you do that, one of three things will happen. One, your present employer will respond with raises, bonuses, and promotions. Two, a new employer will find and grab you. Or three, you'll discover some way to start your own business and write your own paycheck. And if you already own a business and double your paycheck, simply take action to triple the value you offer your customers.

> A producer knows that if she wants to double her paycheck, she will have to do a little bit more to triple her value.

When you do that, most of the time (hey, life isn't always fair) your compensation will catch up to your value. And even if your compensation doesn't catch up as fast or by as much as you would like, you'll still feel a great deal better about doing your best rather than doing just enough to get by.

Characteristic #4: Producers Take Constructive Risks

I speak to thousands of people every year, and I listen to hundreds of their questions. But the number of people who live such small lives continually saddens me. These people are constantly plagued by what-ifs.

What if the stock market goes down or Social Security is not there to help them when they retire? What if their company merges with another and they lose their job? What if they have to keep on working with a difficult boss or team member? What if they decide to marry someone and it doesn't work out?

Plagued by fear and what-ifs, they stay in their comfort zones. They don't realize that everything they want more of—better health, a better relationship, a better job, a better financial portfolio, everything—lies outside their comfort zone.

Show Courage to Get Bigger Payoffs

Producers get bigger payoffs because they exhibit courage. Producers know that success seldom falls upon the fainthearted or the lily-livered cowards. That's why management guru Peter Drucker (1909–2005) says, "In every success story, you find someone who has made a courageous decision."[16] And that's why fear, timidity, and comfort-zone living are incompatible with payoffs.

Dr. Rob Gilbert talks about that in his book, *Gilbert on Greatness* (Bloomfield, NJ: Center for Sports Success, 1988), as he shares the story of a high school senior who had the goal of making it to the state wrestling championships. Unfortunately, when the match was over, the student stood with his head down as the referee raised his opponent's arm in victory. It was not even close. He had lost 14–0. His high school wrestling career was over. There would be no state tournament for him. Not now, not ever. It was his last chance, and he blew it.

Walking off the mat, he heard the applause and cheers for his opponent. But the applause kept growing louder and louder. Then he looked up. All eyes were on him. The eight hundred fans that packed the small high school gym were standing and cheering him. They were giving him a standing ovation. He was overwhelmed. The emotions of the moment became too much for him to handle. He went down on one knee and cried.

Wrestling is a difficult sport for anyone. But it was even more difficult for this high school kid who was born without a left arm. And his right arm was nothing more than half an arm with two fingers growing out of an elbow-length stump. Nonetheless, he had developed his own style of competing as a one-armed leg wrestler, and over the years he had won almost as many matches as he had lost.

Now his wrestling career was over. His opponent was hugging him. His coach and teammates were picking him up and putting him on their shoulders. He saw his mom in the stands crying. And his dad was filming the whole thing with his new video camera. The crowd was still on its feet cheering. They were giving this "losing" wrestler a standing ovation because the one-armed kid had taught everyone a lesson. He taught them that winning is an important thing, but so is courage.

Producers exhibit feelings of courage. But producers also take thoughtful steps and intelligent risks that move them closer to their desired payoffs.

French historian, novelist, and statesman André Malraux (1901–1976) emphasized that. He said, "Often the difference between a successful person and a failure is not one has better abilities or ideas, but the courage that one has to bet on one's ideas, to take a calculated risk—and to act."[17]

In a piece titled "What Happy People Do Differently," Robert Biswas-Diener and Todd Kashdan concluded, "Truly happy people seem to have an intuitive grasp of the fact that sustained happiness is not just about doing things you like. It also requires growth and adventuring beyond the boundaries of your comfort zone. Happy people, are, simply put, curious."[18] To use my language, producers take more risks because they know life is either a matter of risk or regret.

> Producers take more risks because they know life is either a matter of risk or regret.

What about you? Are you taking enough risks? What percentage of your life is spent inside your comfort zone, and what percentage of your life is spent in risk taking? And are you happy with those percentages?

I was deeply inspired by one of my students who demonstrated how producers take risks. His name was Paul. When Paul was born, he was badly deformed. His arms and legs were so badly twisted into knots that he never learned to walk or care for himself. At age eight, Paul heard the doctors tell his parents he wouldn't live very long, so there was no sense in wasting any more time or money on him. His parents were told it would be best to put him in an institution.

So that's where Paul lived—until he was sixty-eight. Sixty years! That was when Paul decided he had had enough. He wanted to live, not just exist. He started to plan out his life, and he decided to take some risks.

That's when I met Paul. He showed up in one of my classes at the university where I was teaching. Paul said he wanted to get a college degree, then a master's degree, and go into the counseling profession. He wanted to help other people who had had a tough time in life.

I had to admire him. Paul had so little. He hardly had any money, no family members, and perhaps only a few years left to live. All he had was the person he hired to push him from class to class, care for his physical needs, and write out the papers he dictated. But he had a plan, and he was taking risks to make his plan come true.

I continued to follow Paul's progress. He enrolled in several of my university classes, so we had many chances to talk. In fact, he joined my family and me for several Christmas celebrations. I watched him as he started a Toastmasters Club on campus, and I watched him as he got elected to a seat on the Student Senate. He was a producer because he chose to take some risks instead of playing it safe and living the remainder of his life in an institution.

Getting The Payoff Principle Working for You

You've read about *The Payoff Principle*. You know "When you find **purpose** in what you do, exhibit **passion** for the outcome, and master the

process to make it happen, you produce the **payoffs** you want, need, and deserve." Following that formula, you become a **producer**.

You know the characteristics of a producer. That is knowledge. And that's good. But education without implementation serves no useful purpose. It's time to start implementing.

PART I

PURPOSE

CHAPTER 3

The Power of Purpose

Where the Payoff Begins

More than anything else, Willem wanted to be an evangelist, but by the time he was twenty-five, he had already been an art dealer, a language teacher, a bookseller, and a failure in love. But beyond all the paintings, words, books, and women, he wanted to devote himself to others.

This calling brought young Willem to the coalfields of south Belgium. During a mine disaster, scores of villagers were hurt, and no one fought harder to save them than he did. Day and night, Willem nursed the wounded, fed the hungry, and clothed the poor.

After the rubble was cleared, the dead were buried, and the sick made well, the townspeople turned to this Dutchman as their spiritual leader. Every Sunday the people packed Willem's services to hear this simple man speak.

But then lightning struck. Some visiting church officials discovered Willem had been living in a simple hut, dressed in old clothes, and had given away most of his salary to the poorest miners. They didn't think it was proper for him to look more destitute than the people he taught, and so he was fired.

Willem was devastated. The career that meant everything to him was suddenly gone. He went through weeks of despair, but one day Willem noticed an old miner bending beneath the weight of an enormous sack of coal.

Fumbling through his pocket, the Dutchman pulled out a tattered envelope and a pencil. He sketched the weary figure that moved him so. The drawing was a crude one, but he tried over and over to improve upon his sketch.

Beginning that day, Willem captured the people he loved in the art he created. And even though Willem was thrown out of the ministry, it did not cause him to throw away his purpose in life. Even though he was not allowed to teach the people, he was able to reach the people through his art.

The man with a calling, the preacher who wasn't to be, became the artist we know as Vincent Willem van Gogh.[1]

It was his **purpose** that gave him the **passion** and led him to the **process** that would eventually deliver the **payoffs** that have been a gift to the world ever since.

Is Purpose Really Important?

Absolutely! Just like Vincent van Gogh, a clear **purpose**, the right purpose, will bring out your best. It will keep you going. It will move you beyond motivation to inspiration and into the big leagues of success. As the former prime minister of Great Britain Benjamin Disraeli declared, "The secret of success is constancy of purpose."[2]

> You *have a* purpose. *You are* here to make *some kind of* positive difference *in the world.*

And the good news is *you* have a purpose. You really do. As Native American author Christine Quintasket (1884–1936), who was also known as Mourning Dove, put it, "Everything on the earth has a purpose, every disease an herb to cure it, and every person a mission."[3]

You have a purpose and it is much bigger than merely going to work, collecting a paycheck, and paying off the mortgage. That's survival, but it's not purpose. *You* are here to make some kind of positive difference in the world. It may be in your family, your company, or your nation, but you're here to make your world a better place.

Now you may not know what your exact purpose is or how to figure it out. You may not even know why on earth you're here in the first place. You may feel like the man in England whose tombstone epitaph read, "Here lies a man who lived and died but never knew who he was."

You're not alone. A lot of people are struggling with those questions. And that's not a comfortable or profitable place to live. *Without* purpose, you will never become a producer. And you may spend your whole life trying to climb the ladder of success to a destination that isn't worth reaching.

With purpose, however, you will gain a lot: three payoffs in particular—better health, greater motivation, and deeper satisfaction. In fact, it will change your ordinary life—if that's what you have—into an extraordinary life.

Purpose Payoff #1: Better Health

Life without a clearly defined purpose jeopardizes your emotional health. In his book, *Halftime* (Grand Rapids, MI: Zondervan, 1994), CEO Bob Buford describes several signs of poor emotional health, signs that your life and work have lost their purpose, or they never had a purpose in the first place. He describes three of them as

> *Life without a clearly defined purpose jeopardizes your health.*

- The thrill of closing a major deal isn't quite what it was ten years ago.

- You spend a lot of time thinking about what it might be like to start over or move "down" to a less responsible position that gives you more control of your life.

- You have a secure position, yet you're scanning the want ads and openings listed in professional journals.[4]

Do any of these signs sound like you? In addition to Buford's signs of jeopardized emotional health, take a look at the following questions that may indicate your life or career is lacking a clear and powerful purpose:

- Do you ever find yourself thinking or saying, "What's the point? Why am I killing myself for this job?"

- Do you envy the guy who decides to follow his passion instead of his pocketbook?

- Are you spending more time daydreaming about "the day I'll get out of this place?"

- Do you ever think that "getting ahead" in life and work should mean more than simply "moving up" in the company?

- Do you ever think about starting your own business or doing what you really love to do even though the pay may not be as good?

- Are your kids and partner asking for more of your time, but you keep putting them off until later when you're not so busy?

If you can relate to any of these signs, it's a good indication that you need to do some work on your purpose, because you know deep down something is missing. And it's a good indication that your emotional health may be under siege.

Well, if you want to change that, noted educator Larry Wilson, author of *Play to Win: Choosing Growth over Fear in Work and Life* (Austin, TX: Bard Press, 1998), said, "Finding your purpose is the most emotionally healing thing you can do." When you're living on purpose, instead of by hit and by miss, you feel like your life and career count for something. And your emotional health is stronger as a result.

The same can be said for your physical health. Study after study connects purpose and lower disease rates, as well as greater longevity.

For example, a study of twelve thousand middle-aged Hungarians found that those who felt their lives had meaning had much lower rates of cancer and heart disease than those who didn't feel this way. Dr. Harold G. Koenig, a professor of psychiatry at Duke University Medical Center, says, "People who feel their life is part of a larger plan and are guided by their spiritual values have stronger immune systems, lower blood pressure, a lower risk of heart attack and cancer, and heal faster and live longer."[5] And Dan Buettner studied the world's longest living people and concluded that having a purpose or "having a reason to get out of bed" was a common trait among those people who lived past the age of one hundred.[6]

> *Without a clearly defined purpose, your motivation goes down because you let the pressures of life beat you down.*

When you clarify your purpose and when you live and work on purpose, chances are you will see positive payoffs in your health.

Purpose Payoff #2: Greater Motivation

Whether you call it energy or motivation, almost everyone seems to want more of it. Indeed, many TV and Internet commercials are pitching some product that promises to do exactly that—give you more energy and motivation.

I can't speak for the efficacy of those products, but I do know that your level of energy and motivation is directly related to the pressures and priorities in your life and which of those two is stronger. And I know that *without a clearly defined purpose, your motivation goes down because you let the pressures of life beat you down.* Do you do that? Do you let the pressures of this world have the upper hand in your life and your work? If so, you'll notice several symptoms. They would include such things as

- **Relational stress:** You're not spending enough time with your partner or children. You know your work relationships could be stronger, but you don't have the time or the skills to improve those relationships.

- **Health issues:** You have some health issues that you know are connected to your crazy work schedule. Or you just don't seem to have enough energy anymore.

- **Time mismanagement:** You're willing to cancel some important personal time for a business issue of any kind. You lack time for yourself, time to read, relax, play, travel, or engage in a hobby. When you go out to dinner with your partner, you automatically answer any incoming phone call. You check your business voicemail when you're running errands over the weekend. And when you go on vacation you still stay in touch with the office.

- **Goal concerns:** You're not sure what your personal or professional goals are, and if you did know, you wouldn't know how to achieve them. You want to be engaged in meaningful work, in a growing career that you truly enjoy, but you're beginning to wonder if this is as far as you're ever going to go.

- **Attitude challenges:** You're feeling increased stress, and your work and life seem to be getting more out of balance with each passing year. You're struggling to keep a positive attitude going all the time. You don't know how to grow spiritually and get the peace of mind you've always wanted. And there are times you feel like jumping ship and moving to some fantasy island.

If one or more of these symptoms describe you, you don't have to stay put. This is simply an indication that you're off purpose. When you get a well-defined and worthy purpose, you increase your motivation because you change your focus from your pressures to your priorities.

There are a lot of pressures in life. If you're not careful, they can easily distract you. There are also a lot of good things in life. Again, if you're not careful, all those good things might divert your attention from the better things or more important things in life. Many people make that mistake and I used to.

For example, some people wear their long hours of hard work or workaholic syndrome as a badge of honor. They brag, "I go to bed at midnight, get up 4:00 a.m., and then head off to my sixty-hour work-week." They may even brag about being successful. They may announce, "Yeah, I got another promotion,"or "I'm making more money than ever before," or "... blah, blah, blah."

Well, I hope to goodness they're successful; all they do is work. As I tell my audiences, it would be very embarrassing to be an unsuccessful workaholic.

If any of that sounds like you, if you're living an overly busy, hurried and hectic life, you may be wasting your life. Oh sure, your calendar may be filled with "good" things, but those good things may be crowding out the "better" things—in particular, your purpose priorities.

I know. I fell into that trap. I used to tell people that I may not be the smartest guy around, but I was by far the hardest worker. No one could outwork me. During my undergraduate college years, I always took the heaviest load of credits the university would allow, and I studied twenty-five hours for every final exam in every class, starting my studies weeks before the exams were given. On top of that I held a part-time job as a shoe salesman to make some extra money. Later, studying for my PhD exams, I would be in the library from 7:00 a.m. to midnight, seven days a week, for months on end, studying the entire time.

Now those aren't necessarily bad things. One could even argue that those were all good things. But it took my focus almost entirely off my higher priorities, such as my health, my marriage, my daughter, and my God. It took a painful,

> *Your calendar may be filled with "good" things, but those good things may be crowding out the "better" things—in particular, your purpose priorities.*

debilitating illness that robbed me of my ability to walk, and it took the loss of several key relationships before I realized I was tragically off base. And when my friend for several decades, Brian Schmall, asked me how all that frenzied activity was working for me, my only response was tears. I realized I had lost my focus on the most important things.

The good news is, when you clarify your purpose and keep your purpose in the forefront of your mind, it becomes so much easier to focus on the things that are most important to you. And that is highly motivating.

I was reminded of that when I was speaking in Europe. One of my program attendees said he had recently visited his grandmother in Germany. The whole time he was there, she never sat down. She was constantly cleaning, cooking, and organizing. She had no time to relax. When he asked his grandmother why she kept up such a frantic pace, she said, "Life is short. There's no time to waste."

Another attendee chimed in and talked about vacationing in Spain. He said he so enjoyed watching a crew transplant a tree, a task that took them three days to complete. He said the crew would dig for a little while, take a breather, sip a little wine, go back to work, and repeat the cycle. When he asked them about the leisurely way in which they approached their work, they said, "Life is short. You've got to slow down and enjoy every moment of it."

Both examples may be extremes, but the one thing they both had in common is "life is short." So you need a purpose that keeps you focused on your priorities. When your purpose allows you to focus, you'll experience a stronger sense of motivation in your life and work.

In addition to that, when you get a well-defined and worthy purpose, you will get an instant and lasting surge of motivation because an effective purpose is compelling.

It makes you want to do something worthwhile. I learned that from my research on the Holocaust of World War II. I wondered how people made it through that horrible event in human history. So I visited such places as the concentration camp at Dachau and Yad Vashem, the memorial to the Jewish victims of the Holocaust in Jerusalem, and I read numerous books on the subject.

The book that really caught my attention was *Man's Search for Meaning* (Boston, MA: Beacon Press, 1959) by Dr. Viktor Frankl. As a young Jewish psychiatrist, he was shipped off to Auschwitz and later to other camps. There in the worst of conditions, with little food, inadequate shelter, and horrendous torture, thousands of Jewish prisoners were forced into excruciating labor that went on month after month.

What amazed Frankl was the fact that some of the laborers survived. While others, in the same conditions, did not. What Frankl found was that the ones who made it through those circumstances—and weren't sent to the gas chambers—had a compelling purpose. They had a purpose that said, "I will do whatever it takes to get out of this place, to find my wife, to find my kids, to reunite my family."

Frankl survived the war and lived into his nineties, writing and lecturing about the power of purpose. Frankl noted that Friedrich Nietzsche, the German philosopher (1844–1900), was right when he said, "He who has a 'why' to live for can bear almost any 'how.'"[7]

If you know your purpose, if you know "why" something is critically important to you, you can make it through almost anything. A compelling purpose gives you incredible motivation and endurance.

Purpose Payoff #3: Deeper Satisfaction

As I discussed earlier, when asked what they want out of life, most people say, "I just want to be happy." And when you dig deeper as to what happiness means to them, they'll rattle off such things as a bigger house, a nicer car, finer clothes, or more exotic vacations. Their definition of happiness is connected to *things* in some way. But that seldom, if ever, brings happiness. A healthy, inspiring purpose is seldom connected to the pursuit of things, fame, or fortune.

Take it from Kevin Anderson, the author of *Divinity in Disguise* (Monclova, OH: Center for Life Balance, 2003). He writes, "Money and possessions are like diet soda—they satisfy momentarily, but they do not nourish." Or take it from Jim Carrey, the movie star. He says, "I believe everyone should become rich and successful so they can see that is not the answer."

The same goes for almost any spiritual philosophy you want to consult. You'll find them saying that real happiness, or a deep sense of satisfaction, doesn't come from things, and it doesn't come with mere accomplishments. It comes from purpose.

You know your purpose is spot on when it pushes you toward activities that not only help others but also satisfy you. That's what the actor Kirk Douglas learned when he was eighty-six years old. After playing the strong, virile, tough guy in eighty-two films, he suffered a stroke, making him totally helpless for a while.

Then he found a new purpose, rebuilding school playgrounds that had become too old, dilapidated, or dangerous to use. He began raising money and even selling items from his personal art collection—including original paintings by Picasso and Van Gogh—to help schools with this project. He and his wife, Anne, went on to rebuild and appear at the reopening of hundreds of playgrounds[8] and, in the process, gained the satisfaction and meaning they were craving.

> Real happiness, or a deep sense of satisfaction, doesn't come from things, and it doesn't come with mere accomplishments. It comes from purpose.

It's what the world-famous psychiatrist Dr. Karl Menninger stressed throughout his life. After giving a lecture on mental health, an audience member asked him, "What would you advise a person to do if that person felt a nervous breakdown coming on?"

Most people expected him to say, "Consult a psychiatrist." To their amazement, he replied, "Lock up your house. Go across the railway tracks. Find someone in need, and do something to help that person."[9]

When you stop thinking about your problems and start thinking about how you could help someone else, you'll have a purpose that will give you the deep satisfaction you need.

If you're like me, all the stories, quotes, comments, experiences, and research studies in this chapter get me excited. I know, I absolutely know, that the power of purpose is the power that kicks *The Payoff Principle* into start mode. So let's move on to what you need to do to discover, capture, and clarify your purpose.

When you stop thinking about your problems and start thinking about how you could help someone else, you'll have a purpose that will give you the deep satisfaction you need.

CHAPTER 4

The Practice of Purpose

Clarify Your Purpose—and Then Live and Work *on* Purpose

A few years ago, one of my mentees, Floyd Holliday, asked me, "How and when did you know your life was going in the right direction?" And my floodgates opened and memory and emotion spilled out.

As I briefly mentioned before, in junior high school, I had decided that I was going into the ministry, which to me meant I would end up being a pastor in a church. I hadn't given it too much thought or sought any other alternatives. It was simply the foregone conclusion of what I thought God and everybody else expected of me. My grandmother even offered to pay all my educational expenses, because it was her dream to have a pastor in the family. The problem was, I wasn't sure it was my dream . . . or ever had been.

Nonetheless, I continued to prepare for my religious vocation as an undergraduate student by taking all the pre-theology classes: Greek, philosophy, and a host of other courses that did not excite me.

As my graduation from college came closer, I knew I didn't want to go to seminary, and I didn't want to become a pastor. It wasn't a matter of losing my faith; I just knew that I didn't want *that* particular job. And I had a dilemma. I was about to graduate and had no idea what I would do for a living. I had prepared myself for a job that I no longer wanted, somehow thinking that a *job* was my *purpose* in life.

To deal with my indecision, to give me time to think, to cover up my guilt, and to escape the seminary, I went on to get my master's and doctoral degrees, even though I had no particular desire to get those degrees and certainly no idea what I would do with those degrees once I got them. But I taught several undergraduate classes while I was pursuing my graduate education so I could pay for my tuition and expenses.

However, something strange happened. I discovered I loved teaching and I was good at it—very good, indeed. But I also felt guilty for tossing aside my "supposed" purpose or calling to the ministry.

After graduate school, and still confused about my purpose and career, I accepted a university teaching position in Kansas for four years to give me more time to think. It felt good when I was selected by the students as the Most Outstanding Professor on campus, but I still felt guilty for not pursuing the religious job I had announced so many years before. Indeed, my feeling of uneasiness continued to grow. I was stuck between what I thought I should be doing and what I wanted to do.

Fortunately, in the midst of the struggle, I attended a weekend workshop on the process of "intensive journaling" taught by Dr. Ira Progoff. He taught me how to relax, think, reflect, visualize, and keep a journal, so that the deeper things inside me might be revealed. It was a life-changing experience. I suddenly realized that there were many ways to serve my God and other people, not just one, like I had thought, in a church setting. So I wrote in my journal, "I *can* serve God and others as a teacher, speaker, and author." Almost instantly, my guilt disappeared, and a sense of peace, direction, and well-being settled over me. I knew I was living my life and working my career on purpose instead of by accident.

Too Many Years of Wasted Time and Guilt

For years I had confused a job with a purpose. My years of confusion were gone now. I finally learned that I could help others or do "ministry" in any job. So it only made sense to choose a job that I really,

Really, REALLY wanted to do *and* one for which I had some aptitude. And here I am, decades later, loving the work I do, feeling thankful that I've been able to touch the lives of thousands of people, because my life and work have lined up with my purpose.

> *The payoffs start to roll in when you know that your life and your work, someway, somehow, are lined up with your purpose.*

The lesson became so very clear to me and hopefully to you as well. The payoffs start to roll in when you know that your life and your work, someway, somehow, are lined up with your purpose—at least some of the time. So that raises a critical question.

How Can You Discover Your Purpose?

It all comes down to the three critical but deceptively simple questions (shown in Figure 4.1). The three legs represent the three questions that will help you discover, determine, or clarify your purpose, and the seat of the stool represents your purpose. In other words, the convergent answer to those three questions. Let's go through the three questions in some detail.

Figure 4.1. Three-Legged Stool

Question #1: What Are You Good At?

No matter who you are or what has happened in your life or career, you do have a lot of talents and abilities. You've got to know that. You may be gifted with numbers or work well with children. You may be good at organizing projects or good at leading others. It's very difficult, if not impossible, to claim and use your strengths if you don't even know what they are.

So search your talents. Ask yourself some talent-clarifying questions. Take time to reflect on and write down your answers to questions such as these:

- What are you already good at?

- What are your dominant gifts?

- What are you best at?

- What natural abilities do you possess?

- What do you do that gets a positive response from people
  you respect?

- What do you do that does not seem like work, regardless of
  the difficulty?

- What do you do that causes doors to open with ease for you?

You get the point. You have lots of things you're good at, whether or not you recognize those things. I want you to dig for those things and write out the longest list of talents you can possibly muster.

In the process of writing, find out what others see as your talents. Don't dismiss their comments. If they keep asking you to do something, it's because they see your talent in that area. Ask them how they would describe you and your talents. Ask them to list the special skills and attributes you bring to every situation and interaction.

I'll even give you an assignment. Ask ten people to list ten talents they see in you. With your list of one hundred items, determine which ones are repeated the most. Once you complete this exercise, you will be on your way to a clear picture of exactly what it is you're good at.

As you learn to clarify what you're good at, let me offer one caution. Do not dismiss any of your talents. Too many people say, "There's nothing special about me. I'm not particularly good at anything. I'm rather ordinary."

A while ago, my wife, Chris, and I were hiking with our friends Mike and Jan Saarela in Glacier National Park. As luck would have it, we found a cafe on the edge of the park that advertised "Good, Old-Fashioned, Home Cooking."

When we finished our meal, the waitress asked what she could get us for dessert. She said, "You really should try a piece of pie. My sister is the cook, and she bakes the best pies west of the Mississippi. In fact, we've got twenty-three different varieties."

So of course we had to try the pie. And it was the best pie we had had in years. So I asked the waitress, "How did your sister become so good at making pies?"

In a few minutes, she returned with her sister, who had the happiest smile I had ever seen. It was obvious she enjoyed her work and took great satisfaction when her cooking was appreciated.

"Experience," she replied. "It's all in knowing how much of each ingredient to put in and baking it for just the right length of time. My pa always said, 'When you learn to do something right, and enjoy doing it, stick with it.' I love baking. Always have. Sure, I've made a few losers. But never twice. When I make something good, that people like, I stick with it. Like my pies. I've been perfecting my pies for eighteen years now."

"Well your pies are so good," we told her, "that we'll take one with us." I really hate to admit this, but her pies were SO-O-O-O good that we stopped by her cafe to buy another pie every day for the next seven days. We wanted to try some of her other flavors—and we had no problem consuming an entire pie each day.

That baker was a winner in every sense of the word because she didn't dismiss her talents. She knew what she was good at and that contributed to her sense of purpose in life.

As consultant Faith Ralston says, "Focusing on talents is not a luxury. It's the key to thriving in today's economy. The old rules aren't working anymore. We can't wait around hoping others will recognize or reward us. To thrive, we've got to recognize our talents and connect them to business results."

That's the first question in your search for purpose—the first leg of our three-legged stool—*What are you good at?* Now we'll move on to the next question.

Question #2: What Excites You?

Take a look at how you're wired. What turns on your energy and what turns it off? Some activities and some causes make you feel alive while other things seem to kill off your spirit.

Tom Bloch discovered this when he resigned his position as the CEO of H&R Block, cofounded by his father Henry Bloch. He gave up running a $2 billion tax preparation firm to become a teacher at St. Francis Xavier Middle School in Kansas City, Missouri. His annual salary dropped to a mere $15,000 a year, a tiny fraction of what he had earned before. But Bloch knew that his hectic

> *What would you do if you knew you could not fail? What would you do if no one would say "no"?*

schedule as CEO had been interfering with his top priority—his wife and two children.

Tom said, "The hardest part was telling my father. But I didn't want to look back on my life and say, 'Gee, you had an opportunity to play a bigger role in your children's lives and didn't take it.'"[1]

What excites *you*? For some of you, that will be an easy question to answer. For others, it may be a challenging question to answer. So let me break that question into a series of smaller questions. I suspect one or more of these questions will unlock a whole series of insights as to what excites you.

What Are Your Dreams?

What did you dream of doing when you were a child? What were your dreams when you graduated from high school or college? What are your dreams today?

If you're not sure, just ask yourself two questions. One, "What would you do if you knew you could not fail?" And two, "What would you do if no one would say 'no'?" Your answers will clarify

> *If you don't stand for something, you will fall for anything.*

your dreams and help you realize what excites you.

Now I realize a dream can be a little scary. That's why so many people quash their dreams before they ever see the light of day. They squelch their dreams with worrisome thoughts such as, "How will I support myself?" "How do I know if this new idea will work?" "What will my spouse think?" or "How will my kids feel about this crazy dream of mine?" It's only natural to be a bit afraid of the unknown, when the future seems fuzzy and vague.

But take comfort in this thought. Once you get a dream, and once you master *The Payoff Principle*, you will have the **passion** and the **process** you need to get the **payoffs** you want.

What Stirs Your Passion?

What do you believe in? What makes life worth living? And what would you die for? You don't want to look back on your life and wish you had lived it differently. As I often tell my audiences, if you don't stand for something, you will fall for anything.

So ask yourself these passion questions. What makes you feel alive? And take time to think about these questions and write out your answers:

- What activities do you enjoy the most at work, at home, or in social situations?

- What are you passionate about?

- What do you love spending time on?

- What desires keep tugging at your heart?

- What is motivating you in the times you are most productive?

- What do you do that makes you feel good emotionally and spiritually?

Of course these passion questions may not sound very corporate. And much of my work is speaking to people in corporations. But don't be too hasty in dismissing these passion questions. When you get right down to it, any good empowerment program, emotional intelligence program, or customer service program boils down to passion . . . or caring about your people and making a positive difference in their lives. And leaders who inspire followership in others demonstrate their passion for the business and those who work in it. Once you've answered those questions, it's time for another.

What Troubles Your Spirit?

The things that upset you are a good clue to your purpose in life. So ask yourself,

- What grieves your heart?

- What infuriates you the most?

Your answers to these questions may point out a problem you want to solve. And that problem, or those problems, will point to your purpose, or a part of your purpose.

Such was the case with one little girl. She stood sobbing near a small church from which she had been turned away because she was told it was too crowded. "I can't go to Sunday school," she sobbed to the pastor as he walked by.

Seeing her shabby, unkempt appearance, the pastor guessed the reason and, taking her by the hand, took her inside and found a place for her in the Sunday school class. The child was so happy they had found room for her, and she went to bed that night thinking of the children who were left out because there was no room.

Some two years later, this child lay dead in one of the poor tenement buildings of her city. Her parents called for the pastor who had befriended their daughter to handle the final arrangements.

As her little body was being moved, a crumpled red purse was uncovered. Inside they found 57¢ and a note, scribbled in childish handwriting, which read: "This is to help build the little church bigger so more children can go to Sunday school." For two years she had saved her money.

The pastor tearfully read the note to his parishioners and challenged them to raise enough money for a larger building.

But the story does not end there. A newspaper learned of the story and published it. A wealthy realtor read the story and offered to sell the church a parcel of land, worth thousands of dollars, for 57¢. Checks came in from far and wide. Within five years the little girl's gift had increased to $250,000—a huge sum at that time, around the year 1900. The little girl's purpose had paid large dividends.

> Something to live on *is the* GOOD life, but having something to live for *is the* BETTER life.

When you are in the city of Philadelphia, look up Temple Baptist Church, with a seating capacity of 3,300. And be sure to visit Temple University, where thousands of students are educated. Have a look, too, at the Good Samaritan Hospital and at a Sunday school building that houses hundreds of children.

In one of the rooms you can see the picture of the little girl whose 57¢, whose purpose in life, made remarkable history.[2]

And as often happens, when you're driven by a purpose, it often ignites a purpose in others. But there's one more aspect to this question of what excites you.

What Work Do You Love to Do?

What pumps you up on a professional level? What would you really like to do? What do you like to talk about and think about professionally? As Jack Jia, founder of Trusper in 2012, an app for sharing and borrowing tips about daily life, says, "If you refuse to do something you believe in, your mind will never leave you alone."[3]

One of my audience members, Tom, talked about that. Even though he was a successful insurance salesman (which is a necessary and noble profession), Tom said he always wanted to be a doctor in a third-world country. But the sales profession promised to give him a great deal more money in a much quicker fashion than pursuing a medical career overseas. So he'd been selling insurance for thirty years.

Tom admitted that he had dragged himself out of bed, five days a week, for thirty years, to do something he didn't care that much about. If he had done what he really wanted to do, if he had become a doctor, he may have made less money, but he almost certainly would have been a happier and more successful human being.

That's why I teach people in my *Journey to the Extraordinary* program that having something to live *on* is the GOOD life, but having something to live *for* is the BETTER life. So ask yourself, "What would I choose to do—even if no one was paying me to do it?" Now you may automatically think of something like shopping, fishing, or golf. But they don't count. Most likely, no one has ever paid you to do any of those things.

So look deeper. Look at all the income-producing work you've done over the years. And ask yourself which parts of that work you liked the most. Then ask yourself, "What would I do if money wasn't an issue?"

In fact, you might try the money-makes-no-difference game. Imagine that every person on earth is paid $20 an hour for work regardless of the job he or she performs. If that were the case, what job would you choose to do? If you choose to be a tree cutter in the forest, you would be paid $20 an hour. If you decide to be a brain surgeon, you would still receive $20 an hour. What would you love to do if money was not involved?

Once you've figured out your answers to the first question (what you're good at) and the second question (what excites you), you've got to ask yourself the third critical question.

Question #3: What Difference Do You Want to Make?

The first two questions are focused on *you*—your talents and your feelings. But the third question focuses on people or situations outside of you.

Of course, we live in an age where we're told to "Go for the gusto" and "Get all you can." But is that the real bottom line in life? Is that what really counts?

When Richard Leider interviewed scores of people over the age of sixty-five, he asked them to share the most important lessons they had learned and what advice they would give younger people so they might have more fulfilling, successful lives. Without hesitation, they said you've got to live a life that matters to others, and you've got to make a contribution to others. Go out there and make a difference in your world, whatever that might be, with whomever that might include.[4]

When physician Raymond Moody interviewed scores of people who had died momentarily and were medically brought back to life and when he interviewed people who had lived through near-death experiences, he discovered the overwhelming necessity of making a difference. Even though his interview subjects had supposedly died or come close to it, every one of them said their minds or spirits were very much alive at that time. They kept thinking about the same issue over and over and over. They kept thinking about the difference they had made in this world and with other people. And they wondered whether they had made any difference at all.[5]

When they were brought back from the verge of death by some medical miracle, they all had the same, but new, bottom line—*making a difference*, making a contribution serving others to some extent, instead of being totally self-serving.

The good news is you don't have to wait until you die before you learn how to live. You don't have to wait for a crisis to happen before you wake up. You can get a purpose right now and start living your life on purpose from today forward.

That's what Troyal learned. Troyal went to Oklahoma State University on a javelin-throwing scholarship, but athletics did not feel like his real calling. So he asked himself a crucial question: "If God came to earth with a box containing the reason for my life inside of it, what words would I most like to find in that box?"

It didn't take long for Troyal to know that the box would contain the word "music." He could pick a little guitar; his voice wasn't too bad, and he had written some songs. So he set off for Nashville.

Troyal did not find instant success in Nashville. He returned to Oklahoma, but two years later he was back in Nashville working at a boot shop. One night he showed up for auditions at the Bluebird Cafe where a Columbia Records scout caught his act. The scout liked what he heard, offered a recording contract, and the rest is history.

Today this singer is known as Garth Brooks, the best-selling country artist of all time. According to PlanetGarth.com, he's sold more records than Michael Jackson or Madonna. But it all started with purpose. When Garth Brooks realized his purpose had something to do with music, when he realized the difference he wanted to make was to bring a bit more joy to the world through his music, happiness and success followed.

What about you? What difference do you want to make? Think about it. It's worth a few minutes of your time.

The difference you want to make may not be as big as rescuing the poor of Calcutta like Mother Teresa. The difference you want to make may not gather worldwide headlines like Dr. Martin Luther King Jr.'s "I Have a Dream" speech.

That's okay. The difference *you* want to make may be in your immediate family, your extended family, your religious organization or charity, your community, your company, or even some part of the world at large. But you must focus some part of your life on making a difference. Otherwise, you may have a good life, but you will never have a great life.

Bring All Three Answers Together

Ultimately, you've got to have all three answers. You have to discover what you're good at. You have to figure out what excites you. And you have to know what difference you want to make. In the *convergence* of those three answers you will find your purpose.

American author and cleric Frederick Buechner said your purpose or "Vocation is the place where your deep gladness and the world's deep hunger *meet*."[6]

And author and CEO Bob Buford writes, "If you look deeply enough inside of you and are honest about *combining* your competence with your passion, you will find the mission that is best suited to you."[7]

Notice my emphasis on the words convergence, meet, and combining. Your answers to the three questions I've just outlined will help you find and/or clarify your purpose.

Once you've figured out your answers, I strongly suggest you write out your purpose statement. In its simplest form, your purpose statement is nothing more than one or two sentences that state why you are here and what you intend to do about it. It's a sentence or two that you live by, and it guides every one of your thoughts, actions, and decisions. It's like the steering wheel of your car or the guidance system installed in a rocket. So it's a really big deal.

Now don't let that scare you. Your purpose statement should be short and clear. It's simple. You don't need a thesaurus to write it. And you don't need a dictionary to understand it. A useful purpose makes instant sense. You know exactly what it says and what it means.

It gets right to the point. Take, for example, the purpose statements for several of my clients. 3M says: "Our purpose is to solve unsolved problems innovatively." Merck says: "Our purpose is to preserve and improve human life." And Sony says: "Our purpose is to experience the joy of advancing and applying technology for the benefit of the public."

Their purpose statements tell you exactly why they are in business and what they plan to do. In fact, their purpose statements are so simple that any one of their thousands of employees could easily memorize and state their purpose, but, more important, they can do a quick "gut check" on whether the work they are doing is consistent with that purpose.

The success of Coca-Cola was due in large part to the purpose statement outlined by Robert Woodruff. As the president from 1923 to 1955, he boldly declared during World War II, "We will see that every person in uniform gets a bottle of Coca-Cola for five cents, wherever he is, and whatever it costs."[8]

After the war, he changed his purpose statement to read, "I want everyone in the world to taste Coca-Cola in my lifetime."

Still not sure what your purpose is or how to write it? Then try this. Write out a sentence that is structured like this.

- **"My purpose in life is to** _____ (insert an action verb . . . to do what?)

- **people who** _____ (specify the types of people to whom your purpose applies)

- **to** _____." (specify the difference you want to make in their lives)

One of the people who attended my *Journey to the Extraordinary* program, thirty-one-year-old Sheila Montgomery, wrote: "My purpose in life is to be a mom that helps her children become confident, self-reliant, effective individuals, partly by being a positive, supportive role model." And ninety-two-year-old Margaret Pederson wrote: "My purpose is to bring interracial harmony to my city through music."

Of course, you may have more than one purpose statement. You might have one for your personal life and one for your professional life. No problem. While my personal purpose statement incorporates my family, faith, and community, my professional purpose statement says, "My purpose in life is to give my clients all the skills they need to achieve all the happiness and success they want—on and off the job."

Once you've got your purpose statement or statements written out, congratulations! You're ahead of almost everybody else on this planet. You've got *The Payoff Principle* off the ground and starting to work for you.

But there's one final issue we need to address. Some people do all the work to figure out a healthy, effective, and motivating purpose for themselves, but then they get off track. They live a life or perform work that is not in sync with their purpose. So how can you make sure you live your life and perform your work *on* purpose?

Purpose Practice #1: Listen to the Right People

Everybody has opinions. But just because somebody has opinions does not mean you should pay attention to them.

As entrepreneurial expert Dan S. Kennedy says, "The reason a lot of people never get ahead is they keep soliciting and paying attention to the opinions of the ignorant." He's so right.

Your brother, for example, may be a wonderful man, a good husband and father, and a great gardener, but that narrows the range of his opinions you ought to pay attention to—marriage, parenting, and gardening. That leaves out business growth, team building, and leadership development.

If you want to know how to fix your car, I'm the wrong guy to ask for advice. And I'm the wrong guy to take advice from . . . if I offer it. I hardly know the difference between a fan belt and a seat belt.

If you want to know how to build a positive attitude in yourself or your organization, or if you want to know how to motivate your team in times of change, I'm a great guy to get advice from. I've helped thousands of people do exactly that.

> "They have a constitutional right to their ignorant opinions, but you have an entrepreneurial responsibility to ignore them."
> —Dan S. Kennedy

People are quick to dispense advice on any subject, regardless of their qualifications to do so. It makes them feel important. They rarely give any thought to their qualifications. They just spout out their opinions. They don't even distinguish between their opinions and true knowledge. That's why you must make sure you are listening to the right people.

As an author and professional speaker, I often help my clients create strategies that will make them more positive, productive, and profitable. But then those same clients are assaulted with ignorant opinion providers. Their spouse, their coworker, or another department will gang up on them and harshly criticize the strategies we have created. They'll say, "That would never work," "It costs too much," or "I just don't like the idea."

Unfortunately, none of those opinion givers has any real knowledge or expertise in personal and professional development. None of them has spent thirty years of time and research on the topic like I have. As Dan S. Kennedy would say, "They have a constitutional right to their ignorant opinions, but you have an entrepreneurial responsibility to ignore them."

To stay on purpose, choose wisely the people to whom you will listen. And choose to ignore the negative opinions of the uninformed naysayers.

Purpose Practice #2: Start Your Day with a Six-Pack

We all have a million things we could put on our to-do lists. That's never a problem. The problem is how you spend your time on a daily basis. If you spend your time reacting or overreacting to things as they pop up, you've got a problem. If you allow distractions and interruptions to steal your focus, you've got a problem. And if you end up wondering where the day went or wondering why you never get anything done, you've got a problem. In every one of those cases, most of your day was spent off purpose.

To get away from those problems, get a six-pack. Identify the six most important things—or the six highest-value items—on your possible to-do list, and focus on those six things for the day. Make sure that at least three or more of them have something to do with your purpose.

Forget about those to-do lists that are longer than your arm. Remember, there are only twenty-four hours in a day. You can't get it all done, so focus on your six-pack.

Efficiency expert Ivy Ledbetter Lee (1877–1934) understood this when he pitched his consulting services to a steel mill that was struggling with profitability and survivability. He told the company's stone-faced president,

Charles Schwab (1862–1939), "If you allow me the chance to help, I'll teach you and your executives to manage better. You'll know how . . ."

Schwab cut him off. "Look, Mr. Lee, I'm sure your services are great, but we don't need them. We don't need any more 'knowing' around here. I don't manage as well as I know how to now." He shook his head. "We already know what we should be doing. If you can show us a way to get it done better, I'll pay you anything you want."

Lee stepped toward the president's desk. "What if I could give you something in the next twenty minutes that would raise your efficiency by 50 percent?" Schwab raised an eyebrow and tilted his head slightly. "Go on."

Lee rifled through his briefcase for a moment, pulled out a small blank piece of paper and slid it toward Schwab. Schwab looked slightly confused. He glanced up at Lee and then stared at the paper. Lee asked, "Do you see this paper?" Through a furrowed brow, Schwab looked up again. "Of course."

"Take that paper and write down the six most important things you need to do tomorrow." Schwab thought for a couple of minutes and scribbled down six items. After he finished, he tossed his pen back onto the desk. "Now what?"

Lee folded his arms and looked down at the paper. "Now number them in order of importance." Schwab reached across the desk to grab the pen he had just flung. It only took a moment to put them in order. This time he laid the pen on top of the list. He gave a nod. "There."

Lee smiled. "Now, tomorrow when you get to work, I want you to work on the first item until it is done. Distractions will arise. Ignore them. Work on number one until it is done. Then move on to number two, then when that's all finished, number three, and so on. At the end of every day, make a new list. Don't worry about the things that don't get done. You will know you have been doing the most good possible for your company, and if you can't get all items done using this method, you couldn't get them done using any other system either. Once you've had time to prove to yourself the value of this, have your people try it out as well. In fact, try it out as long as you like. Then, you send me a check for whatever you think it is worth."

The steel mill president stood up and extended a hand, but he looked lost in thought. Several weeks later, Lee received a letter in which Schwab informed him that his "list of six most important things" idea was the most profitable thing, from a money standpoint, that he had ever learned. Enclosed in the letter was a check for $25,000.[9]

How much will it be worth to you to stay on purpose?

Purpose Practice #3: Keep Your Six-Pack Visible

You know the old slogan "Out of sight, out of mind." It's so true when it comes to living your life on purpose. If you don't keep your six-pack clearly in view, you'll be tempted to work on other things and never get to your six-pack. You've got to keep your purpose in the forefront of your mind.

Try Jim Meisenheimer's method. He's one of the most effective sales trainers and time managers I've ever come across. When I visited his office, I noticed a 2-foot by 3-foot whiteboard mounted on an easel directly across from his desk. On the board, prominently displayed, were his six purpose-driven priorities for the day. It's no wonder he gets so much done; his purpose and his goal-related activities are staring him in the face all day long. And the same thing should be said about your purpose and supporting goals.

Purpose Practice #4: Pause and Reflect

Even though people are constantly complaining about the lack of peace and quiet in their lives, they indiscriminately give away what little peace and quiet they still have left. They give away their cell phone numbers to just about any Tom, Dick, and Harry "just in case you need to get a hold of me" or to every customer "should you have any questions." Even though Meisenheimer is in sales, he says that's crazy. "You may as well go to a tattoo parlor and get 24/7 printed on your forehead when you give everybody your cell number."

Even if you have your written purpose within eyesight much of the day, you're still going to be tempted to stray off task. You're going to be confronted with dozens of supposedly urgent crises that need to be handled immediately.

When that happens, pause. Catch your breath. Call time out. Disconnect from the frenzy. Don't allow yourself to be caught in the riptide. Stop running and take time to pause and reflect on your purpose. Clarify what's really important.

When you take a moment to look at your current pressures in light of your lasting purpose, you'll be able to choose the wisest course of action. You'll be able to focus on the vital few instead of the trivial many.

Purpose Practice #5: Engage in Purpose-Fulfilling Activity Every Day

I learned that lesson years ago. For years, I kept saying my kids were important to me. They were a part of my purpose in life. That was my *talk*.

But my *walk* was quite different. I was out speaking to groups, all the time, across the world and was seldom home. I missed most of my kids' events. But I rationalized my behavior. I was important, I was in demand, I had to work to pay the bills, and I had a professional purpose that overshadowed—or should I say, "blotted out"—any personal purpose I claimed to have.

> There is simply no way you can have self-esteem, integrity, or peace of mind if you profess one set of values but live another.

But there came a time when I realized I could no longer say one thing and do another and feel good about myself. I could no longer say my kids were important to me and continue to miss out on so much of their lives. If I was going to be a man who lived his life on purpose, a man who walked his talk, if I was going to be a man of integrity, I would have to cut back on my travel schedule so I could spend more time with my kids. And I did.

So I ask you, "Are there any gaps between your

talk and your walk? And do you need to make any changes in your life or in your career to close those gaps?"

There is simply no way you can have self-esteem, integrity, or peace of mind if you profess one set of values but live another. And there is simply no way you can be at your best and produce your best if you're not living your life *on* purpose and engaging in some purpose-fulfilling activity *every day*.

If you're going to be a producer, you've got to have a purpose, and you've got to take action on your purpose.

After attending one of my seminars, Jill Weston, who works at the world's most renowned medical clinic, did exactly that. She got a purpose of creating a more positive family environment and went to work on it. She wrote me the following note:

> There was such a spirit of negativity and ungratefulness in my home that I knew I had to do something different or else die trying. I decided to start a journal with my children. *Each night* I asked each one of my kids to spend two minutes with me and fill out a piece of paper that had a few questions on it. I asked them to list: (1) at least one thing they were good at or liked doing, (2) one thing that they did to help someone else that day, (3) how it made them or the other person feel when they gave the help, and (4) one thing they were grateful for. I also asked them to pick a family member and jot down one strength or one good thing about that person.

Notice how Weston not only defined her purpose but she worked on her purpose every day. It was a critical part of the success she experienced. As Weston put it,

> It was amazing what happened. After a few weeks, all of us were seeing opportunities to help others that

we hadn't seen before. Helping others blessed others, brightened our day, and made us feel good. Self-esteem skyrocketed because my children were seeing and affirming the goodness in themselves and others. The contention in our home lessened, and we had more peace and happiness in our home and in our lives. Of course, my children found it hard at first to even admit that their siblings possessed any good qualities, but each one of my children has asked me to revisit the answers and tell them the good things their brothers or sisters have said about them. They loved it, even though they didn't want to participate at first.

In a sense, the Weston family learned what author Johnetta B. Cole taught. In her words, "While it is true that without a vision the people perish, it is doubly true that without action the people and their vision perish as well."[10]

With Your Purpose in Place . . .

Purpose is where the payoff starts. Indeed, classic author Joseph Addison (1672–1719) wrote, "There are three grand essentials to happiness in this life." They are "something to do, something to love, and something to hope for."[11] These sound somewhat like my three questions for clarifying your purpose, don't they? When you clearly answer those three questions, your life and work begin to have meaning and purpose.

To get your purpose off your paper and working for you, it's time to unleash the second element of *The Payoff Principle*. It's time to apply passion to your purpose.

PART II

PASSION

CHAPTER 5

The Power of Passion

Where the Payoff Gets Fired Up

Purpose is the first ingredient in *The Payoff Principle*. And it is, without question, critically important. But purpose is only the first ingredient. In and of itself, it will never bring you the payoffs you want, need, crave, and desire. You also need the power of **passion** working for you.

John Mahoney learned that. He had a purpose—helping others with the English language. But somewhere along the way he lost his passion. "When I was thirty-seven," Mahoney recalls, "I had gone through a career as an English teacher and a medical editor. But I was very dissatisfied with my life. So I thought, 'What did I ever do that brought me real joy?' Immediately I knew the answer. It was when I was acting. I thought, 'I've got to give it a try so at least I can say that I tried.'"[1]

He did. He reclaimed his passion, and it was at that point that Mahoney began a successful stage and film career as an actor. And chances are you know him for his portrayal of the father in the hit sitcom *Frasier*.

The power of passion! Sounds kind of sexy, doesn't it? It conjures up images of zeal, fervor, spirit, energy, romance, and excitement. It makes you think of a person who is all fired up. And it's true; passion has all those emotionally intelligent nuances.

But passion is so much more than that. Passion is not some nice-to-have soft skill without any bottom-line significance. Early in his career, author and consultant Price Pritchett had a mentor who was a very skilled management psychologist. Time and again, Pritchett heard him say, "In my opinion, the single most important factor for success in the business world is a high energy level."

From the mentor's point of view, energy—or passion, as I'm calling it,—contributed more to career success than intelligence, personality, advanced degrees, social skills, or any other factor. And after twenty-five years of consulting, Pritchett now says, "I can't guarantee that energy level is absolutely the single most important factor for career success. But I have become convinced it belongs in that small handful of most critical factors."[2]

> There's little need to know what your purpose is if you don't have the energy to do anything about it.

Business adviser and author Mark C. Thompson concurs. After he interviewed dozens of corporate and government leaders around the world, Thompson concluded there's one distinguishing characteristic of successful leaders everywhere. He said, "It is passion that makes the difference. Being passionate about work transforms the best in us."

In fact, I consider my passion or energy level to be one of the secrets to my success. Anyone who knows me will comment on my energy level. I am filled with it almost all the time. I seldom sleep more than four or five hours a night, seldom get tired, never get jet lag, and work or play from early morning to late at night. I pack a lot into every day, and I live life to the fullest. It's the power of passion working in me.

And yet, I realize that lots of people do not have the passion or energy they need for greater success at work or at home. Maybe you're one of them. Maybe you're wondering, "What exactly goes into this passion thing? How do you get all fired up and keep that fire going?" That's what "Passion," or part II of *The Payoff Principle*, is all about. There's little need to know what your purpose is, the material I discussed in part I, "Purpose," if you don't have the energy to do anything about it.

I've learned that good, healthy, lasting, abundant, and effective passion has three components. Let me give you a brief overview before we dig into the upcoming chapters.

Three Components of Fired-Up Passion

For a fire to burn—and produce meaningful payoffs—it needs *fuel*, something like wood, oil, or coal. It needs *oxygen* or it gets choked out. And it needs *guidance,* something like a fire ring or a fireplace, or it can easily do damage (see Figure 5.1).

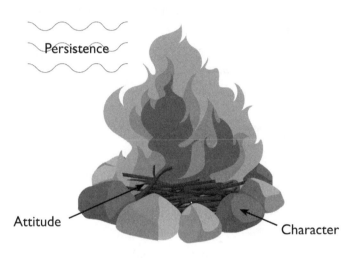

Figure 5.1. Three Fired-Up Passion Components

Attitude, the Fuel

The first one is *attitude*, which is similar to the fuel needed by a fire. Written some five thousand years ago, Proverbs 26:20 says, "Fire goes out for the lack of fuel."[3] And passion goes away without attitude.

The more attitude you have—positive attitude, that is—the longer your fire will burn. Elizabeth Edwards spoke eloquently about this. Despite the fact that she was the wife of a presidential candidate, despite the fact that her husband betrayed her with a lover and a secret love

> For passion to work, for a fire to burn, and produce meaningful payoffs, it needs fuel, oxygen, and guidance.

child, and despite the fact that she was battling cancer, she said, "A positive attitude is not going to save you. What it's going to do is, every day, between now and the day you die, [is a guarantee] that every day you're going to actually live."[4]

Entrepreneur Rachel Elnaugh added a business twist to Edwards' comment. Elnaugh said, "I would say that success is much more about a state of mind and an attitude than any sort of business skill. It's about keeping positive."

Persistence, the Oxygen

The second component of passion is *persistence*, which is like the oxygen needed by a fire to keep on burning. Unfortunately, too many people let their fires get choked off. You hear it in their words when they say, "If only I would have . . ." "I wish I had . . ." "I should have . . ." and "Why didn't I . . . ?"

Persistence is absolutely essential if you're going to get the payoffs you want. As President Calvin Coolidge noted, "Nothing in the world can take the place of persistence. Talent will not; nothing is more common than unsuccessful men with talent. Genius will not; unrewarded genius is almost a proverb. Education will not; the world is full of educated derelicts. Persistence and determination alone are omnipotent."[5]

He couldn't have been more correct. When you read about persistence in an upcoming chapter, you'll learn exactly what you have to do to keep on keeping on whether you feel like it or not.

Now this is where almost every success, self-help, business, and motivation book stops. They try to get you fired up with attitude and persistence and leave it at that. But that's dangerous. As I tell my audiences, "If you motivate an idiot, all you get is a motivated idiot." And our society already has too many gruesome, exasperating examples of that.

To make sure your fired-up passion works for you instead of against you, to make sure your fire doesn't make you act like some motivated idiot, you need to guide your fire. As you know, if you don't guide a fire, it can consume a home, a business, a neighborhood, a relationship, and everyone inside.

Character, the Fire Ring

I refer to that needed guidance as *character*. And character is the third component of passion, serving as a fire ring to make sure your fire burns smart. Unfortunately, I had to learn about character in an embarrassing way. I had lots of attitude and lots of persistence, but I didn't always have the character I needed to guide the use of my passion.

For example, I never played sports in high school. I could tell you that I had no interest in sports, which was partially true, because I was much more interested in debate, theatre, radio, television, and competitive speaking. But the deeper truth was, even if I did have an interest, I would never have been chosen to be on one of the teams. I was too fat, slow, and awkward.

However, I was selected to announce the basketball games at my high school for three years. I knew something about the game, rather enjoyed it, and was able to use my speaking talents. I felt pretty good about myself. I figured if I couldn't be "on the court," I could at least be "on the air." It gave me a bit of recognition and a bit of a big head. But it didn't take too long to realize that my big-headed passion was missing the guiding element of character.

When I entered college, I was immediately asked to be the sports announcer for my university football team. My reaction was, "Yeah. Wow. A bigger crowd, a bigger arena, more recognition, and more prestige." I had passion, to be sure, but I was also a motivated idiot.

It wasn't until after I accepted the job as the football announcer that I realized I knew nothing about football. Absolutely nothing! I didn't know any of the rules, moves, plays, or anything else.

As the first football game approached, the game I was to announce, panic set in. How could I possibly announce the game? So I asked my brother David, who played football throughout his high school years, to come to the game with me. Together we sat high above the stadium, where the sports announcers sit, and my brother would tell me what was happening in the game. He literally told me what to say, and I repeated it over the PA system and the radio. I don't know how many people in the stands noticed the delay between what was happening in the game and my comments on it. But I knew my performance was lackluster at best, and I knew the people deserved better. I resigned the announcer's job after the first game.

Sure, I had two of the three components of passion. I had a positive attitude toward the job, and I had the persistence to pursue the job. But I lacked the character component to guide that passion and tell me that I wasn't the best person for the job. I needed all three components, and so do you.

CHAPTER 6

The Attitude of Passion

Attitude: The Fuel Supply for Your Fire

Little Jason loved his Grandpa Ernie, but he also loved to play tricks on people. So when Grandpa sat down for a nap after lunch, Jason put some stinky Limburger cheese on Grandpa's large handlebar mustache.

When Grandpa woke up an hour later, he started sniffing in bewilderment. He walked around the bedroom sniffing, and then he said, "This bedroom stinks."

He went to the kitchen, sat down for a cup of coffee, and started sniffing once again. He said, "This kitchen stinks too!" In fact, it stunk so much that he went outside to get some fresh air. As he took a deep breath, he hollered, "The whole world stinks!"

Well, you and I both know some people who have Limburger cheese spread across their attitudes. It doesn't matter what they do, who they see, or where they are, everything smells bad to them. And the payoffs they get, or you get, with a negative, Limburger-cheese attitude will be minimal.

However, when you have a positive attitude as the fuel for your fire and passion, your payoffs are huge. For example, in the early 1900s, one of the pioneers of modern-day psychology Dr. William James (Harvard University even named a building after him) proclaimed, "It is our attitude at the beginning of a difficult task which, *more than anything else*, will affect its successful outcome."[1]

Around that same time, French literary theorist Tom Blandi wrote, "Our attitudes *control* our lives. Attitudes are a secret power working twenty-four hours a day, for good or bad. It is of paramount importance that we know how to harness and control this great force."[2]

And the most recent research from Jon Gordon, the author/speaker, goes a step further. He writes, "The research is clear. It *really does pay* to be positive . . . Being positive is not just a nice way to live. It's *the* way to live."[3]

To be precise, the **attitude** of passion is vitally important. And if you have it, or build it, you can expect two major payoffs.

Attitude Payoff #1: You *Attract* Significantly Better Personal Results

Notice the emphasis on the word "attract" in this heading. As the father of positive thinking, Dr. Norman Vincent Peale (1898–1993), declared, "There is a basic law that like attracts like. Negative thinking definitely attracts negative results. Conversely, if a person habitually thinks optimistically and hopefully, his positive thinking sets in motion creative forces, and success . . . instead of eluding him . . . flows toward him." In plain terms, good attitudes attract good results and bad attitudes attract bad results. It's that simple.

To be precise, *you* attract more opportunities. That's partly because a good attitude helps you *see* opportunities you would have missed with a more negative attitude. Earl Nightingale, the twentieth century's foremost authority on success, said, "A great attitude does much more than turn on the lights in our worlds. It seems to magically connect us to all sorts of serendipitous opportunities that were somehow absent before we changed."[4] A positive attitude opens your eyes and fuels your energies.

> A positive attitude opens your eyes to opportunities you wouldn't have seen otherwise.

For example, the person with a negative attitude thinks, "It's never been done before." A producer with a positive attitude sees an opportunity and says, "We have the chance to be first." The negative thinker says, "It's good enough," while the positive producer sees it differently and says, "There's always room for improvement." As a result, a producer attracts opportunities or better personal results.

Just as important, with a positive attitude firing you up, you attract better health. Remember earlier in the book when I talked about the connection between purpose and better health? A similar research-proven connection exists between your attitude and your health.

For example, Dr. Daniel Goleman reported on a study that compared pessimistic and optimistic men who had heart attacks. In the first group, twenty-one of the twenty-five most pessimistic died within eight years of a heart attack. Only six of the twenty-five most optimistic men died in that time.[5] That's a *big* and positive difference.

A while ago, one of my customers, a manager from The Boeing Company, wrote me about his daughter who had made some very poor, self-destructive choices during her late teen years, resulting in the birth of a premature baby, preeclampsia, the HELLP syndrome, and the complete shutdown of her liver and kidneys. She was on life support and hospitalized for eighty days while the doctors told everyone to prepare for her death. Nonetheless, his daughter defied all odds and was released to the care of her parents for her long road to recovery.

To help pass the time, his work colleague gave her a copy of my book, *PIVOT: How One Turn in Attitude Can Lead to Success* (Peak Performance Publications, 2006). To the father's amazement, she read the book three times, even though she had never read an entire book in her life! The father finished his note by saying, "My daughter continues to remain strong and positive and has turned this experience into something that has transformed her life. She is now a successful and focused college student . . . and a loving, wonderful mother to her healthy, happy three-year-old daughter. Your book on attitude was a huge part of her inspiration."

It's obvious. With the attitude of passion working for you, you attract significantly better

> With the attitude of passion working for you, you attract significantly better personal results.

personal results. But . . . attitude can also have a major impact in your professional life.

Attitude Payoff #2: You *Create* Significantly Better Professional Results

This time, note the emphasis on the word "create." There are numerous studies indicating that positive leaders and positive team members behave in ways in which they create . . . or receive . . . more pay raises and more promotions than those with a negative attitude. With a positive attitude firing up your passion, you tend to create a higher level of income.

In one particularly fascinating study, Dr. Martin Seligman reported on 1,500 people. Group A (or 83 percent of the people) chose their jobs because they believed they could make a lot of money. Group B (only 17 percent) chose their jobs because they had a positive attitude toward the job.

Twenty years later, Seligman noted the two groups had produced 101 millionaires. But only one millionaire came from group A (people who chose a particular job to make a lot of money). The other one hundred millionaires came from group B (people who chose their jobs because of a positive attitude toward the job). Attitude had made a huge difference in their eventual incomes.

Speaking more broadly, Seligman even noted that salespeople fueled by a positive attitude sell more, and make more money, than pessimistic salespeople. Well, of course. Who wants to buy anything from a grouch? And that only makes sense because positive attitudes lead to positive behaviors, which lead to more productive work relationships.

To be specific, when you're fired up with a positive attitude, you tend to notice the good in other people and you tend to comment on those things, frequently. As Dr. Ken Blanchard wrote in his book, *The One Minute Manager* (New York: William Morrow, 1982), it's not enough to say that you're fair and balanced, that you try to balance out your praise and criticism. "In a corporate study where criticizing and praising were actually tabulated and the reactions measured, where there was one criticism for each praising, people felt as though they had a totally negative relationship with the boss. When the ratio was changed to two praisings for each reprimand, people still thought their boss was all over them. It wasn't until they got to four praisings for each criticism that people began to feel as though they had a good relationship with their boss."[6]

It's clear that if you don't start giving a lot of praise, the people you work around will be gin to think of you as negative and unfair. But if you are fueled by a positive attitude, you will naturally give out more praise— honest, appropriate, and motivating praise. And almost without exception, that will build a more positive work environment filled with more effective, cooperative work relationships. The information I've shared so far in this chapter is important—very important. But let's get personal.

> *If you are fueled by a positive attitude, you naturally give out more honest, appropriate, and motivating praise.*

A Checkup from the Neck Up

Take a look at your attitudes to see how well they are serving you. Are you more positive or more negative? There are a few ways you can get an answer to that question.

Survey Some People Who Know You

Ask ten of your closest friends and family members if they would rate you as "more positive" or "more negative." Ask the same question of another ten people at work. If you get more than six of the twenty people saying you're "more negative," it's time for you to fuel up your attitude. You're too negative.

Check Out Your First Reaction to Any Bit of News You Get

If, for example, you get an email from your boss that says, "See me immediately," what is your first reaction? Is your first reaction, "Great, the raise is coming early this year"? Or is your first reaction, "What did I do wrong this time?" Eighty-five percent of people expect the negative and, therefore, are more negatively programmed.

Observe Your Daily Comments

See if you can go twenty-four hours without uttering one single negative comment. That's right; see if you can go twenty-four hours without making any negative remarks about the weather, your workload, a particular customer, a family member, an item in the news, or anything else.

> If you can't go twenty-four hours without complaining about something, worrying about someone, griping about something, or putting someone down, you're addicted to the negative.

You may be addicted to negative thinking and negative talking without even knowing about it. If, for example, you can't go twenty-four hours without a cigarette, you're addicted to nicotine. If you can't go twenty-four hours without an alcoholic drink, you're addicted to alcohol. And the same principle applies to your communication. If you can't go twenty-four hours without complaining about something, worrying about someone, griping about something, or putting someone down, you're addicted to the negative. You need to fire up your attitude.

See How You Stack Up Against a Checklist

People with a positive attitude, or people who are overall positive in thought, word, and deed, exhibit some fairly consistent behavior patterns. Inspired by author Craig Jarrow,[7] I developed the following checklist. Go ahead and circle each item that describes you, most of the time:

- Smiling and laughing frequently

- Being happy even when you have little to be happy about

- Being happy for someone else's success

- Giving more than you expect to get in return

- Having a good time even when you are losing

- Not getting what you want and not pitching a fit

- Always having an uplifting word to share with others

- Refusing to let other people's negativity bring you down

- Getting back up no matter how many times you fall down

- Understanding that people are more important than things

- Refusing to complain, no matter how unfair things appear to be

- Expecting good things to happen, even if your present situation is difficult

If you circled seven or more of these behaviors, you tend to fall on the positive side.

You Can Change Your Attitude

For a long time, one of my pet peeves was hearing people say, "I can't help the way I feel . . ." "That's just the way I am . . ." "I've always been that way . . ." or "I can't change." I thought they were wasting their lives. They were missing out on so many of the good things in life because they were saddled with a negative, self-limiting attitude.

Well, I no longer feel peeved by those people. I'm actually saddened

I'm here to tell you that you absolutely can change your attitude.

by their comments. I now realize they're simply ignorant. They don't know *how* to change their attitude. I'm here to tell you that you absolutely *can* change your attitude.

Of course, some people joke about that, like journalist David Frost. As he was describing a person he had interviewed, Frost noted, "He's turned his life around. He used to be depressed and miserable. Now he's miserable and depressed."[8]

You don't have to be miserable and depressed. You don't have to gripe and groan. You can be positive and victorious . . . no matter what your circumstances are.

Take your job, for example. You may be upset or disappointed about changes in your organization. You can concentrate on what's going wrong and become preoccupied with the things that are aggravating or upsetting you. But how long are you going to let those feelings go on? One week? One month? One year? Ten years?

It's up to you. You can change your attitude. In that same frustrating job situation, you could *choose* to put your energy into making things better. You could choose to be positive, optimistic, and enthusiastic in your attitude.

But you may ask, "Dr. Zimmerman, how can I possibly *change* my attitude when things at work or at home are so bad?" I just gave you a hint in the last paragraph. It's found in the word "choose." You control your attitude by *choosing* the attitude that will serve you best.

I learned that lesson years ago during a catastrophic weekend when I got a call I never expected and never wanted. My father phoned, sobbing uncontrollably, to say that he had found his wife's (my mother's) body. She had ended her life. I was twenty-nine, with a beautiful wife and daughter, and a career that was going like gangbusters. But all of that was about to change.

Shortly after the funeral, my wife announced that she was leaving me. My first reactions included anger and disbelief. I began to think, "How could anyone give such horrific news at a time like this? How could anyone be so tacky or so inappropriate?"

My negative attitude wanted to blame her for her calloused announcement and a host of other "things she had done wrong" . . . which was just as inappropriate and ineffective as some of my behaviors. I had to admit that in almost every divorce situation . . . including mine . . . there's always plenty of blame on each side.

I'll never forget sitting in my empty house a few days later—my wife and daughter had already left—and making a decision that would change my life forever. Instead of focusing on how wrong it was for my wife to leave me during the most difficult time in my life, instead of focusing on how bad my situation was, I literally decided this was a good thing that was happening. It would have been far worse if my wife had pretended she still cared about me and continued to pretend for the next several months. It would have been far worse if she told me she was leaving me after I had had a few months to heal from my mother's death. I would have had to go through the entire grieving process again.

> I decided to be thankful for the truth so I could deal with it, learn from it, and move on.

So I made a conscious choice at that very moment to change my attitude. I knew my mom's death and my wife's departure had the potential of making me better or bitter, and I was determined to become better. I decided that if I had to go through lots of pain sooner or later, then sooner was better than later. I decided to be thankful for the truth so I could deal with it, learn from it, and move on.

No matter what your situation is—personally or professionally—I absolutely know that you *can* change your attitude, and that will change the payoffs you get. Here are seven ways you can do that.

Attitude Practice #1: Decide to Have a Positive Attitude

That was the secret of my healing during the worst episode of my life. And that was how one ninety-year-old man learned to live a new life after his wife of seventy years passed away and he was forced to move to a nursing home. Even though he had to wait several hours in the lobby of the nursing home, he smiled sweetly when he was told his new room was ready.

As he maneuvered his walker to the elevator, the nursing assistant provided a visual description of his tiny room, including the eyelet curtains that had been hung on his window. "I love it," he stated with the enthusiasm of an eight-year-old having just been presented with a new puppy.

"Mr. Jones, you haven't seen the room; just wait," urged the nursing assistant. "That doesn't have anything to do with it," he replied. "Happiness is something you decide on ahead of time. Whether I like my room or not doesn't depend on how the furniture is arranged, it's how I arrange my mind. I already decided to love it."

Mr. Jones continued, "It's a decision you need to make every morning when you wake up. You have a choice; you can spend the day recounting the difficulty you have with the parts of your body, your life, or your job that no longer work, or you can get out of bed and be thankful for the ones that do."[9]

Our very first first lady, Martha Washington (1731–1802), said the same thing. She said, "I am still determined to be cheerful and happy, in whatever situation I may be, for I have also learned from experience that the greater part of our happiness or misery depends upon our dispositions, and not upon our circumstances."[10]

As silly as it sounds, the only time you're going to have a good day is when you decide to have a good day. Happiness is an inside job. It starts in your head . . . with the attitude you decide to have.

Unfortunately, negative people think happiness comes from the outside. They think their happiness is dependent on certain things happening in their lives, such as a raise in pay or the acquisition of a customer. But if other things happen, such as a drop in the stock market or a conflict with their spouse, they're unhappy.

That is a lousy way to live. If you wait for happiness, if you wait for certain things to happen, you become the victim of circumstances, rather than the master of them. And you simply cannot do that if you want to be in charge of the payoffs you receive in your life and career.

You've got to decide to have a positive attitude no matter what is happening all around you. You've got to decide that today and every day is going to be a good day.

I can already hear the skeptics saying, "Yeah, Zimmerman, that's easy for you to say. Just decide to have a positive attitude. You couldn't possibly understand how difficult my parents, spouse, children, finances, health, company, boss, job, coworkers, or customers are."

Wait a minute. I do understand. Firing up a positive attitude didn't come easily for me. I've come through a debilitating illness, divorce, and financial strain. I've seen my loved ones affected by abuse, alcoholism, imprisonment, and suicide. And I've encountered betrayal from coworkers, incompetent direction from bosses, and idiotic change from the executives above. I know what it feels like to face lots of challenges and still maintain a positive attitude.

You may feel like the thirty-year-old woman who wrote in her diary: "My God, what will become of me? I have no desire but to die. There's not a night that I do not lie down on my bed wishing that I may leave it no more. Unconsciousness is all that I desire."[11]

This woman's depression was overwhelming. Yet I would be willing to bet that you would never guess who wrote those words.

In fact you might be quite surprised to learn that when she died sixty years later, she was said to be one of three people in the world who did the most to alleviate suffering in the nineteenth century. Her name was Florence Nightingale, the founder of the modern nursing profession.

When Florence decided to have a positive attitude—instead of wallowing in her negativity—her world, indeed the entire world, turned around. She learned that even though she had to go through seasons of pain, it was still possible to make significant gains in life.

The same is true for you. You can make a lot of progress in life. You can achieve some major payoffs, even if life throws you a few curveballs, if you *decide* to have a positive attitude.

Attitude Practice #2: Feed Your Mind a Steady Diet of Positive Inputs

Everyone wants to be healthy. That's a given. And it's also a given that there are six major ingredients that ensure vibrant physical health: (1) what you eat, (2) the liquids you drink, (3) the air you breathe, (4) the exercise you take, (5) the rest you get, and (6) the thoughts you think.

Unfortunately, most people don't realize that the sixth one is the most important. If you manage the first five ingredients well, but the sixth element stinks, you're going to be in trouble. That's why I tell my audiences, "What you feed your body is *nothing* compared to what you feed your mind."

Yes, *feed*. You would never think of putting yourself on an all-candy diet if you were training for a marathon. You know that the fuel you put in your body, to a great extent, will determine your performance. So you would feed your body the best foods you could get.

And yet, when it comes to feeding the mind, most people disregard this basic piece of wisdom. They unconsciously let negative garbage into their minds, and they consciously do little or nothing to feed their mind the positive thoughts it needs.

I know. I was one of the guilty ones. For many years, my morning ritual began with a thorough reading of the newspaper and then listening to the radio news as I drove to the office. After filling my mind with the day's murders, rapes, indictments, invasions, and all the other bad news, it shouldn't have come as a surprise that my attitude was less than positive.

I gave up this stupid morning ritual many years ago and replaced it with a steady diet of positive inputs. And it paid off in every part of my life. So, I highly recommend the following procedure.

Spend Five Minutes Every Day Thinking about Good Things

Think about good things in your job, your life, your family, the world around you, or whatever. It's what the Apostle Paul recommended about two thousand years ago when he wrote, "Fix your thoughts on what is true and good and right. Think about things that are pure and lovely, and dwell on the fine, good things in others. Think about all you can praise God for and be glad about."[12]

Spend Ten Minutes Every Day Reading for Inspiration

Read things that will make you a better person and a better professional. And sorry, but newspapers and novels don't count when it comes to fueling your passion. Oh, you may learn something from a newspaper, and you should enjoy a good fiction read once in a while, but they will seldom do anything to help you build and maintain a positive attitude.

The most passionate people—the producers at work and in life—don't depend on yesterday's motivation for today's challenges. They spend at least ten minutes a day putting positive, inspiring information into their minds.

Practice Word Therapy

Say such words as *indomitable, unsinkable, undefeatable,* and *victorious* throughout your day. Say them out loud if possible. And if you're going through an especially tough time, or if your attitude has been too negative for too long, add a bit of discipline to your word therapy. Instead of merely verbalizing these strong, self-empowering words once in a while, speak them three times a day, every day, for the next thirty days.

Surround Yourself with Positive People

Seek the company of upbeat, optimistic people. Eat lunch with coworkers who are more positive if your present luncheon companions are constant gripers. Surround yourself with nurturing people who build you up, believe in you, and encourage you. Attitudes are contagious; so make sure you're around people whose attitudes are worth catching.

That's why I continue to meet with six other highly skilled, highly respected, and highly confident professionals in my industry. I've taken the time and spent the money to connect with these people for two days, four times a year, for more than twenty years. Oh sure, there are times they challenge me, but I always know these people are in my corner and rooting me on. And I will continue to meet with these kinds of people all my life because I know the difference they have made in my life, in my work, in my attitude, and even in my family.

Attitude Practice #3: Keep a Motivation Journal

Instead of keeping a diary of your days, keep a journal. Use it to write down all the good "stuff" you see, hear, find, learn, or experience. In your journal, record great ideas, inspiring quotes, key insights, important lessons, key phrases, what worked and didn't work, and all kinds of daily observations that are worth remembering.

In fact, have some fun with your journal. Write down the humorous lines you hear or read. They'll give you a laugh, and the laugh will add to your overall positive attitude. For example, I came across the following line and put it my journal: "The evening news is where they begin by saying 'Good evening' and then proceed to tell you why it isn't."

At the end of each day, before you retire, think of three or more good things that happened during your day. Write them down. And take a moment to reflect on why those good things occurred.

You get the idea. Keep a journal of the positive. And go back and read what you wrote once in a while. You'll be amazed at the wisdom you accumulate and the high it will give you.

Attitude Practice #4: Practice an Attitude of Gratitude

There's an old song that says, "Count your blessings, one by one." Evidently that advice was not only theologically correct but scientifically correct as well. Research shows that when you count three or more blessings a day, you get a measurable boost in your energy, your spirit, and your overall happiness. There are two ways you can do that.

Be Thankful for What You Have

Don't wait for a crisis to be reminded of what you have. And don't wait for the tough times to practice an attitude of gratitude.

One of my students, Lisa Blaum, reminded me of that when Hurricane Katrina destroyed her home. They had to evacuate to her sister's place in Atlanta. While there, her young nephew asked her if she got all the important things out of the house before she left. Lisa said, "While my mind raced through thoughts of important papers and photos and jewelry and sentimental items, my sister was quicker to respond to him than I was. She simply said, 'Yes, she got her husband and her children!'"

To get yourself started, take two minutes to list all the things you're thankful for. And take another two minutes every day to list some more things for which you're thankful.

And just so you are clear, this is not an exercise in denial. I'm not suggesting that you bury your head in the sand and pretend that everything in your world is good and wonderful. I'm not suggesting that you ignore the relational, occupational, emotional, and financial issues in your life. Not at all! You simply cannot spend too much of your time focusing on how bad things are. Remember: the more thankful you are the less stress you'll feel.

Be Thankful for What You Don't Have

Personally, I like the way one anonymously written poem puts it. It says, in part, "Be thankful that you don't already have everything you desire. If you did, what would there be to look forward to? Be thankful when you don't know something, for it gives you the opportunity to learn."

> Consciously spend some time practicing an attitude of gratitude. It's one of the most energizing forces in the world.

Consciously spend some time practicing an attitude of gratitude. It's one of the most energizing forces in the world. After all, it is not happy people who are thankful. It is thankful people who are happy.

Attitude Practice #5: Choose a Perspective That Serves You

People tend to think their way of seeing something is the *only* way to see it. Not so. There's *always* more than one way to see something, and the perspective you choose will make all the difference in your professional success and personal happiness.

> There's always more than one way to see something, and the perspective you choose will make all the difference in your professional success and personal happiness.

I see it happen all the time in the workplace, where two people with the same job take different perspectives and, as a result, they get very different results. Salesperson A constantly complains that his company's prices are too high; his supporting sales materials aren't up to date; he doesn't have the latest software on his computer; his territory is too small; there are too few good prospects; and his support staff is inadequate.

Salesperson B has the same set of challenges. Instead of whining about it, he concludes he'd better spend more time than ever making face-to-face contact with his prospects and customers. He knows the success of his sales will depend, to a large degree, on the quality of the relationships he builds.

Given those two perspectives, guess who has the better track record in sales?

The truth is, some perspectives invigorate you while others depress you. So ask yourself, "How well is my perspective *serving* me?" Does your perspective help you accomplish more? And feel better? Does your perspective give you lift and motivation? Or does it drag you down and hold you back? If your perspective is *not* serving you or is *not* making your life better, then you need to change it.

I learned the importance of having a perspective that served me when I was a young man. I had just left the funeral of a two-year-old child and went into the parking lot to get my car . . . which wouldn't start. It was late; it was dark; I was in a bad neighborhood; and everyone else had left. Of course I called AAA to come and help me start my car.

Due to a number of circumstances, AAA couldn't get there for a couple of hours. The AAA mechanic was very helpful and extremely apologetic about the delay. I was calm; I was okay with the entire ordeal, but the mechanic wondered why I wasn't upset.

I'll never forget the answer that came to me and has stuck with me all these years. I thought, "How dare I be upset with a car that wouldn't start or a two-hour wait when I just came from the funeral of a two-year-old?" Put in perspective, my situation was nothing more than a minor inconvenience. It meant nothing.

I can't tell you how many hundreds of times I've thought about that situation. And every time I think about it, my attitude becomes a bit more positive. I simply refuse to let the little things get me down. I ask myself how important those little things will be in a week, in a year, or in the light of eternity. Most of the time, those little things won't matter at all, and so my attitude stays positive.

Choose a perspective that serves you well when difficulties come. Learn to be like the woman who said to her husband, "Our vacation is not a total loss, dear. Most people go an entire lifetime without ever seeing icicles on palm trees."

Attitude Practice #6: Act As If You Are Positive

Suppose there was a magic pill that gives you more energy, makes you less stressed, gives you more confidence, and makes you more productive. You'd probably take that pill, just like I would. In fact, you'd probably want a lifetime supply.

Well, the good news is, there is such a pill on the market right now. And you don't have to go to a doctor, get a prescription, or worry about any side effects. The pill is found in what I call "the three most powerful words in the English language." All you have to do is *act as if*.

In the mid-twentieth century, the world-famous personal development specialist Dale Carnegie (1888–1955) commented on those three words. He wrote, "Act as if you were already happy, and that will tend to make you happy."[13]

If you're wondering if this really works, look at Dr. Dale Anderson's research in the early twenty-first century. Anderson studied actors and actresses and discovered an amazing thing. When the actors and actresses played the role of a happy character, their internal chemistry changed dramatically. They not only felt better but their bodies exhibited all the signs of a healthier person.[14]

As a medical doctor, Anderson gave his patients a simple prescription: "Act positively." Act as if you're enthusiastic. Jump. Smile. Put an extra skip into your step. Add a lilt to your laugh. Fake it until you make it. And it doesn't matter what is happening in your life or how you feel—just act positively, and you will, without a doubt, feel better. And if you act positively, you will become more positive and passionate in your attitude.

Attitude Practice #7: Deflect the Negative

In the natural world, the law of gravity says what goes up must come down. In the psychological world, the law of exposure says what goes in must come out. If you're exposed to a lot of negatives, if you allow those negatives to *get into* your mind, they will *come out* in a more negative attitude.

The good news is you can choose which negative inputs will stay put. As entrepreneurship consultant Gladys Edmunds says, "Picture your thoughts as people passing by the front of your home. Just because they're walking by doesn't mean you have to invite them in."[15]

And in a similar sense, just because you're exposed to a barrage of negative news or negative people doesn't mean you have to dwell on them. You can let them pass on by. It will do wonders for your attitude. Try these strategies for deflecting the negative.

Limit Your Exposure to Negative Information

Obviously, you want to be informed about what is happening in the world, in the country, in your company, and in your family. You want to know enough so you can make the best judgments as to what you should do.

But once you know the news, shut it off. Cut back on the time you spend with a newspaper or watching the nightly broadcast of horrors, because overexposure to negative input has no redeeming value. It will not make your life better, help you sleep more soundly, make you more money, or improve your relationships. Negative input will only depress you. After all, the news now—like the news five, ten, or fifty years ago—is almost always negative and almost always repeated.

Limit Your Contact Time with Negative People

Your mama was right. Be careful about who you hang around with. If you spend too much time with negative people, it will be very difficult for you to stay fired up.

Perhaps you've noticed some folks at work talking on and on about how bad the economy is. Or you've heard some coworkers express their anger over the changes in the company. Be careful of spending too much time with gripers and complainers or moaners and groaners. If you're not careful, they'll drag you into their pit of despair. Or they'll suck you into the discussion, where you may start adding your own comments about how rotten everything is. And as you do, you'll kill off your own positive attitude, and you'll end up feeling worse than you did before.

Of course, some of you will protest, "I can't limit my contact time with some of the negative people in my life. That includes my spouse or boss, and I've got to be around them." If that's the case for you, then practice taking their negativity with a grain of salt or a healthy dose of skepticism. You can't let somebody else's negativity kill off your energy. You could even take it a step further.

Challenge the Negativity of Others

Challenging others' negativity may stop, or at least diminish, the other person's negativity so you don't have to hear so much of it in the future.

Personally, I like the way one of my clients, Reggie Clifton, dealt with it. He told me he had a small office filled with employees who talked behind one another's backs and who were continually whining. He got so sick and tired of babysitting or policing them that he put up a complaint jar. Clifton said, "Whenever an employee would complain about an office policy, another employee, or anything else, they had to follow up with a constructive solution. If not, they had to put a quarter in the jar. I let the employees police themselves, and it cut way down on the petty complaints. Then we used the money for pizza and drinks at the next staff meeting."

Another one of my clients, Tracey Medves, has a great way of challenging negative people as well. She says, "When people tell me how bad their day was, I tell them, 'If that is the worst thing that happened today, it must have been a pretty good day!' Amazing how that makes people stop and think."

There you have it, seven practices for building and keeping a fueled-up, fired-up, passionate, positive attitude. But you may still be wondering if a positive attitude *really* works. The answer is yes!

Positive Attitudes Always Work

That statement always raises a few eyebrows. In fact, a lot of people tell me, "I tried to adopt a more positive attitude, but it didn't work."

Oh really? Then I suspect you've got a messed-up definition as to what a positive attitude is and how it works. I know I struggled with the definition for several years. For a while, I thought that a person with a positive attitude would always be happy. Then I realized that was nonsense. It's not possible to live your life having only one emotion.

Later, I had the misconception that a positive attitude would eliminate all problems in life. I soon realized that was nonsense as well. Life will always give you plenty of problems, no matter how positive you might be.

Finally, I learned that a positive attitude is all about energy or fuel, and that energy or fuel helps me see things in a better light and do things in a better fashion. I learned that even though I may not *have* the best of everything, with a positive attitude, I can *make* the best of everything I have. And so can you. That's why a positive attitude always works.

What really pulled it together for me were the words of William Arthur Ward (1921–1994). In his book, *Fountains of Faith* (Anderson, SC: Droke House, 1970), Ward gives the most useful, realistic, and empowering definition of a positive attitude I've ever come across. He wrote, "Real optimism [or a positive attitude] is aware of problems but recognizes solutions, knows about difficulties but believes they can be overcome, sees the negatives but accentuates the positives, is exposed to the worst but expects the best, has reason to complain but chooses to smile."[16]

> *Even though you may not* have *the best of everything, with a positive attitude, you can make the best of everything you have. That's why a positive attitude always works.*

If you've got a positive attitude, you may still get down once in a while, but you won't stay there as long. You may still have some problems, but you'll get through them much more quickly. Your positive attitude propels you upward and pushes you forward. It's passion in its purest form.

As you integrate *The Payoff Principle* into your life and work, you've learned about the power and practice of purpose. It's all about where you're going. But you also need passion to get you there, starting with the attitude of passion.

To keep on keeping on, you'll also need the *persistence* of passion. Read on.

CHAPTER 7

The Persistence of Passion

Persistence: The Oxygen Supply for Your Fire

I've compared passion to fire, and like any fire, it needs three components to work for you. The first component is fuel. That's your attitude. We talked about that in the last chapter. But to keep your passion fire burning, it also needs oxygen. That's **persistence**. With those two components in place, you're well on your way to capturing the payoffs you want.

Great minds throughout the ages have confirmed that. About two hundred years ago, the great American philosopher Ralph Waldo Emerson (1803–1882) said, "Every great success is ultimately the triumph of persistence."[1]

CEO and best-selling author Harvey Mackay says, "I've known entrepreneurs who were not great salespeople, or didn't know how to code, or were not particularly charismatic leaders. But I don't know of any entrepreneurs who have achieved any level of success without persistence."[2]

In 1985, the *Los Angeles Times* surveyed 120 top performers in business, sports, politics, entertainment, and academia. The one characteristic all these producers had in common is that they persistently worked to reach the top.[3]

Two of my former students, Scott Anderson and Chip Kudrle, who went on to form the Diamond Performance Group, have gotten very specific with this attribute as it applies to sales. They've found that 92

> *Persistence is keeping on even when you don't feel like it. You keep on taking the right actions, move in a positive direction, and pursue your payoffs, even though it may be easier to quit.*

percent of salespeople give up after the fourth "no." Think about that. Ninety-two percent quit after the fourth "no"; however, 60 percent of customers say "no" four times *before* they say "yes." That means the majority of the sales go to the few salespeople who are persistent enough to hang in there and stay in contact with the prospect.

And my own experience in working with hundreds of thousands of people confirms that. The truly successful person or professional keeps on trying, persistently, despite the rejections, difficulties, and obstacles.

One of those customers, Jean Rush, the president of CIGNA, one of the most successful Medicare providers in the country, told me, "In today's world, a successful leader or individual contributor must have persistence: persistence to weather the multitude of challenges that confront companies and individuals today."

If all the authorities seem to agree on the significance of persistence, then it must be extremely important and worthy of discussion. So what is it?

Keeping On, Even When You Don't Feel Like It

In the simplest of terms, persistence is keeping on even when you don't feel like it. So what if you fall down? So what if you make a mistake? So what if you lose a customer, a business, a home, a relationship, or anything else that is vitally important to you? It's terrible, of course, but it's not the end of the world—if you practice persistence. You keep on keeping on no matter how you feel. You are determined to take the right actions, move in a positive direction, and pursue your payoffs, even though it may be easier to quit. That's exercising persistence. When you do this, you can expect two significant payoffs.

Persistence Payoff #1: Freedom from the Lies

After watching years and years of TV commercials, sitcoms, and dramas, we've been deceived. We've come to believe that most of our health and beauty problems can be solved in thirty to sixty seconds. And we've come to believe that our career problems and family difficulties can be solved in thirty to sixty minutes. That's what the commercials, sitcoms, and dramas tend to imply, but they're just telling lies.

Overnight Success? That's a Lie!

It's simply a lie that you can be or can have overnight success. So it's no wonder so many people get depressed, bottom out, or give up when the tough times come. They mistakenly assume the payoffs they want should be quick and easy. And if they don't come quick and easy, well, it just wasn't meant to be.

The truth is, the achievements you and I see in truly successfully people are almost always preceded by a lot of blood, sweat, and tears. We *see* what looks like an overnight success, but we don't *hear* about the twenty years of persistent guts and gumption that preceded it.

Take one man, for example. His track record gave him every reason to quit. And if you looked at his resume, you probably wouldn't have hired him. The resume read as follows: 1832—defeated for political office in the State Legislature, 1833—failed in business, 1834—elected to the Legislature, 1835—sweetheart died, and 1836—had a nervous breakdown. During the next twenty-four years, he was defeated in his run for speaker, defeated in his nomination for Congress, defeated in his run for the Senate, defeated in the nomination for vice president, and defeated again in his run for the Senate. He only made it to Congress once, and in nine out of his eleven tries for office, he failed.

But in 1860, he—Abraham Lincoln—was elected as the sixteenth president of the United States, because he was focused on his purpose of abolishing slavery. He knew exactly what he wanted to accomplish, and his persistence helped him achieve exactly that.

No Work Required? That's a Lie!

The second big lie is that you can have whatever you want without doing anything. Some people even go so far as to say that one of the great secrets of success is to simply think about what you want and the results will magically appear. I disagree. I believe that's one of the great misconceptions about success.

Oh sure, my research and experience tell me that it's critically important to *think* about the payoffs you want in a certain way in order to achieve them. We'll talk more about that in part III, "Process." But I also know that thinking is a *part* of the process, not the *entire* process.

The truth is, payoffs come when you think the right thoughts *and* do the right things. It takes both elements. We all know people who are big thinkers and big talkers, but they're mighty small on follow-through. Focusing merely on the right thoughts is a recipe for failure, or at the very least, mediocrity.

More often than not, producers try and try and try, and they work and work and work . . . until they become extremely successful. They are persistent. Producers persist like long-distance runners run. They know that when they run and their sides hurt, they may want to quit. But they also know if they keep on running they'll get a second wind.

Producers are mature people who have learned the art of follow-through. As one wise person put it, "Maturity is perseverance, sweating out a project or a situation in spite of opposition and discouraging setbacks."

Left-behinders—the polar opposite of producers—quit. They've bought into the lie that they can have whatever they want without doing anything. So when it gets a little tough or unpleasant, when they don't get the results they want as quickly as they'd like they say, "I'm outta here." They bail out of jobs, careers, businesses, relationships, and life in general.

Of course, left-behinders may try to cover up their bailout or lack of persistence by using fancier words than that. As one person wrote on the bottom of his job application, "Please don't misconstrue my fourteen jobs as 'job hopping.' I have never QUIT a job."

You're going to get discouraged once in a while. That's normal. You're going to have some setbacks. But if you refuse to buy into the two lies, you're going to get some big payoffs, in your life, your job, your company, and your relationships.

Persistence Payoff #2: An Insurance Policy for Results

When you read the stories of those who achieve the biggest payoffs in life and at work, when you study the patterns that precede incredible success, you can't help but conclude one thing: *Persistence is a major contributing factor in the results that are achieved.*

In fact, most of the time, persistence ensures your success. Some authors, like H. Jackson Brown Jr. in *Life's Little Instruction Book* (Rutledge Hill Press, 1991), take it even further. He says, "In the confrontation between the stream and the rock, the stream *always* wins—not through strength but by perseverance." It's the combination of baby steps and persistence that brings about most victories in life.

Take Bill Porter, for example. By anyone's reckoning, he could've been considered a major candidate for "least likely to succeed." But his persistence ensured his rise to the top as the leading salesperson in the entire northwest for Watkins, Incorporated.

Bill had cerebral palsy. He got up every morning at 4:45 a.m. to catch the 7:20 bus. He needed that much time to get dressed, but he left his cuffs unbuttoned, his wing tips loosely tied, and his tie in his briefcase. Some friends at the bus stop helped him with those items.

Then Bill went door-to-door selling Watkins' home remedies and spices. Bill hit the streets for eight hours or more, telling himself the next customer will say "yes."

One winter day, a storm was forecast for Portland. To Bill, the weather report was good news. "Perfect for a door-to-door salesman," he said. "Everybody's home." So he bundled up and made his rounds until he'd made his quota.

By then, the buses had stopped running because the roads were so bad. He had to hitchhike home, only to discover the steep driveway leading to his front door was a sheet of ice. He tried to get up it again and again but kept falling down. Finally, he got down on his hands and knees and crawled to the front door, thoroughly satisfied with his day's work.

Bill Porter's success could not be attributed to "lucky breaks" or "knowing the right people." It could only be attributed to persistence. He said, "There are no obstacles, only challenges."[4] He lived a life of persistence when quitting would have been so much easier. He proved the truth of author and businessman Robert Half's quote: "Persistence is what makes the impossible possible, the possible likely, and the likely definite."[5]

> The truth is, most victories, on and off the job, are the result of persistence, rather than genius.

Ignorant people and jealous losers attribute the success of others to lucky breaks or knowing the right people. But they're wrong, of course. Other never-going-to-make-it types attribute the success of others to some special gift they were born with. They see those winners as being endowed with genius, talent, and superhuman powers that nobody else has. Again they're wrong.

The truth is, most victories, on and off the job, are the result of persistence, rather than genius.

The great singer Ray Charles (1930–2004) knew that. In fact, his whole life was a testament to the power of persistence. When he was six years old, he lost his eyesight. And to a young, poor blind child, the future didn't seem very promising.

But his mother told him, "Ray, you've lost your sight, but you haven't lost your mind. You can still create a productive life for yourself."

Ray began dreaming about becoming a music star. So he would practice the piano and practice his singing every day. One schoolteacher told him, "Ray, you can't play the piano, and God knows you can't sing. You'd better learn to weave chairs so you can support yourself."

That kind of feedback would have stopped most people dead in their tracks—but not Ray. He continued to focus on his goal of being a music star, even though time after time, audition after audition, he was told he couldn't carry a tune in a bucket.

But here's the rest of the story. Ray Charles insisted on persisting. Eventually, he won twelve Grammys and was inducted into the Rock and Roll Hall of Fame for his musical talents. He performed for millions of ordinary people and hundreds of dignitaries around the world.

Certainly, Ray Charles was a gifted singer. But the world is filled with gifted singers who never go anywhere or become anybody, or as some would like to say, never make the big time.

So let me ask you: Was it Ray Charles' talent that brought him the Grammys? Yes, of course. But would he have gotten those Grammys if he hadn't persisted? Of course not.

More often than not, genius comes disguised as persistence. Even Albert Einstein (1879–1955), who is always praised for his brilliance, said, "It's not that I'm so smart; it's just that I stay with problems longer."[6]

So yes, persistence is an insurance policy for the results you want. But even more important, it is something you can learn.

Persistence Can Be Learned

On one hand, the quitters, the left-behinders, and the never-going-to-make-it types use their circumstances as a reason to give up. They don't take the time to learn persistence or even realize they can learn it.

Instead, they say they never had a chance to succeed. They are the wrong age, color, or gender, or they had the wrong parents at home, the wrong teachers at school, and the wrong bosses at work. Other people, of the same age, color, or gender, and with similar parenting, schooling, and managing, are doing quite well. The difference is their persistence, or lack of it.

On the other hand, producers use their circumstances as a reason to get going or to get more education, training, and coaching. This gets them whatever they need so that they can keep on keeping on, above and beyond their present circumstances.

I'll never forget the time I was tempted to quit. It was my first paid speaking engagement at a major Fortune 500 company. I was hired to conduct a two-day seminar, at least that's what I thought. Two hours into the program, the boss of the group called for a break, pulled me aside, and said, in effect, that I was a terrible speaker, offering none of the content he wanted. He proceeded to take over and teach the seminar for the next two days, as he relegated me to a seat in the back row. Talk about humiliation and failure.

> *Left-behinders use their circumstances as a reason to quit; producers use their circumstances as a reason to get going.*

I could have shut down my new, budding career as a professional speaker. I could have closed shop and gone back to my safer tenured career as a university professor. But I had a father who had taught me that even though I might fail at certain things in life, I was not a failure. I knew it was okay to fail, but it wasn't okay to give up.

My persistence paid off. Sometime later, another leader in that same company invited me for an interview. He wanted to discuss the possibility of hiring me to conduct a number of seminars for managers throughout their company. Before he continued the discussion further, I told him, in the spirit of total openness and honesty, that I had already spoken to another group in his company and had been promptly fired on the spot. He responded by thanking me for my disclosure, said he already knew about that incident, said the other guy was a "real jerk," and proceeded to give me a six-figure contract.

If I had folded up my company after that previous setback and humiliation, would I have gotten this big contract? Certainly not.

I had to learn more about and get better at persistence as my speaking career continued. In my professional association, the National Speakers Association, the highest earned designation is the Certified Speaking Professional (CSP). To earn it, I had to give at least fifty presentations a year, to at least fifty different clients, over a period of five years, at a certain fee level, and receive an "excellent" rating in every one of those engagements. It would have been easier to let it go and not work toward the achievement of my CSP, but I was persistent. I earned it. That not only felt good, but it also brought me additional business.

My persistence was heavily tested when that same association nominated me for the Council of Peers Award for Excellence (CPAE), the highest honor they bestow on a speaker. Only a mere handful of people in the past thirty years have received this lifetime honor, including such notables as President Ronald Reagan; General Colin Powell; TV personality Art Linkletter; and best-selling authors such as Dr. Ken Blanchard, Jack Canfield, and Randy Gage. Receiving this award is a huge honor for anyone. And to top it all off, the CPAE ceremony is very much like the Oscars with the tuxedos, gowns, and the awe-inspiring surroundings.

What tested my persistence was being nominated ten years in a row without receiving the CPAE. I began to doubt my competence and worthiness, and my confidence was challenged. That must be the way some people feel at the Oscars, when they sit there year after year, knowing they were nominated for best actor or actress, but the award keeps going to someone else. But I learned to be even more persistent, working on my content expertise, my presentation skills, and the difference I wanted to make in the lives of others. And the day came where I was called up on stage to receive my CPAE, one of the highlights in my career.

Persistence may not always bring you the exact payoff you want, but it does bring payoffs that are so much better than you would ever get when you quit. And persistence can be learned. So what can you do to develop passionate persistence? Check out the next five practices.

Persistence Practice #1: Tap Into the Power of Desire

When you really, really want something—a particular goal at work, or a certain payoff at home—your desire turns into persistence. And persistence has power. Not some quick spurt of power that easily fades away, but a source of power for the long steady climb.

Hulda Crooks knew that. She wanted to stand on top of the tallest mountain in North America. She wanted to see the beauty of the world from that perspective.

Age slowed her down a bit, but her goal was so personally important that it ignited her persistence, and she made it to the top at age ninety. Featured on a television news program, she was asked about her age. The news anchor asked, "When do you think you are going to grow old?" Hulda answered, "I haven't really considered that very much."[7] Her goals and her persistence made her age irrelevant.

Desire comes when you have some "gotta-haves," not some "nice-to-haves." Buddha knew that. When a young man came to seek his advice, to discover the path of deliverance, Buddha led him down to the river. The young man assumed he was to undergo some ritual of purification. So they walked out into the river, and suddenly Buddha grabbed the man and held his head under the water.

The man struggled and fought. After a great deal of effort, the young man wrenched himself loose and brought his head above the water.

Quietly Buddha asked him, "When you thought you were drowning, what did you most desire?"

The young man gasped, "Air."

Buddha said, "When you want salvation as much as you want air, then you will get it."[8]

Likewise, when you really, really want something, when you *desire* your goal, you will have the persistence you need to achieve the success you crave. So think about your goals. Dream about them. See them.

Feel them. Taste them. Smell them. The more you desire your goals, the more persistence you'll have.

My neighbor, seven-year-old Brian Cole from Mankato, Minnesota, taught me that. As a first grader, he heard about a swim marathon to raise money for cancer research. He wanted to help because his cousin had died of cancer two years earlier.

So he went out collecting pledges. He asked people to pledge a certain amount of money for each lap he would swim. He told them he hoped to swim ten laps, the number his teacher had instructed him to tell his potential sponsors.

Come the day of the marathon, Brian jumped in the pool and started swimming. He swam up and down, back and forth, stopping for the first time when he completed one hundred laps—and only then to put on his goggles because the chlorine was stinging his eyes. After putting on his goggles, he swam another eight laps.

Brian's parents were astonished by their son's accomplishment. But they were also a little embarrassed. How would they tell Brian's sponsors that their son had swum 108 laps when those sponsors only expected to pay on a fraction of that?

So they called Brian's sponsors to explain the situation and release them from their agreement. It was no problem. Almost everyone paid in full, and some non-sponsors even threw in some money. Brian simply said he was "swimming for sick people. Maybe if someone had done this before, my cousin Mary would still be alive."

Brian's swim for "sick people" demonstrates a goal, backed up by desire, which turned into persistence. And you can achieve the same thing.

Persistence Practice #2: Develop Resiliency

Persistence isn't something that somebody else can give you. Persistence isn't something you're born with. Plain and simple, it comes from a set of practices such as the ones we are discussing. And another one of those practices is a decision you make.

Decide to Get Back Up

When you're down, you decide to get back up. You may be at the bottom; you may land at the bottom; or you may have had others push you there. But you also know that if you stay at the bottom, that's pretty much your decision, and it's certainly your responsibility. But a passionate persistent producer decides to get back up.

> *You may be at the bottom; you may land at the bottom; or you may have had others push you there. But if you stay at the bottom, that's your decision and your responsibility.*

You see it over and over again. The first prizes don't always go to the most talented. They often go to the most determined. As the prolific journalist and civil rights activist Roscoe Dunjee (1883–1965) put it, "Some people succeed because they are destined to, but most people succeed because they are determined to."[9] They get back up.

Your getting-back-up ability plays a bigger role in your success than almost anything else. Business consultant John Baker has seen that so many times that he now says, "Durability is stronger than talent, better than luck, more real than potential, and more valuable than intellect." A great drive, or the decision to get back up, will easily compensate for little or limited talent.

And your resilience will be especially tested when you're faced with unfairness. After all, we all know deep down in our gut and high up in our head that life *should* be fair, but it isn't. But when it's not fair, it's easy to get sad, angry, demotivated, and depressed—all of which can kill your persistence.

So take a look at how you respond to unfair treatment. Someone else got the job or promotion that you deserved. Someone else got the credit for the work you did. And someone else got to take the trip you earned. Do you get down and out or up and going?

Refuse to Be a Victim

Producers, when they're the victim of unfair treatment, decide to keep on going anyway. One young lady learned that. While she was at Ohio State University, she set the goal of becoming Miss Ohio, not only for the title but also for the scholarship that would finance her college education. So she entered three pageants, three years in a row, and lost every one of them. But two days after the last event, the state pageant office called and said, "Laurel, the judges did not understand the ballot. We recounted and you won. But we've already crowned the other girl as the winner, and there is nothing we can do about it." How unfair.

Laurel could have sued. She could have spent months of negative energy plotting how to respond to the situation. But that's not what Laurel did, because she understood at an amazingly young age that life is not always fair. The best person doesn't always win. Mistakes can happen.

Rather than fret and stew, Laurel did something quite remarkable. She decided to try one more time. During her senior year in college, she entered the local pageant and won. She won Miss Ohio (1971), went to Atlantic City, and became Miss America (1972) . . . Laurel Schaefer.[10]

The lesson is clear. You're more likely to get the payoffs you want when you accept the fact that life is not always fair and keep on keeping on anyway.

Use Positive Phraseology

One of the best ways to reinforce your resiliency is to use "I can" language. What goes on in your head and what comes out of your mouth has a huge influence on your overall persistence. If, for example, you go around thinking, "It's too hard" or "It will never work," or if you find yourself saying, "I just can't do it" or "I can't hang in there any longer," you're in trouble. You've just shot down any measure of persistence you might have going for you.

However, when you talk to yourself positively, affirming the persistence you want and need to have (whether or not you already have it), you're going to become more persistent. There's incredible power in the use of affirmations. It's that simple and that magical. I cover more on that in later chapters.

For the time being, to pump up your persistence, practice a lot of positive phraseology. Say, "I feel good" instead of "I can't complain." Say, "I'm pleased" instead of "I couldn't ask for more." Say, "Let's do it" rather than "I don't see why not." Say, "It's a pleasure" instead of "No problem." And say, "We can . . ." instead of "Why don't we . . ." Your choice of words does matter.

Persistence Practice #3: Embrace Hard Work

Hard work is seldom popular. Most of us would like easy wins and instant successes. And if the payoff seems too far off in the future, many people just throw in the towel.

Producers embrace hard work by recognizing that the size of the payoff is what really counts, not the length of time it will take to accomplish.

Patsy Meisel taught me that. She was a fellow professor of mine at the university many years ago. And even though she had been teaching for decades, she had the dream of going beyond her master's degree to earn a doctorate.

> Producers embrace hard work by recognizing that the size of the payoff is what really counts, not the length of time it will take to accomplish.

Everyone told her she was foolish. After all, she was in her sixties and would probably only teach a few more years, so why bother? Besides that, the schooling would cost her more money than she would ever have the chance to recoup.

But Patsy was a person who believed in hard work. She didn't let the amount of time it would take to finish the degree dampen her enthusiasm. She took a leave of absence from her job, went back to school, got her doctorate, came back to the university as Dr. Patsy Meisel, taught two more years, and retired.

A waste, you think? No way. Patsy achieved her dream and continues to live and work into her eighties, knowing the pride and satisfaction that comes with hard work.

Going beyond that, producers are able to embrace hard work because they know success is not measured by being the very best at something. That would leave most of us out. They embrace hard work because they know success is measured by doing your best with what you have.

Do Your Best with What You Have

Take Joe Frazier (1944–2011), for example. As a young boy, Joe dreamed of becoming a boxer. He got an old sack and filled it with sand. That was his punching bag. And that was the beginning of his disciplined plan to reach the success he wanted. Eventually, he won the gold medal for boxing at the Olympic Games.

When asked about his secret, he said that success depends on your roadwork. You must be willing to do your roadwork, week after week, month after month, and hurdle after hurdle. You can get anywhere you want to go if you are willing to work hard.

What many people don't know is that Joe had a handicap. His left arm was injured when he was a small boy. The injury left him unable to completely extend his left arm.

As John Shumway, a former amateur boxer, told me, "I can tell you with confidence that one of the most important assets a boxer has is his left-hand jab. The jab is not only an indispensable defensive weapon, but it is the cornerstone of a boxer's offense. At the incredibly competitive and dangerous world-class level of professional boxing, a left-hand jab is crucial."

If you watch the way Joe Frazier fought, you see that Joe did not effectively utilize his left jab. The limited range of motion of his left arm was not suited to the jab. Instead, he did the best he could with what he had.

So as a boy, punching a bag of sand, he threw thousands of left hooks—a punch for which his left arm was suited. He also believed that if he could develop superior endurance, he could win in the ring.

Because of Joe's persistence, his tireless hard work, and his willingness to adapt, he became a great champion. Joe combined his lethal left hook with a fearless and unrelenting style to get to the top of the boxing world.

When Joe Frazier fought Muhammad Ali, he was up against the best left jab anyone had ever seen. Nonetheless, for fifteen rounds, Frazier stalked Ali, firing his deadly left hook while tirelessly bobbing under Ali's lightning-fast punches. Frazier wore down Ali, actually dropping him to the canvas with his wicked left hook late in the fight. Although Ali was able to fight to the end, he was unable to sustain an effective offense. Joe Frazier became the Heavyweight Champion of the World and one of the most respected fighters to ever step into the ring.[11]

Frazier did the best he could with what he had. This is one of the keys to persistence. Are you doing the best with what you have? If so, you're in line to be a producer.

Unfortunately, many people aren't doing the best they can with what they have. They compare their talent to someone else's, and when they find themselves lacking, they give up. This is the student who thinks, "I'll never be as smart as Theodore, so why even bother to try?" Or it's the salesperson who thinks, "I'll never be in the top 10 percent of this company's sales force, so why should I be working so hard? I'll just get by, and that's good enough."

No, it isn't. If you don't make the best of what you do have, you'll have even less—less self-esteem, less self-respect, less happiness, less success, and less of everything else that might be valuable.

> If you don't make the best of what you do have, you'll have even less— less self-esteem, less self-respect, less happiness, less success, and less of everything else that might be valuable.

Practice and Then Practice Some More

Producers embrace hard work because they know practice precedes payoff. Even before he became a professional basketball star, Bob Pettit understood the power of practice. He knew that the payoffs he wanted would come as the result of practice, practice, and more practice. Even though he became one of the highest scoring players in the sport, it wasn't that way in the beginning.

As a freshman in high school, Bob was weak, frail, and uncoordinated. All he had going for him was the determination to practice until he became a quality athlete.

Bob began with a wire coat hanger that he bent into the shape of a basketball hoop. Hour after hour, day after day, he threw tennis balls through his makeshift basket. Eventually, his father got him a real basketball and hoop.

Bob would throw baskets after school every day, go to dinner, and then go back to practice. It wasn't too long before he became the star of his church team, then his high school team, college team, and finally a professional team. He became the first recipient of the NBA's Most Valuable Player Award. And he won the NBA All-Star Game MVP award four times,[12] a feat matched only by Kobe Bryant.

It's the same for you and me. You've got to embrace hard work, which means you've got to practice your craft over and over again. So ask yourself, "Am I practicing enough?" If your answer is "yes," congratulations! You know something about the power of persistence.

But you may be saying, "I don't even know how to practice. And even if I did, there are times I don't feel like practicing." Then try this. The next time you're working on a task you know you have to do but don't want to, give it your all for ten minutes. No matter how distasteful the task, I know you can give it your best for ten minutes. The next time you're back on that or any other disliked task, give it your all for fifteen minutes. Keep on adding five minutes to these practice sessions, and you will often find that you want to go on longer. Then you'll know that you are in the process of mastering persistence.

From all these stories, you probably realize one thing. Persistence pays off in the long run. Your success may not come immediately, but your success is fairly certain if you persist. That's why it's very important to also practice patience.

Persistence Practice #4: Apply Patience

It's a toughie. Most of us are like the person who prayed to God, "I want patience, now!" It's difficult to stay calm and patient, but it's a vital part of persistence.

If you have a hard time staying calm and patient, take a lesson from the successful businessman Donald Bennett. Even though he was an amputee, he always wanted to climb Mount Rainier. The mountain was so enticing, so beautiful, but very few ever climb it because the weather makes it impossible most of the time—especially on one leg.

Donald trained and trained, until he was given permission to climb the 14,410-foot mountain. The time eventually came, and he climbed 14,000 feet. But the weather forced him to turn back, which meant he had to wait another year.

Many people wouldn't have had the patience to try again, and they would've quit saying, "I gave it a try, but it just didn't work out."

Not Donald. A year later, Donald Bennett stood on the top of Mount Rainier—on his one leg. He was the first amputee to make it to the summit. When a reporter asked him how he did it, Donald said, "One hop at a time."[13] Talk about patience.

If you want to be a champion, if you want phenomenal success, it will be hard. What else could you possibly expect? If it wasn't hard, everyone would be doing it. Just remember, champions do not become champions in the ring—they are merely recognized in the ring.

Refuse to Be Sidetracked

If you're not the patient type, you can learn to be patient and apply patience . . . by refusing to be sidetracked. Pain, setbacks, tragedies, disappointments, sickness, and other adversities are always chasing you. At least three or four times a year, one or more of those things will catch up to you or someone you care about. And if you're not careful, they'll distract or sidetrack you, taking your persistence with them.

You can't allow that to happen. You can stay patient and on course if you refuse to be sidetracked. Senator Robert Taft (1889–1953) demonstrated that. Early in his political career, he went into hostile territory to make a speech. Someone threw an overripe tomato at him. It hit the senator in the chest and burst all over his face, glasses, and hair.

What did he do? React with anger? Lash out? Quit? No. He didn't wipe his face, glasses, or hair. He just went on giving his speech and never even referred to the tomato. When he finished, he stepped down from the platform and said, "Good-bye boys," in a friendly manner. As Senator Taft walked down the aisle toward the door, the once-hostile crowd gave him a standing ovation.

That's what I call class on the senator's part. And that's how persistent people get through adversity and onto the payoffs. They refuse to get sidetracked.

Could the same be said of you? Do you stay calm and remain patient? Do you refuse to give up? Do you endure?

Or do people, secretly behind your back, say you bail out when things get a little tough? Do they say you give up way too easily or throw in the towel too quickly? Do they point out the fact that you seldom finish what you start?

If you answer "yes" to any of these questions about how others view you, let me tell you once again—you can learn patience.

Do a Cost and Benefit Analysis

Try this exercise. Write the name of your challenge or desired payoff at the top of a sheet of paper. Put a line down the middle.

At the top of the left-hand column, write down the words "What it will cost me if I quit." Write down all the losses you will incur if you quit. Maybe you will lose some time, money, energy, promotions, and relationships. At the top of the right-hand column, write down the words "What are the benefits I will receive if I persist?"

You'll discover, most of the time, that you have a lot more to gain and very little to lose by not quitting and applying patience to your situation. As Benjamin Franklin put it, "He that can have patience can have what he will."[14]

Persistence Practice #5: Reject Defeat

Failure and defeat aren't easy. I know. I've failed in relationships. I've failed in business. And I've failed in a dozen other ways, as well, on various occasions. And maybe you have too.

Well, so what! Far worse than failure and defeat is failing to persist because you *might* fail. Yes, that's possible, but that's also a stupid way to approach life.

To keep on keeping on, you must learn to reject defeat. Sounds nice in theory, but how do you do that?

> You are going to fail once in a while. That's a given. But far worse than failure is failing to persist because you might fail.

First, Give Your Feelings a Vote but Not a Veto

Of course, there will be times when you will not *feel* like doing what you need to do. There will be times when you don't feel like hanging in there. But be a little wary of your feelings. They can sometimes be useful in decision making, but they should never have the final say in whether you continue doing what needs to be done. The final say should come from a thoughtful consideration of your purpose and the payoffs you want to achieve as well as a look at what your head and heart are telling you about whether to keep on or quit.

That's what Lucille did. Even though she didn't feel like going on, she rejected defeat by not allowing her feelings to veto her dreams.

It all started when she told her friends she was going to be an actress. So she went off to drama school in New York City at the age of sixteen. But it wasn't too long before her mother received a letter from the school saying, "Take her home. She has no acting ability whatsoever."

Her feelings said, "Quit. Forget about it." But how could she go home? She had told all her friends she was going to be an actress.

So she auditioned as a showgirl in a musical and got the job without pay. Four weeks before opening night she was fired. She then auditioned for three other musicals, and each time she was hired and fired before opening night. Talk about obstacles. In two years she had not earned one penny as an actress.

Finally, she got a job as a model, but that didn't last long. She came down with pneumonia, which resulted in severe, long-term pain in both legs. The doctor said she might never walk again and sent her to a New York City hospital as a charity case, where she spent the next several months. While there, she hobbled around on crutches then used a cane, having to wear twenty-pound weights on her shoes. It was two years before she was well again.

Talk about defeats. She had gone to New York City at sixteen, and now, by age twenty-two, she had nothing to show for herself except a track record of persistence and the lessons she learned from rejecting defeats.

And yet some years later, in 1953, according to a June 2, 2013, entry on the National Media Museum blog, twenty million people watched the coronation of Queen Elizabeth on TV. Twenty-nine million people watched TV as Dwight Eisenhower was inaugurated as president. And yet forty-four million people watched this star of the TV show

I Love Lucy in the much-anticipated episode from season 2, "Lucy Goes to the Hospital."[15]

The actress, of course, was Lucille Ball. From the very first episode, when she was forty, her show was rated as one of the top ten TV shows in America. And within twenty episodes, it became the number one show in America, which it remained for four years.[16]

So was Lucille Ball a success or a failure? If you read her fascinating life story, you realize she was both. But ultimately, she was a success because she rejected defeat by giving her feelings a voice in her career but not the final word.

Renounce Negative Self-Talk

Taking it a step further, to actively and vigorously reject defeat, renounce negative self-talk. You and I will have some failures along the way. That's a given. But don't ever tell yourself, "I'm a failure." You are not defined by an incident or two or three, or even an ongoing bad habit. As psychologist Dr. Bev Smallwood tells her clients, "You are definitely not a 'failure,' *unless* you bail out, give up, or quit trying." And I might add, "Unless you *call* yourself a failure."

Producers renounce negative self-talk. Bruce Lee (1940–1973), the martial artist, actor, and author, is a prime example of this. He said, "Defeat is a state of mind. No one is ever defeated until defeat has been accepted as reality."[17]

When I'm tempted to give up and throw in the towel, when I begin to think negatively—that I'm never going to make it—I give myself a firm reprimand. I renounce the negative self-talk by telling myself, "Stop it! Now just stop it!" And I replace the negative self-talk with a positive affirmation. I tell myself, over and over again, "Never let up when you're ahead; never give up when you're behind."

That's how one high school student did it—and made national news at the same time. He loved wrestling, and during his junior year, he had an amazing season, winning the second-place trophy in the state championships.

Now that was good, very good indeed. But the day after the state finals, he was back in the same old gym working out in the same old sweats with one small change. He had placed white tape on each of his middle fingers, and on each piece of tape was a letter—M-I-H. His friends, family, and teammates all repeatedly asked about the letters, but he refused to divulge their meaning.

He kept the letters on his fingers all year, and he trained harder than ever, until he again found himself at the state tournament. This time the outcome was different and not a surprise to anyone who had witnessed his daily determination in the gym. He was crowned state champion.

Finally, he was able to share with everyone that while they cheered his second-place finish the year before, he vowed to get better, to be the best. Displaying vision beyond his years, he developed a clear goal, designed a plan to achieve it, and created a tool to keep up his persistence. He knew that if he really wanted to be the best, it was up to him. He was determined to MIH—Make It Happen.[18]

What a powerful affirmation! And what a great way to renounce any and all possible negative self-talk. Ask yourself, "What am I saying to myself to renounce negative self-talk and replace it with an empowering affirmation? What am I doing to MIH?"

Your Challenge

As we finish this chapter, I'm reminded of the coach who was talking to his football team. He was talking about the kind of players he wanted to recruit. He asked them, "Men, do we want the kind of player who gets knocked down and stays down?" They all shouted, "No!"

The coach asked, "Do we want the player who gets knocked down, gets up once, gets knocked down again, and stays down?" Again the men shouted, "No!"

So the coach continued, "Do we want the player who keeps getting knocked down and keeps getting up?" The players said, "Yes!"

Of course that's not too bad. But the coach said, "No. I want the player who keeps knocking him down."

You need to be both of those players—the one who keeps on getting up and keeps on knocking down the obstacles that get in your way. And you can be those players if you've got the power of persistence working for you.

CHAPTER 8

The Character of Passion

Character: The Guidance System for Your Fire

If I asked you to name one of the biggest con artists of the past one hundred years, or if I asked you who operated one of the biggest Ponzi schemes of all time, you'd probably name Bernie Madoff. He scammed thousands of people out of billions of dollars and was eventually sent to prison. While he was there, he was asked how he felt about his past as a con artist and his present as a jailbird. His response was alarming as well as refreshing. He said, "I've never been at more peace in my life. My lack of character was killing me."

Madoff *looked* and *sounded* like a man of passion, which is the second element in *The Payoff Principle*. He had plenty of attitude—the fuel to feed his fire. He had an abundance of persistence—the oxygen that kept his fire burning. But he lacked the third component of passion—the **character** or the guidance system for his fire. As a result, his fire burned out of control and devastated the futures of countless people and organizations, as well as his own.

As I've said in the last three chapters, passion is very similar to fire. It needs fuel or attitude to get you going. It needs oxygen or persistence to keep you moving. But it also needs a guidance system, like a fire ring or a fireplace, to keep you moving in the right direction. That's the role of character.

What Is Character?

Many famous people have talked about the importance of character. Kitty Carlisle Hart (1910–2007), the film and TV star, said, "A career takes more than talent. It takes character." And evangelist Billy Graham preached, "When wealth is lost, nothing is lost; when health is lost, something is lost; when character is lost, all is lost."

I believe your character will prove to be more important than your career. After all, your character is one of the few things you take with you wherever you go in life. And some would argue it's the only thing you take with you when you leave this life.

In the 1700s, abolitionist John Woolman equated it with walking your talk. He said, "Conduct is more convincing than language."[1] A person of character walks his talk. What he says and what he does are in sync with one another.

During the Great Depression, humorist Will Rogers (1879–1935) equated it with upright, moral behavior. He told people to "live in such a way that you wouldn't be ashamed to sell your parrot to the town gossip!"[2]

In the late twentieth century, theologian Dr. Charles Swindoll equated character with courage, but not the heroic acts of courage witnessed on the battlefield. He equated character with the quieter forms of courage, such things as "remaining faithful when nobody's looking, like enduring pain when the room is empty, like standing alone when you're misunderstood."[3]

Character has several ingredients. But when it comes to *The Payoff Principle*, I define character as *doing the right thing*.

William Clay Ford Jr., chief executive at the Ford Motor Company, demonstrated that a while back. When Ford Motor stock was downgraded, Ford told the company shareholders that he would not accept any compensation until profits from the automotive division improved.

Wow! Usually we read just the opposite. When a company's fortunes fall, the leadership team members still earn huge amounts of money at the same time the employees lose jobs, benefits, and pensions—the very opposite of character. Not Ford. He did what was right.

The same was true of Ted Williams (1918–2002). When he was closing out his career with the Boston Red Sox, he was suffering from a pinched nerve in his neck. "The thing was so bad," he later explained, "that I could hardly turn my head to look at the pitcher."

For the first time in his career, he batted under .300, hitting just .254 with ten home runs. And that was an embarrassment for Ted, because he was the highest-salaried player in sports, making $125,000.

Nonetheless, the Red Sox sent him the same contract the following year. But when he got the contract, Williams sent it back with a note saying that he would not sign it. He said, "They were offering me a contract I didn't deserve. And I only wanted what I deserved." So he cut his own salary by 25 percent.[4]

As is often the case, good things come to people of good character. During the next season, Williams raised his batting average by sixty-two points, and he closed out his brilliant career by hitting a home run in his final time at bat.

That's character. Williams did the right thing, even when it cost him. And if you aspire to be a person of character, that's what you have to do.

Of course, you may be saying, "How do I know what I'm *supposed* to be doing?" Coach Lou Holtz said, "It's not real complicated. Do what's right. Don't do what's wrong." You don't need a PhD in ethics, religion, or philosophy to figure out what is right.

But I'll give you a simple answer that is correct 99 percent of the time. You're doing the right thing if you're comfortable having other people know about your behavior—the thought process behind it and the decision process that went into it. Or put another way, if your behavior was broadcast on TV or printed on the front page of the newspaper, you would be okay with that.

> *You're doing the right thing if you're comfortable having other people know about your behavior—the thought process behind it and the decision process that went into it.*

If you would prefer to have your behavior kept private, chances are you've got a character problem. The more you want to hide your behavior, the less right it's likely to be. The more willing you are to have your thoughts, decisions, rationales, and behaviors exposed, the more right they're likely to be.

Your character is tested in private. As British historian Thomas B. Macaulay (1800–1859) wrote, "The measure of a man's real character is what he would do if he knew he would never be found out."[5] Congressman J. C. Watts Jr. declared, "Character is doing what's right when nobody's looking."[6] And one of my clients, Hearth and Home Technologies, demands that their salespeople demonstrate "personal integrity," which means doing what is right even "when no one is watching." Your character may be tested in private, but everyone around you is usually already familiar with your character.

Checking Out Your Character

They see the example you set—your coworkers, your subordinates, your customers, your spouse, and even your kids. As Joseph M. Tucci, the CEO of the information management firm EMC, a US-based information storage equipment business, says, "Every move you make, everything you say, is visible to all."[7] And management consultant Darcy Hitchcock says, "Employees are professional boss watchers."[8] They don't miss a thing you say or do.

What about you? Are you truly aware of the character you're displaying? And how can you check out your character? Get some feedback. Ask some Brave Questions (we'll learn more about these in chapter 13). Find out how you're coming across to the people you lead, live with, and work with. It takes courage to ask these kinds of questions, and it takes guts to sit and listen to the answers without getting defensive. But you need to ask them nonetheless. Ask some of your colleagues, coworkers, customers, friends, and relatives such questions as

- On a scale of one to ten, where ten is the best, how would you score my trustworthiness—to tell the truth and do what I say I'm going to do?

- What words would you use to describe me to someone else? Where would the words "character," "integrity," "honorable," and "upright" fall on that list?

- What does my example "tell" other people?

- Where do I seem to be lacking in character? Or where does there seem to be a gap between what I say and what I do?

- What is there in my character that automatically earns your trust? And what is there in my character that automatically alerts your danger signals?

- If I were to have a character makeover, what changes do I need to make?

- What three things in my character do you find to be the most admirable?

Take the time to check out your character. If you like what you discover, great. If you find that your character needs some development, you can develop your character. Let's get started.

Character Practice #1: Engage in Behaviors that Build Your Self-Respect

There's a lot of energy to be found in self-respect. In fact, energy and self-respect go hand in hand. Every time you do something that makes you feel good about yourself, you increase your energy and passion. And every time you do something that makes you feel bad about yourself, you decrease your energy and passion. So what behaviors will build your self-respect? There are two behaviors in particular.

Accept Yourself

Remember the movie *Forrest Gump* (1994)? I was especially touched when Forrest was asked the biggest, most important question anyone can be asked. "What are you going to be when you grow up?"

Dumbfounded, Forrest replied, "Well, I'm going to be me, aren't I?" Great answer. Despite the fact that the world had labeled him slow or retarded, Forrest intuitively knew the importance of being himself. That's the mark of a healthy character.

> You can't possibly respect yourself if you don't even want to be yourself.

People with poor self-esteem often try to be like somebody else. And that only leads to self-loathing. You can't possibly respect yourself if you don't even want to be yourself. As romance author Doris Mortman said so well, "Until you make peace with who you are, you'll never be content with what you have."[9]

Of course, that doesn't mean you're perfect. Nobody is. It doesn't mean you can't and shouldn't improve. Everybody needs to. It simply means you accept yourself as a person of value.

Lou Holtz, one of the most successful football coaches of all time, reinforced that when the two of us were speaking to a large audience on the topics of success and performance. Lou got right to the bottom line when he said, "The most important thing I can tell you is to believe in yourself. Have faith in yourself." In fact, he said that was the secret to his teams' winning records. The more they believed in themselves, the better they did.

That's exactly what Carl Jordan learned. A fleet analyst at the Wagner Equipment Company, Carl wrote,

Replacing my low self-esteem with confidence in my abilities was my primary reason for attending your *Journey to the Extraordinary* program. Before your seminar, I often thought how much I hated myself when things didn't go the way I thought they should. It got to the point that I would verbalize those thoughts in front of both my family and friends.

I followed your self-esteem building steps. Every morning, I started telling myself what a great person I am, and every evening I list the positive things I accomplished that day. I started to believe what I was saying, and now I have the confidence and security that I have desired for so many years. I can honestly say the most rewarding days of my life have all come after taking your *Journey*. Thank you very much for opening my eyes to what I can do if I believe in myself. I now look forward to every day's challenges with anticipation rather than dread.

You may have made some bad choices in your life, and you may be deflated and dishonored in your own eyes. You may have a difficult time accepting yourself. But character is not built on the fact that you are perfect. Character is built on a decision you make—that you are a person of value, period.

Perform with Excellence

When you do what's right, you engage in behavior that builds your self-respect. If you're paid $40 an hour to perform a certain job, you give back at least $40 worth of effort each hour. It's not only the right thing to do; it's also the self-respecting thing to do, to perform with excellence.

> *Character is not built on the fact that you are perfect. Character is built on a decision you make—that you are a person of value, period.*

> You can't feel good about yourself if you do just enough to get by or turn in work that is barely acceptable.

After all, you can't feel good about yourself if you do just enough to get by or turn in work that is barely acceptable. You can't goof off when the boss is gone and think it's okay just as long as you don't get caught. Deep down you know it is not right. Oh, you may feel clever or sneaky for a while, but that's totally different from having a deep respect for yourself.

And I suspect your best teachers knew that secret. They were the ones who made you work, work, work. They were the ones who said, "You can do it, and you're going to do it." You may have complained about those teachers at the time, but those were the teachers you held in highest regard because they brought out your very best. They knew, and intuitively you knew, it was good for your character when you performed with excellence.

The same truth applies to your work situation. You respect the boss who brings out your best, who believes in you and your ability to deliver quality work, and under his or her leadership you almost automatically perform with a higher degree of excellence. And that, in turn, gives you a powerful injection of self-respect.

To build your character, you must perform with excellence—whether you consciously choose to do so or are encouraged by someone else to do so. And you must perform with excellence all the time. As the great philosopher Aristotle put it, "You are what you repeatedly do. Excellence is not an event—it is a habit."

So character is doing what's right, which comes, in part, from engaging in behaviors that build your self-respect.

Character Practice #2: Engage in Behaviors That Respect Others

The comedian Rodney Dangerfield made his living by talking about the fact he never got any respect from anyone. We can laugh, but in reality it's not funny if you feel disrespected by others. However, when you're a person of character—doing what's right—you make deliberate behavior choices that demonstrate your respect for others.

Give Rather Than Take

First, you show respect for others when you give to them rather than take from them. The great actress Katharine Hepburn (1907–2003) talked about that. She said, "Love has nothing to do with what you are expecting to get—only what you are expecting to give."[10] The same truth applies to respect.

Givers think about others, and their thoughtfulness shows up in their respectful behavior. One of my esteemed customers, Deb Wittenberg, the manager of Learning & Development for the Digi-Key Corporation, was like that. When I asked her for her definition of a giver, she said, "It's all about 'paying it forward.' I feel successful when the way I behaved, the way I spoke, and the way I listened to someone's concerns affected another person's life in such a way that he or she made better, more positive decisions."

Alternatively, you're more of a disrespectful taker if you're a leader who seldom thinks about how the corporate changes will affect your staff or seldom asks for their input. You're more of a taker if you're a customer service provider who treats customers as an interruption of your work instead of being the main reason for your work. And you're more of a taker if you're so preoccupied with your iPod, iPad, Facebook, Twitter, and TV programs that you fail to connect with your family members. This is taking, disrespectful behavior focused on me, me, me and what I want.

It's like the father who was asked by a young man if he could marry his daughter. The father asked, "Can you support a family?"

The young man said, "Yes."

"Good," replied the father. "There are six of us."

The father was a taker, fixated on his needs. He didn't give a thought to the needs of his future son-in-law.

Assume People Have Good Intentions

Second, you show respect for others when you assume good intentions on their part. It's easy to get upset with people who irritate us. And it's easy to give them disrespect in return. But producers assume good intentions instead of planning ways they can get back at the other person.

The author and student of human behavior, Stephen Covey (1932–2012), gave an example. He reminds us that we often do not or cannot know what is causing a person to behave in a way that we don't like.

Covey writes about a Sunday morning subway ride in New York City. As a few people sat quietly reading newspapers, a father and his young children entered the subway car. The father sat down and seemed to drift off in thought as his children ran around the car, screaming and distracting other passengers. After a few minutes of restraint, and after it became obvious the father wasn't paying any attention to his children's behavior, Covey asked the man to control his children.

The father's response is an important lesson to all of us in assuming good intentions. The father said, "Oh, you're right. I guess I should do something about it. We just came from the hospital where their mother died about an hour ago. I don't know what to think, and I guess they don't know how to handle it either."[11]

As Covey points out, his feelings instantly changed from irritation to compassion. And the same thing will probably happen to your feelings if you assume good intentions the next time you deal with a difficult person. You'll respond as a person of character instead of being a character in an unpleasant drama.

Chances are, you have to work with or interact with a variety of people. So you're bound to deal with some complaining people on occasion. If you automatically label those complainers as difficult, deceitful, or manipulative, you'll have a very difficult time assuming good intentions on their part. And if you're not careful, you may allow those complaining people to diminish your passion.

Producers start with an assumption that the other person has good intentions. They welcome complaints and try to see things from the other person's point of view, rather than immediately react to the other person's offensive behavior.

Of course, you may be thinking, "That's the last thing I want, a bunch of customers with problems and complaints." But did you know that the most loyal customers, the biggest spending customers, are the ones who had a complaint and had it fixed promptly by an individual or an organization? They're the customers who go around talking about the good service they received when times were tough.

At Charles Schwab, the investment company, they know that a well-handled complaint turns into extra sales for the company. So they aim to do more than simply satisfy the complaining customer. They aim to keep that customer and increase the amount of business they do with him or her.

To measure this, their complaint department does not measure success by attempting to lessen the number of complaints they receive. Instead, they look at the amount of business a client gave them six months before a complaint and six months after. So they assume good intentions and welcome complaints at Charles Schwab. And the results speak for themselves. More than half of their complaining customers give them even more business after their complaint. They can actually monetize the payoff they're receiving.

Practice Kindness

Third, you show respect for others when you are kind. As author Michael Josephson points out, "The way we treat people we think can't help or hurt us (like housekeepers, waiters, and secretaries), tells more about our character than how we treat people we think are important. People who are honest, kind, and fair only when there's something to gain shouldn't be confused with people of real character who demonstrate these qualities habitually, under all circumstances. Character is not a fancy coat we put on for show. It's who we really are."[12]

> "The way we treat people we think can't help or hurt us (like housekeepers, waiters, and secretaries), tells more about our character than how we treat people we think are important. People who are honest, kind, and fair only when there's something to gain shouldn't be confused with people of real character who demonstrate these qualities habitually, under all circumstances."
> —Michael Josephson

I know what he's talking about when he refers to how we treat those "less important" people. In the early days of my career, when I was in my twenties, when I was finishing my doctoral studies and writing my doctoral dissertation, I worked as a part-time instructor at the university to make some money to support my wife and child. And not to boast, but I was a natural at teaching. I was really good at it. Students sat there in rapt attention and furiously took notes on all the brilliant things I had to say. I felt respected.

But money was very short. So I got another part-time job as a desk clerk at a hotel working from 11 p.m. to 7 a.m. I was stunned by the way some of the customers treated me. I experienced everything from condescending tones of voice and rolling eyes to verbal putdowns. This was anything but kindness. I couldn't believe the contrast in treatment. A few hours before I had been *the* respected rising star in academia being quoted by others, and now, I was one of *those* lowly servants.

What about you? Do you treat everyone with kindness, no matter what his or her title, position, or profit potential might be? Or do you sometimes treat people as things to be used in the pursuit of your goals?

Serve Others

Fourth, you show respect for others when you serve them. Sounds something like "servant leadership," doesn't it? And it sounds very much like some fourth grade children Robert Roberts writes about where the teacher introduced a game called "balloon stomp." A balloon was tied to every child's leg, and the object of the game was to pop everyone else's balloon while guarding your own. The last person with an unpopped balloon would win.

The first group wasted no time in entering into the spirit of the game. Balloons were relentlessly targeted and destroyed, and the entire battle was quickly over. It's hard to win at a game like balloon stomp because you're almost forced to be pushy, rude, and offensive.

But then a second class was introduced to the same game. Only this time it was a class of intellectually disabled children. They were given the same explanation as the first class, but the game was played very differently. Perhaps the instructions were given too quickly for children with learning disabilities to grasp them. The one idea that got through was that the balloons were supposed to be popped. So it was the balloons, rather than the other players, that were viewed as enemies. Instead of fighting each other, the children began helping each other pop balloons. One little girl knelt down and held her balloon carefully in place, like a holder for a field goal kicker. A little boy stomped it flat. Then he knelt down and held his balloon for her. It went on like this for several minutes until all the balloons were vanquished, and everybody cheered. Everybody won.[13]

Who got the game right, and who got the game wrong? In our world, we tend to think of another person's success as one less opportunity for us to succeed. There can only be one top dog, one top banana, one big kahuna. If we ever find ourselves in that enviable position, we will fight like mad to maintain our hold on it. A lot of people and a lot of companies fail to enjoy prolonged success because they have this balloon stomp mentality, instead of a character-minded mentality of serving others.

How are you playing the game? It's worth a moment of your time to reflect on the question.

Be Generous

Finally, you show respect for others when you're generous with them. I always figured I had this one nailed down. I was in the habit of giving away 10 percent of my gross income every year to people and causes that tugged at my heart. And then my wife and I increased that amount by 1 percent every year, for several years. It felt good, as giving to others should feel. I have to admit, I even felt a little proud of that giving, until . . .

Until I was backpacking in the jungles of the Philippines. (I love adventure travel. It's one of the ways I keep my energy up and my stress down.) After hiking for some distance, I came upon a little village of thatched-roof huts. The natives were obviously poor but thrilled by the excitement of a new person trekking through their village because they had very little contact with the outside world.

After some small talk and after giving them a few simple items I had brought with me, one of the elders asked if I would like a Coke. Absolutely yes! That sounded wonderful, as it was extremely hot and humid, and I was dripping with sweat. So the elder said a couple of the kids would get one for me. And off they ran.

Some four hours later, the children came back with a single bottle of Coca-Cola. They placed the bottle on a table in the middle of an otherwise empty, dirt-floored hut, as dozens of children filled every window of the hut to watch me drink it.

What I didn't know is that the two children had to run two hours to another village to buy the Coke, and then run back to give it to me. They couldn't run to the refrigerator as we often do; they didn't have such things. And they couldn't afford such luxuries as a bottle of Coke in their village. But they wanted to give me one. I was so humbled by their generosity that I wanted to cry, but knew I shouldn't. I wanted to give the Coke to the children who were so eager to have one, but knew I couldn't refuse their gift.

That was the day I learned that you show great respect for others when you give to them generously—not to enable them but to honor them.

What about your levels of giving and generosity? What are you doing to show respect and give honor to others? Once you've mastered this second element of character, of showing respect for others, you still have work to do.

Character Practice #3: Engage in Behaviors That Show Respect for the Truth

The first thing other people want to see in you is *you,* not some superficial image you've created and tried to project.

Be Authentic

That's why the first way you show respect for the truth is by being authentic. Of course, this practice might seem so elementary that I shouldn't even have to mention it. But we're living in a time when looking good seems to be more important than being good and being real.

> We're living in a time when looking good seems to be more important than being good and being real.

As a professor teaching a communication between the sexes class, I was forever cautioning my students about the way some of them approached their dating relationships. Rather than being themselves, some of them would try to figure out what kind of person would be most attractive to someone of the opposite sex, and then they would pretend to be that kind of person.

That approach always fails on two counts. First of all, you won't like yourself for doing it. In fact, you can't possibly like yourself if you don't even accept yourself. (Go back to my first point on accepting yourself earlier in this chapter.)

Second, the other person won't like you either. You can't be the Great Pretender forever. Eventually, your real self will be revealed, and from then on, the other person will automatically question everything you say and do because you're not engaging in behaviors that show a respect for the truth.

To be authentic, you have to be absolutely clear about who you are and what you stand for. You have to know your values, and you have to live your values.

Be Honest

If you're going to be a producer, you can't play games with the truth. You must be absolutely honest. No distortions. No little white lies. No false fronts. No bravado. No parsing of words, such as the definition of "is." Character comes out in plain, simple, but tactful, honesty.

The strange thing is, most people think they are honest, but they don't think there's anything wrong with a little dishonesty. They rationalize that white lies, exaggerations, or minor distortions of the truth are okay.

But what would you think of a manager who says, "My staff is really upset about the company's new quality initiative," but later you discover there had been only one minor complaint? Obviously, you wouldn't trust that manager quite as much in the future. As the German philosopher Friedrich Nietzsche (1844–1900) said, "What upsets me is not that you lied to me, but that from now on I can no longer believe you."[14]

> The cold stark reality is—anything other than absolute honesty does not exhibit character and does not build trust.

The cold stark reality is—anything other than absolute honesty does not exhibit character and does not build trust. It doesn't and it shouldn't. I tell sales groups, "If the truth can't sell, nothing should."

That's how I live my life and run my business now and how I have for the past several decades. But there was a brief time in my life when I failed that test. I was working my way through my undergraduate degree as a shoe salesman in a women's department store. I sold out my character on those nights I stayed late so we could mark *up* all the prices on our shoes before the big sale the following day. My coworkers and I put a "New Sales Price" label on each box of shoes that was the same as the old, original, full-price offer. I sold out my character when I lied to my customers about how much money they were saving when they bought the shoes. I couldn't look my customers in the eye; I couldn't speak to them with confidence, and I couldn't live with myself behaving that way. So I quickly decided I would treat the truth with the respect it deserved.

> *People don't know when a lie is so small that it's okay and when a lie is so big that it's not okay. They simply want you to be a person who respects the truth by telling the truth.*

To make things worse, business paralysis sets in when people are afraid to tell the truth. As Margaret Heffernan, former CEO at CMGI, states, "I've seen countless deals hang in midair because no one had the honesty to say out loud what everyone was thinking privately: 'This is really stupid' and 'It will never work.' And so millions of dollars and countless hours of work were lost somewhere between intent and execution, with people in the know hoping that the whole mess will simply go away, but remaining unwilling to address the problem head on."[15]

Some people have a problem with honesty. Do you? Do you find it easier to tell the embellished truth? Do you craft your words to "give the right impression" . . . even though that impression may not be accurate? If so, you're not giving truth the respect it deserves. If you are going to show respect for the truth, you have to be honest. That doesn't mean you're cruel, brutal, and tactless because that would violate our second practice of showing respect for others.

You have to be honest, nonetheless. It is at the foundation of every good, healthy, and effective relationship. Other people don't know when a lie is so small that it's okay and when a lie is so big that it's not okay.

They simply want you to be a person who respects the truth by telling the truth.

Keep Your Word

Producers always do this: they make commitments, and they do what they say they're going to do.

And, "Yes, keeping your word is sometimes difficult, expensive, and inconvenient," according to Michael Hyatt, the former chairman and CEO of Thomas Nelson Publishers, and author of *Platform: Get Noticed in a Noisy World* (Thomas Nelson, 2012). "But the cost of not doing so is even *more expensive*. It will ultimately cost you your leadership."[16]

Underachievers use noncommittal language instead. They'll say, "I'll see..." "I'll think about it..." and "Well, maybe..." And if they ever do make any commitments, what they really mean is, "Sure, I'll do it, if nothing else comes up, if I don't get a better offer, and if I feel like it." This is a far cry from showing respect for the truth. And it's far different from keeping your word.

If you're going to be a person filled with passion and guided by character, if you're going to lead a team or an organization, if you're going to lead a family, you've got to keep your word. No excuses. You know that a promise is a promise. It doesn't matter if you no longer "feel" like doing what you said you were going to do. Unless all hell breaks out, if you're a person of character, you keep your word. You follow through on every promise you make.

As one person noted, "Character is the ability to follow through on a resolution... long after the mood in which it was made... has left you." Producers don't rule their lives by their feelings;

> A promise is a promise. It doesn't matter if you no longer "feel" like doing what you said you were going to do. Unless all hell breaks out, if you're a person of character, you keep your word. You follow through on every promise you make.

they rule their feelings by thoughtful, conscientious decision making and follow-through.

Admit Your Mistakes

Even if you do what you think is right, you're going to be wrong some of the time. And people of character admit their mistakes. Don't pass the buck. And don't blame anybody else or anything else *if* you are indeed responsible. When you admit your mistakes, you show your respect for the truth.

I remember one high school principal who made a serious mistake, and everyone in the school knew he made a serious mistake. He got on the intercom and apologized to the entire student body even though he was concerned about losing everyone's respect as a result of his mistake and his apology. He became the most popular and respected high school principal in the district. Months afterward, students came up to him and said they wished they had a father like him, as their fathers couldn't ever admit they were wrong.

Katie Paine, founder and CEO of the Delahaye Group, instinctively knew that. She instituted the "Mistake of the Month Club." She says, "Several years ago, I overslept and missed a flight to a big client meeting. I walked into my next staff meeting, plunked $50 down on the table, and said, 'If you can top this mistake, that money is yours.'"

Katie continued, "People started to own up to mistakes, and suddenly we had a flood of them. At every staff meeting since, we've set aside thirty minutes to write up the mistakes of the month on a whiteboard. Then we cast a vote. Since then we've recorded more than two thousand mistakes. Once a mistake hits the whiteboard, it tends not to happen again. It has become a bonding ritual. Once you go through it, you're a member of the club."[17]

> Admitting your mistakes takes guts. But it also builds character and demonstrates your respect for the truth.

Admitting your mistakes takes guts. But it also builds character and demonstrates your respect for the truth.

The Good and the Bad News About Character

The Bad News

As journalist Richard Reeves notes, "All leaders face some crisis where their own strength of character is the enemy." He should have said, "*Everybody* will face crises where their own strength of character is the enemy." Your character will be tested.

You're going to have those times when it would be quicker and easier to criticize a coworker in public rather than wait for a more appropriate and private moment. Your character will help you decide which way you go—with expediency or respect.

You're going to have those times when you're tempted to tell your salespeople to say whatever they have to say to make the sale, even though it means "stretching the truth." Your character will help you decide which way you go—with profit or honesty.

You're going to have those times when you want to say you're out of the office when you're there, or you didn't receive a message when you did. Your character will help you decide which way you go—with a cover-up or transparency.

You're going to have those pressure-filled times when doing the right thing may seem too laborious. Does your character push you toward doing the right thing all the time? Or do your character and your actions take a nosedive when you think no one is looking and you won't get caught?

The Good News

You get to choose the kind of character you want. As Heraclitus of Ephesus says, "The content of your character is your choice. Day by day, what you choose, what you think, and what you do is who you become. Your integrity is your destiny."

Character is doing what's right, all the time, whether or not it's cool, popular, expedient, or politically correct. You must go beyond looking out for yourself and do what is right for all concerned, as much as possible. It keeps your passion from turning into greed, selfishness, or fanaticism. That's good news.

The other bit of good news about character is the payoffs it will bring you:

- **It becomes easier and easier to keep on doing the right thing.** As the saying goes, "Opportunity may knock once, but temptation bangs on your front door forever." But if you keep on doing what is right, it becomes an integral part of who you are, guiding your passion toward the payoffs you seek.

- **You gain the respect of others.** Dan Zadra, CEO of the Creative Director Compendium, says, "Live your life so your children can tell their children that you not only stood for something wonderful—you acted on it."[18] It's what people of character, leaders filled with integrity, and value-driven parents do.

- **You gain the trust of others.** Journalist Walter Lippmann (1889–1974) noted, "A man has honor if he holds himself to an ideal of conduct even when it is inconvenient, unprofitable, or dangerous to do so."[19] Quite simply, people trust you when you do the right thing, not the easy thing or the self-serving thing.

So far, we've talked about the power of purpose—where the payoff begins. And we've talked about the power of passion—where your payoff gets fired up. But it's time we look at the power of **process**, which will turn your payoffs into reality.

PART III

PROCESS

CHAPTER 9

The Power of Process

Where Your Payoffs Turn into Reality

You remember *The Payoff Principle*: "When you find purpose in what you do, exhibit passion for the outcome, and master the process to make it happen, you produce the payoffs you want, need, and deserve." In effect, you become a producer.

We've spent considerable time talking about purpose, which is all about direction, and passion, which is all about energy. So let's dig into the third and final element—**process**, which is all about the skills or methods that turn your desired payoffs into reality.

How I Learned the Producer's Processes

My introduction to the power of **process** came at age seven. I was visiting with Judy, my nine-year-old next-door neighbor and my secret crush. As we were sitting on the lawn talking, I noticed a medium-sized cardboard box sitting next to her, with a collection of smaller boxes strewn around it. Of course, I was curious and asked her what that was all about.

Judy explained that she had ordered a sample collection of greeting cards that she had seen advertised in a comic book. The ad said all she had to do was go knocking on doors, show the person who answered the door her selection of cards, take orders for those cards, and make *big* money. But she had changed her mind and no longer wanted to do that.

No problem. I wanted to do it! I wanted to make some of that big money, which was probably not more than $20 to $30 back then. So I asked Judy if I could sell her sample collection if she wasn't going to. She readily agreed.

Within ten minutes I was knocking on doors, talking to people, showing them my greeting cards, and taking orders. When I got home that night for dinner, I was mighty proud of myself. I told my parents about my new business and showed them the number of orders I had gotten. I never even thought about asking for their permission or guidance; I just did it.

Although my parents were impressed with my initiative, my father was particularly interested in how I was going to manage my business. So he asked me a number of questions about how I had conducted myself with my prospects, how I would fulfill the orders I received, and what thought I had given to profit margins. Of course, I had not given any thought to any of those business issues. I just knocked on doors and said, "You wouldn't want to buy any cards, would you?"

My father questioned me to make sure this was what I really wanted to do—spend some or all of my summer vacation selling greeting cards. I let him know that I was serious. I was in business to be successful and make some money. I had a goal—to buy the awesome three-speed Schwinn bicycle I saw in the window of the Montgomery Ward department store. It was a child's dream bicycle, but I also knew it was a bike my truck-driver father and homemaker mother could never afford to buy me.

Once my father was convinced of my commitment, he let me know there was a better way to run my business than the way I had done it that very first day. He told me there were several *processes* I needed to learn and use if I was going to maximize my profits and produce the success I wanted.

And so my training began. It started with my presentation. My father indicated that too many salespeople fail to sell because they haven't worked on their presentation. They don't know how to communicate with their prospects to get the cooperation they want. (You'll hear more about this in chapter 12—"The Process of Connective Communication.") I couldn't simply go to a door and "wing it." I had to have a prepared presentation instead of just saying whatever came out of my mouth.

So we began to work on my presentation, word for word, sentence by sentence, writing it all down. Then it was my job to practice my little presentation over and over again until it was memorized, smooth, and conversational. I was involved in the **process of continuing education** (see chapter 11 for more information). And even though that training session took place more than fifty years ago, I still remember my presentation. I was to knock on a door, and when the resident opened the door, I would start my comments by saying, "Good morning, Ma'am. May I have two or three minutes of your time to show you the latest selection of greeting cards? I can assure you that I have some of the very best cards at the very best prices."

My closing rate shot up instantly and dramatically. Almost everyone said "yes," that they would like to see my greeting cards, and almost everyone purchased. I don't know if my sales improved because my presentation was refined or because my housewife prospects were impressed that a seven-year-old sounded so professional. I suspect it was a bit of both. That was the first summer with my new business.

When the following summer vacation came around, I told my parents I wanted to continue my business. My parents were okay with that, but my father said it was time to learn another strategy in the process of continuing education that would save me time and increase my profits.

To be specific, my father taught me that my approach to the business was costing me twice as much time without giving me any more profit. My approach was to knock on a door, talk to a prospect, take her order, go back home, send in the order, wait for the cards to arrive, and then go back to the customer's house, sometimes repeatedly, to deliver the cards and pick up the money.

My father suggested a different approach. I could order a huge quantity of greeting cards at one time, before I even sold them, because I could buy them in bulk at a much cheaper cost. In addition to that, I could carry the cards with me when I called on prospects. If they wanted to purchase some of my cards, they could do so and pay me at that very moment. I adopted that process, but not without some fear.

To purchase my inventory in bulk, I had to empty out my savings account, my entire lifetime savings of $272. I spent every penny of it ordering hundreds of boxes of greeting cards. Indeed, when the delivery came, a huge semitruck backed into our driveway filled with my merchandise. The truck driver carried dozens of great big cardboard boxes down to the basement of our house. I was a bit concerned, to say the least, seeing our basement filled with cards that I would have to sell, or lose my savings.

No problem. I was committed to selling them. And unbeknownst to me, I started to use the **process of affirming achievement** (for more info see chapter 10), talking to myself over and over again, telling myself I could do it, which built my confidence and kept me going.

My father had given me wise counsel. I tied a wagon to my old bicycle, built up the sides of the wagon so I could carry a large inventory of greeting cards with me, and began to tow my merchandise from house to house. I began selling and delivering the cards and picking up the money on my very first call. My father had taught me a great time-saving process. It increased my profits because I could now call on more prospects, and it saved me time, so I had plenty of time to play as well as work during my summer vacation.

At age nine, when my third summer vacation came around, I still wanted to be in the greeting card business. But it was time for some additional teaching. My father emphasized the **process of compassionate listening** (for more info see chapter 13), that if I wanted to get more from my customers, I would have to listen for their expressed or unexpressed needs.

My customers had been telling me they would be interested in such things as wrapping paper, and my vendor had a very attractive, full-color catalog that featured everything from wrapping paper to kitchen gadgets, wall plaques, knickknacks, and a host of gift items. In the matter of days, I was selling such a variety of items that I could no longer tote them around all by myself.

It was time to hire my first employee, which happened to be my younger brother. I paid him 5¢ for every box of greeting cards I sold, and his job was to merely drag another wagon of merchandise behind his bicycle. He was a great help as my "transportation assistant," but I didn't treat him with the respect he deserved. At that time, I didn't know anything about coaching and developing people.

My business continued to prosper. When I was ten, I was the richest kid in the neighborhood. Indeed, I was buying so many products from my vendor and selling so much merchandise that the president of the company called my house. She spoke to my mother, asking if she could speak to Alan Zimmerman, who had become their company's biggest customer. She wanted to know what my secret was; she wanted me to share it with their other customers so they could learn from me.

Of course, she had no idea she was about to speak to a ten-year-old kid. I couldn't articulate my secret then as I can now, but I had been using *The Payoff Principle*. I had a **purpose**, no matter how meager it may have been originally (getting a bicycle), then moving on to the larger purpose of saving for a car, and then pursuing the substantial purpose of saving for college. I had plenty of **passion** to keep me going, and my father was teaching me the **processes** I needed to know to bring it all together.

I was on fire, and I was seeing the **payoffs**. So I started researching "businesses I could do from home in my spare time." (You've seen the ads. They're still out there.) I decided to add an import division to my little door-to-door business. I began importing cuckoo clocks from Germany, watches from France, shoes from the former Czechoslovakia, and a host of other goods. I could buy them for pennies on the dollar and reap a very nice profit. It was an early and valuable introduction to *The Payoff Principle*.

The Four Critical Processes

If you ever wonder why you don't see more of your hopes, wishes, and dreams fulfilled in your life, you may be overlooking this third element in *The Payoff Principle*—process. There are some processes you need to use, no matter how much purpose, clarity, or passion energy you have.

> There are some processes you need to use, no matter how much purpose, clarity, or passion energy you have.

And if you don't know *what* processes you have to use, you can get mighty discouraged in the pursuit of your payoffs. You may quit your job—in fact or in theory. (As I mentioned earlier, we all know people who have retired but haven't told the Personnel Department yet.) Or you may leave your dreams, friends, family, and everything else that is important to you behind. That's the bad news.

As much as I hate to say it, I've got some other bad news for you. There isn't one for-sure, guaranteed no-fail process that you can use on every challenge that crosses your path. There isn't one single process or step-by-step program that you can use for strategically planning the future of your company, building your team at work, selling more products to your customers, improving your marriage, bettering your health, and everything else you want.

However, and this is good news, I have discovered four major processes behind every success story. Somehow or other, the producer has consciously or unconsciously, deliberately or accidentally, tapped into the power of one or more of these processes. It was the proper use of these processes that turned their purpose and passion into reality. And that's what part III, "Process," of the book is all about—helping you understand and then implement these processes as quickly, easily, and effectively as possible.

The even better news is, these four processes are fairly quick, easy, and simple. That's encouraging because if you're like a lot of my customers, you may be thinking, "I don't care about the theory. Just tell me what I have to do to get the results I want."

Process Is Personal and Interpersonal

Two of these processes are personal and two of them are interpersonal. Together they will turn your purpose and passion into payoffs.

The personal processes are things you need to do for yourself. You need the **process of affirming achievement** (see chapter 10) so you accomplish more goals in less time with less effort. And you need to adopt the **process of continuing education** (see chapter 11). You can't expect to achieve tomorrow's dreams with yesterday's skills.

You can't use yesterday's skills to win today's victories. And you can't use today's motivation to achieve tomorrow's dreams.

The interpersonal processes are things you have to do with others. You need to learn, practice, and implement the **process of connective communication** (see chapter 12). Many of the payoffs you want on and off the job will require the willing cooperation of others. That cooperation starts with your communication competence and is completed by the **process of compassionate listening** (see chapter 13).

As you move through these four processes, *please* don't read them and move on. Devour them. Use them. Practice them. Master them. Just knowing about them won't do you much good. In fact, they'll be as useless as a car without a steering wheel.

I know. My failure to use these four processes almost killed me.

The Crash, Burn, and Rescue

When I resigned my secure, lifetime, tenured position as a university professor to start my own speaking, training, and consulting business, I was filled with purpose and passion. I wanted to take the transformation that was taking place in my classrooms into the marketplace. But I had no process to make that happen.

For several years while I was teaching, I was speaking on the side—quite a bit, actually. But I also turned down a lot of requests for speaking engagements because I was already "booked" with my classes. What I didn't realize was that I was building up a following.

When I finally resigned, I figured it would take me a couple of years to build my business. Not true. I booked 167 programs the first year I was in business as a full-time professional speaker. And that was without marketing, calling, or brochures. Word of mouth advertising jam-packed my calendar. But 167 programs, plus travel, also meant I was never home.

I was filled with purpose and passion. I was proud of myself. I was making a difference. And I was receiving accolades galore. But I had ignored the processes of managing my business and nourishing my health and my relationships, all at the same time. I was just winging it.

That's what I did until it was impossible to wing it or ignore the processes any longer. My speaking and travel schedule decimated my body, so much so that I could barely walk for two years. My wife got tired of being number two, three, or ten on my list of priorities and divorced me. And my daughter and I barely spoke for several years. I crashed and burned.

I became a dinosaur in danger of extinction. In fact, it really hit me, in the midst of all that, when I saw a cartoon of two dinosaurs standing on the last bit of land as they watched Noah's ark sail away to safety. One dinosaur asked the other, "Oh crap, was that today?" Without the proper processes, some of the important ships in my life had sailed on and left me behind.

Personally, my life was in trouble. And professionally, I had developed a business that was so large I didn't have the time or expertise to manage it and continue delivering keynotes and seminars everywhere, almost every day. I ignored, or didn't know, the processes that could have prevented my crash and burn.

The rescue came with Chris Gibson, an expert on process. She led a major division of a health-care company, had more than four hundred employees, and managed a multimillion-dollar budget. In fact, she was so talented at process that she led one of the few health-care organizations in the country that passed rigorous Medicare audits time after time with zero deficiencies.

She agreed to come in and help me establish the processes that would ensure the continuing growth and health of my company and myself. Using a nursing model of documentation, she created a process that made sure every incoming and outgoing call was clearly documented. Sounds like common sense now, but it wasn't common practice for me. Using a nursing model of triage, she created a process that clearly identified every potential customer, their degree of interest in our services, and our strategy for follow-up.

Chris went on to create job descriptions, policies, and procedures for every one of my team members. Prior to her arrival in the company, everyone was so busy with his or her own work in his or her own silo that our work was less than efficient. She established regular staff meetings and strategic planning sessions so we could tap into the best ideas of everyone else in our organization and use those ideas. And every employee was given continual education so they could be proactive rather than reactive in our work with customers.

And yes, like any other company, there was some initial resistance to the changes she was making in the company, but the results were indisputable. Within a year, she cut back my speaking and travel schedule by 40 percent, so I could have plenty of time for new research, a healthier work-life balance, and flourishing relationships. She increased our revenue by 112 percent, so everyone could be compensated more generously. And together, as one team and one organization, we created the processes for long-term sustainability.

I found out that the crash, burn, and rescue were totally unnecessary. I didn't have to crash and burn. And you don't either. I knew the right processes to follow. I had used them with great success as a youngster in my first businesses.

But I had made a common mistake that you may be making as well. I got so busy doing my work that I forgot about managing my work, taking care of myself, paying attention to the people in my life, and planning for the future. As the old saying goes, I couldn't see the forest for the trees.

The Payoff Principle makes it clear that the big payoffs in life or on the job come when you have all the elements of purpose, passion, *and* processes working for you. Let's dig into the four processes that will turn your payoffs into reality.

CHAPTER 10

The Process of Affirming Achievement

You Change Your Life When You Change Your Mind

Imagine that you're in a boat and the autopilot is set for east, but you decide you want to change directions and go west. You take hold of the wheel and using all your might, you force the boat west. As long as you hold the wheel steady, the boat keeps on going west. But pretty soon, you get tired of fighting the boat's inclination and let go of the wheel. And once again, you're heading east—because that's the direction the boat is programmed to go.

As John Baker notes in *Life's Healing Choices* (New York: Howard Books, 2013), "That's how it is when you try to fight against your own internal autopilot. By your own willpower, you try to force new behavior. You try and you try, but pretty soon you get tired . . . and you let go of the wheel . . . and you revert back to the way you've always acted."[1]

If you don't know *where* your autopilot is set, and if you don't know *how* to reset your autopilot for the payoffs you want, you will revert to any one of a hundred nonproductive behaviors. That's why most people do not come close to reaching their full potential. They don't achieve the goals

> Most people don't achieve the goals they'd like to achieve or live the life they'd like to live because their autopilot is stuck on the wrong setting.

they'd like to achieve, and they don't live the life they'd like to live. Their autopilot is stuck on the wrong setting.

And that may be of true of you as well. Your autopilot or mental programming may be the victim of the exposure-adoption-addiction cycle, and you didn't even know it.

When you were young, for example, you may have been *exposed* to the negative comments of others, thousands of times. You were told repeatedly such comments as "No, you can't do that." "You'll never amount to anything." "You never listen to me." "You're no good at math."

Unfortunately, this type of negative programming from others didn't stop when you left home, graduated from school, or became an adult. When you got a job, your exposure to negative conditioning continued and sometimes accelerated. You were exposed to a variety of comments that implied other people didn't believe in you or your ideas. Author Jack Canfield calls them "Killer Statements" because they kill off your energy, your enthusiasm, your initiative, and your effectiveness if you don't know how to respond to them.

There are hundreds of Killer Statements that get in the way of you becoming the producer you want to become. I'm sure you can relate. You bring up an idea at work, and people respond to you by saying such things as: "We've never done that kind of thing before," "That wouldn't work here," "We tried that five years ago," "That's not my job," "We're too busy for that," or "You're right, but . . ."

After you've been exposed to enough negative feedback, you may unwittingly *adopt* a narrower, smaller, more limited outlook or mindset. In a sense, you throw up your mental arms or throw in the towel and get used to getting by instead of getting ahead. You allow your mental autopilot to be stuck on the wrong setting.

However, and this is critical, what people are saying out there—at home or on the job—is not nearly as important as what you're telling yourself.

> What people are saying out there—at home or on the job—is not nearly as important as what you're telling yourself.

After you've adopted enough of the negatives, you can actually get *addicted* to that way of thinking and start telling yourself your own set of self-defeating negative comments. I call them "Mind Binders," and the more you think them or say them, the less successful you're going to be in those areas of your life and work.

Again, there are lots of them. I'm sure you've heard people say some of the following, or maybe you tell yourself some of these Mind Binders:

- I can't remember people's names . . .

- I always attract the wrong kind of people . . .

- I'll never get ahead . . .

- I just can't seem to save any money . . .

- I can't lose weight . . .

- I can't stick to a diet . . .

- I've got too much work to do . . .

- I'll never get caught up . . .

- I always get a headache at 3:00 p.m. . . . .

Mind Binders are absolutely disastrous because they keep your auto-pilot stuck on the wrong setting, preventing you from getting the payoffs you want and need.

That's what happened to Karl Wallenda when he let the Mind Binders get to him. Back in the 1960s, the flying Wallendas were seen as the finest circus act in the world. They took the art of tightrope walking to the great extreme and the very dangerous. In fact, Karl Wallenda loved it so much, in 1968 he said, "Walking the tightrope is living. Everything else is working."[2]

His wife noted that never once in all his life, in his entire career, did Karl even think about falling. But in Puerto Rico, with his rope stretched between two skyscrapers, and with thousands of people watching, Karl fell to the pavement and his death.

His wife later said that for the last three months of his life, Karl had been consumed by one thought—"I'm going to fall." He never thought of it before, but now that was all he thought about.[3]

Karl did not understand that worry is negative goal setting. He did not understand that you are drawn to the very thing that fills your mind. As Mrs. Wallenda later said, Karl put all his energy into falling rather than walking, and the minute he did that he was destined to fall.

The good news is you can reset your autopilot to achieve what you want to achieve.

Give Your Autopilot a Temporary Reset

Take a moment, once in a while, to check out your thoughts. Notice how often you're thinking negative thoughts about yourself, your life, your job, your relationships, or anything else. In fact, if you find yourself sinking, *pay attention to what you're thinking*. Be especially careful of thinking any of the four most common, self-defeating Mind Binders:

- I am not _____ (good, smart, attractive, etc.) enough.

- I am a victim of _____ (my past, my upbringing, my genes, my boss's whims, etc.).

- I cannot trust _____ (myself, my decisions, my opinions, my preferences, or whatever).

- I am not worthy of other people's _____ (love, respect, time, recognition, help, etc.).

These statements are all indications of an autopilot that will hurt you instead of help you. And they're all indications that you need to give your autopilot an immediate, albeit temporary, reset. Use one or more of the following techniques.

Refute Your Mind Binders

As soon as you think one of them or speak one of them, talk back to yourself. Tell yourself, firmly and authoritatively, to "Stop it. Now just stop it!" Or follow up any negative thought with a command that says, "Cancel. Cancel." With repetition, you neutralize the negative thoughts and reset your autopilot, at least for the moment.

> *If you find yourself sinking, pay attention to what you're thinking.*

Reject Your Mind Binders

Avoid the use of such words as "can't." As industrialist Henry Ford (1863–1947) put it, "Whether you think you can or think you can't, you're right."[4]

Eliminate the word "impossible" from your vocabulary. One of my students helped me do that when she gave me a poster that read, "An impossibility is nothing more than a big idea striking a small mind." And the business books and the sports pages are filled with stories of people who did the impossible because they refused to speak the word "impossible."

Reprimand Your Mind Binders

Just keep a rubber band on one of your wrists, and whenever you think a negative thought or utter a negative comment, snap the rubber band. Sure, it will hurt a little, but it's a simple way to cut down on your old, negative, self-destructive thoughts and give your autopilot a temporary reset.

Replace Your Mind Binders

For example, if you find yourself thinking something like "I'll never be able to handle those difficult coworkers," replace that with a more constructive thought. Tell yourself something like "I can take a seminar on dealing with difficult people, and I can improve my skills when I'm talking to them." Instead of saying, "I'll never amount to anything," tell yourself, "I'm getting better and better."

Your thoughts are not some innocent innocuous bystander in your life. Indeed, what you think about you tend to bring about. As author Florence Shinn (1871–1940) wrote, "The game of life is the game of boomerangs. Our thoughts, deeds, and words return to us sooner or later, with astounding accuracy."[5]

You give your autopilot a temporary reset when you use these techniques. Using the process of affirming achievement, you could also give your autopilot a *permanent* reset.

Give Your Autopilot a Permanent Reset

This is where you get the biggest payoffs—when you follow a proven process of setting and using affirmations, which are carefully crafted declarations of the goals you want and expect to achieve, and which are deployed through a step-by-step system.

> *You get the biggest payoffs when you follow a proven process of setting affirmations and then deploy them step-by-step.*

Of course, affirmations are not new. They've been around a long time. You've probably heard of them, and you may even have tried them. But if you're like a lot of people, you didn't know the exact process to follow, and so your results were mixed, at best. That's why comedian Al Franken satirized affirmations for years on *Saturday Night Live*. Playing the character of Stuart Smalley, he was known for his signature ever-present affirmation, "I'm good enough, I'm smart enough, and doggone it, people like me."

When you follow the **process of affirming achievement**, you can permanently reset your autopilot to achieve amazing payoffs. Mary B. Johnson, my marketing director for eighteen years, can testify to that.

She wanted to improve her posture as well as her customer service skills. So she began to tell herself, "I stand tall in my love and service to others."

Some months later, coming back for her annual physical examination, her doctors were baffled. In fact they were so shocked that they checked her height again and again, and they checked her records from the past several years. Since her last physical, she now stood one inch taller than ever before.

Indeed, my files are filled with similar testimonials from hundreds of my students. Using the same process of affirming achievement, Barbara Heiden from Cargill, the largest privately held company in the United States, accomplished amazing things as well. She writes, "Using your affirmation techniques, I am eating well-balanced meals, losing weight, and have more energy than ever! I got a new job that pays a great deal better, and even applied your techniques to our family finances for a net gain of $125,000. As you can tell, I have made some very positive changes. Thanks!"

Better yet, it doesn't take weeks and weeks and months and months to reset your autopilot permanently. Mike Sojka of Fastenal, the leading fastener distributor in North America, learned that. Within a mere month of attending my program, Mike was seeing amazing results. As he says, "I used your affirmation process to successfully start my own business. And I used your techniques to eliminate worry, which has made life a lot less stressful."

The process of affirming achievement works equally well in your professional and personal lives. Marilyn Schilling, an administrative office manager at the world's number one medical clinic, said she was stuck in a rut of low self-esteem, had lost her ability to be assertive at work, and overall had lost her focus in life and work. But she said, "Your affirmation process changed all that. I started a weight-loss program and lost ten pounds. At work, I learned how to work with difficult people, when necessary, and I've made progress on projects that I didn't think I could do before. I am no longer letting the negative talk get into my head, and my positive attitude is coming back because of what you taught me. If I don't watch out, I might start humming out loud again!"

So how do you get the process of affirming achievement working for you? Here are four steps you can follow.

Affirmation Step #1: Define Your Goals

The process starts with clarity. If you aren't clear about your goals, chances are you won't like the payoffs you get.

For example, one of my acquaintances talks about her goal to lose weight and be physically fit, but she smokes two packs of cigarettes a day, drinks six beers a night, and never exercises. She's good at talking the talk but totally lacking in credibility when it comes to walking the walk. Her real goal, deep down, is to keep on smoking, drinking, and avoiding the inconvenience of regular exercise. And she's getting the exact payoffs that go along with that goal—excess weight and diminished self-esteem. Even though she thinks she's clear about her real goals, she's *not*!

Another acquaintance says his goal is improved relationships with his wife and kids. But he works two jobs and fifty-five hours a week, but not out of economic necessity. He just likes the feeling of being important and in demand. As a result, his payoffs are fairly predictable. His wife is angry with him, and his kids have replaced their dad with electronic gadgets that now occupy their time. Again, there's a huge gap between what he says his real goal is and what he does to reach that goal. Let's start the process of defining *your* goals. Ask yourself the following questions.

What Do You Really, Really, REALLY Want?

Remember our discussion from chapter 1? Start the process by brainstorming your wants and desires. Decide what you want—not what you think you want, or might want, or what someone else thinks you should want, but what *you* really want! So get out a piece of paper and write down *everything* you want, desire, wish, and hope for. Brainstorm. The longer your list the more useful it will be.

Your wants might include improvements in certain areas of your life. You may want to improve your golf score or increase the number of sales you close. You may want to modify your behavior in certain situations. You may want to be more assertive with your coworkers or more open with your family members. You may want to change a personality characteristic or drop a bad habit.

How Much Balance Do You Have in Your List?

Once you've brainstormed your list of possible wants, whether it takes you ten minutes or ten days, make sure you've listed at least five wants in each of the eight dimensions of life: physical, recreational, financial, occupational, social, mental, emotional, and spiritual.

If you have one goal, such as making a million dollars in a year, and if you dedicated every bit of your time, energy, and thought into that one goal, the chances of you achieving that goal are pretty good. But chances are also good that your life, your health, your relationships, and everything else would be a mess. So a healthy, balanced, effective producer has at least five positive goals in each of the eight dimensions of life.

What Would You Want If You Knew You Could Not Fail?

Don't waste your time wondering whether your wants and desires are practical or possible. That's premature. In most cases, when you follow the process of affirming achievement, you will be able to acquire most, if not all, of the things you desire. So don't let fear hold you back from making your long, extensive, and thorough list. Just write down everything you want.

What Do You Want to Subtract from Your Life?

Maybe you want to get rid of your procrastination, your disorganization, your inability to cope with certain people, or a bad habit such as the excess use of food, nicotine, and alcohol. Write them all down.

Thus far, everything you have written down probably falls into a "get" category. You want to get yourself financially stabilized, get that promotion at work, get your marriage on stronger footing, and get yourself in better shape. And that's great. You should have some "get" goals to work on.

What Are Your "Be" Goals?

Two, three, five, ten, twenty years from now, you will be a different person. Have you figured out what you want that person to be? Or are you just drifting through life, thinking whatever happens, happens?

A producer would never take that approach. A producer knows that goal setting and achieving involves a lot more than *getting* a bunch of stuff; it's also about *becoming* the right kind of person.

So you need to list everything you want to be. Close your eyes and imagine your ideal self, possessing all the qualities you would like to have. List eight to ten qualities that describe the kind of person you want to be now and the kind of person you want to become in the future. Maybe you want to be more self-confident, be more skilled in selling your product, be more effective in managing your team, or be a bigger risk taker.

What Do You Want to Be Remembered For?

Of course, we talked about this in the chapters on purpose. But let me suggest a little homework. Write out a description of how your life would look if it turned out *exactly* the way you hoped it would. You'll get some clarity on what you want to be remembered for. Do you want people to say, "He led the district in sales six years in a row?" Or do you want them to say, "She treated everyone with the greatest respect?"

Affirmation Step #2: Write Your Goals as Affirmations

The research is clear. If you're not willing to put your goals on paper, you probably won't achieve them. The act of writing shows your commitment. You are doing more than wishful thinking. And writing gives your mind a sense of direction. You're telling your subconscious mind that of all the millions of possibilities out there, these are the few you would like.

This is one of the most important, self-motivating practices of all time. Put all of your personal and professional goals in writing. And if you're not currently doing this, let me assure you it will literally change your life.

> *If you're not willing to put your goals on paper, you probably won't achieve them. But writing down your goals gives your mind a sense of direction and tells your subconscious mind to go to work on achieving them.*

For example, I had a goal for eighteen years to write a book, and that goal was buried deep in my subconscious. As a subconscious goal for eighteen years, I did not write a single word. Once I put my goal in writing, it only took me two years to complete that first book. And I've written several books since then, all as a result of writing down my goals as affirmations.

Of course some of you are whining. You'll tell me you're not the writing type. Or you don't have the time to write out your goals. Well maybe, just maybe, that's why you haven't achieved all you are capable of achieving. As Sir Francis Bacon (1561–1626) advised, "If we are to achieve results never before accomplished, we must employ methods never before attempted."[6]

Think about it. If you're a manager who wants to ensure an employee's follow-through, you might ask him to write down your instructions. If you're giving directions over the phone, you might ask the other person to read back what she has written. You wouldn't let the other person off the hook without making sure they got the message. So why would you let yourself off the hook by not writing out your goals as affirmations?

This is a critical part of the process of affirming achievement. Your mind responds to certain language structures. If you don't write your affirmations correctly, they won't work the wonders you want. So please, please, please do the following as you write out your affirmations.

Use a Present Tense Verb in Your Affirmations

Say, "I am filled with energy and vitality," rather than "I will be energetic." And say, "I am confident in my telephone sales," rather than "I will be confident." Your mind will do its best to fulfill a present verb statement, but it will ignore future "will" statements.

Use the Word "I"

Personalize your affirmations. Write something like "I am the top sales person in my region," or "I weigh a slim, trim 150 pounds." Remember, affirmations are used for *your* goal accomplishment, not somebody else's. You can't have an affirmation for somebody else. You can't say, "The children will behave" and expect it to work. Affirmations focus on what *you* are going to do.

State Your Affirmations Positively

Avoid words like *no*, *not*, or *never*. Write down what you want instead of what you don't want. Rather than telling yourself, "I don't lose my temper," say, "I am cool and calm in difficult situations." It simply works a great deal better to focus on what you're going to do . . . instead of what you're not going to do. At the same time, avoid *overly* positive sentences such as "I can lose 40 pounds in two weeks." It would be more appropriate to say something like "I am achieving my ideal weight by controlling my eating habits and improving my exercise program."

It's a matter of focus. Your mind and behavior move toward your focus. When I told myself, "I won't get nervous when I'm making cold calls to prospective customers," guess what I focused on? Getting nervous, speaking ineffectively, and saying some stupid things. And that's exactly what I did.

However, when I changed my affirmation and focus to the positive, my mind and behavior followed along. Now I tell myself, "I speak with confidence and communicate clearly when I'm talking to prospective customers." Again, that's exactly what happens. So state your affirmations positively.

Be Specific

Your mind does not relate to vague goals or generalized hopes. If you want to improve your memory, you might say, "I have an excellent memory with clear and easy recall." That's specific. If you want to earn more money, tell yourself, "I am earning $_____ this year," and fill in the exact amount you want to make. That works a whole lot better than telling yourself, "I'm making more money."

The more specific your affirmations, the quicker you will reach your goal. Specificity gives you focus. It clarifies the target. It points you toward the bull's eye. There's an old saying, "When a ship misses the harbor, it is seldom the harbor's fault." And when your mind fails to achieve a goal, it is seldom your mind's fault. It's the vagueness of your target that causes the problem.

Use Words with Feeling

Even though you may not initially believe your affirmations will work, say them like you mean it. Better yet, put a feeling word into the affirmation itself. There's more power in an affirmation that says, "I am eagerly preparing and calmly delivering presentations at work" than "I am preparing and delivering presentations at work." Adding feeling words like "eagerly" and "calmly" makes a huge, motivating difference.

Affirmation Step #3: Deploy Your Affirmations

Once you've consciously written your affirmations, you need to move them into your subconscious. Because that's where your negative auto-pilot or your negative mental programming resides. So you want to make sure you've got your subconscious working for you and not against you. To move your affirmations into your subconscious, use the following process.

Relax

Let your body relax because tension blocks the information flow between the conscious and subconscious levels of thought. You might try sitting up straight in a comfortable chair, placing your feet flat on the floor, resting your hands on your lap, and closing your eyes. If you simply don't have the time or the place to be that relaxed, say them anyway—in the shower, walking the dog, or driving to work. And by the way, if you say them in the car on the way to work, I suggest keeping your eyes open.

Repeat

The best way to move your affirmations into your subconscious is through repetition. Repeat your affirmations to yourself over and over again. Say each one of them four or five times, either silently or out loud, during three different times throughout your day. For most people it works best if you say them the first thing in the morning, sometime around lunch for midday correction, and as the last thing before you go to bed.

Don't skip this step. It's absolutely critical that you be persistent in saying your affirmations if they are to work.

Review

After you've said your affirmations, take a few seconds to *view* them or visualize each of them. Just imagine each of them as having come true. There is a strange but powerful force that works to create what you affirm and what you imagine.

If you're not used to visualizing, try this. Visualize each of your affirmations for ten seconds each. Vividly imagine yourself in situations where you are acting out, practicing, and/or living the affirmation. *See* yourself bonding with your children, inspiring your staff, working out for ninety minutes each week, or whatever achievements your affirmations indicate.

All goals are mind accomplished before they are materially accomplished. If you can't see yourself in a happy marriage, you may never have one. If you can't see yourself closing more sales, you probably won't. But if you can *see* yourself doing, having, or being your affirmations, you will be taking a major step toward their accomplishment.

Remember

You've heard the conventional wisdom that it takes twenty-one days to form a new habit . . . such as saying your affirmations every day and then getting the payoff you want. That's bunk. Scientists who study habit formation say there isn't a magic number—and even if there was, it would be more like sixty-six days, according to one recent study led by University College London research psychologist Phillippa Lally. For some people, she says, new healthy habits can be established in a mere eighteen days—while others may take as long as 254 days.[7]

The point is, you must remember to declare your affirmations until you no longer need them. Until you've achieved the payoffs you're looking for. You probably won't make a million dollars or lose 100 pounds in those mythical twenty-one days. But if you're saying your affirmations every day, it does mean you're on the right path, doing the right things, and getting closer to your goals. Some affirmations take longer, but they still work. It took me two years of affirmations to overcome the pain and immobility of rheumatoid arthritis, and it took me five years to acquire my dream house on the lake.

Affirmation Step #4: Ensure the Success of Your Affirmations

As I mentioned earlier, many people have heard of affirmations and tried them . . . without all the success they were hoping for. That's because they messed up the process. To ensure the success of your affirmations, there are two "do's" and two "don'ts" you must follow.

Do Establish Some Triggers

You may think you don't have time to say your affirmations, or you may forget to do them. Well, you can't skip them or forget them and expect to succeed. Fortunately, there's a way to do them where you never forget and it takes no time whatsoever.

Establish triggers or little reminder events. When those events occur, you will remember to do your affirmations. A trigger may be your morning shower, your commute to work, waiting for your computer to boot up, or walking to lunch. Every time you do those activities, you will know it is your time to say your affirmations.

Do Make Sure Your Affirmations Are Physically Possible

I could write a well-written affirmation that declares, "I am the next King of England." It fits all the guidelines I gave you earlier, but it's never going to happen. I'm not in the royal family, and there's no chance of me inheriting the throne. It's not physically possible for me to achieve that affirmation. Don't forget: I'm teaching you a method, not a miracle.

Don't Share Them with Dream Spoilers

Some people write their affirmations and post them on their bathroom mirror or near their computer screen. That's okay, *if* you live with and work with positive people. But if you're around folks who say, "What is this silly garbage . . . that you can lose 50 pounds? You've never been able to keep the weight off," then keep them private. Or if someone says, "Your affirmation, how ridiculous, that you are an upbeat and optimistic person. You're the biggest grouch I know," again, keep them private. After all, the most powerful force in the world is a new idea, but it can be so fragile at birth that it can be killed by a single sneer.

However, if you work or live with positive, supportive people, feel free to post your affirmations where you can see them and be reminded of them. My staff members, for example, use their affirmations as screen savers, so whenever they step away from their computers and come back again, they can review their affirmations consciously or subliminally. It works in our office because everyone I hire is not only highly competent but also extremely positive, supporting one another in whatever has to be done.

Don't Be Fooled by Progress

This is by far the biggest way people mess up the process, and as a result, go around telling people, "I knew these affirmations wouldn't work." They were fooled by progress. They wrote out their affirmations and began to say their affirmations, day after day, making some progress. They closed a few more sales, improved their customer service a little bit, got along better with their families, or ate a few less junk-food snacks. They weren't anywhere near the completion of their goal or affirmation, but they made progress, felt better, and no longer craved the goal quite so much.

That's exactly where most people *stop* saying their affirmations. And what happens? They always go back to start. That's why people have to start and restart diets, exercise programs, and every other change initiative over and over again. They were fooled by progress and failed to keep on saying their affirmations all the way through to the completion of the payoffs they were seeking.

But let's get more specific. If you adopt the process of affirming achievement, what exact payoffs can you expect?

Affirmation Payoff # 1 : Focus

As American novelist Chuck Palahniuk puts it, "If you don't know what you want, you end up with a lot you don't."[8]

Sister Esther Boor taught me that as well. Through marriage I was related to her and had the privilege to visit with her and learn from her on a few occasions. Sister Esther died at the age of 107, and she'd been very alert and mobile her entire life. In fact, Sister Esther didn't retire from her teaching position until she was ninety-eight. After that, she only taught occasionally. Later, she and her fellow nuns were the feature in *Time* magazine when they reported on a study of Catholic nuns who were living well into their nineties and hundreds.[9]

So I wondered, "What do these vigorous old nuns have to teach us?" When interviewed by *Time* magazine, almost every one of them said, "Plan your life. Set your goals." Or putting it in my terms, "Get focused." Affirmations will do that for you.

The sad reality is, many people don't even bother to plan out their lives or their careers until they're hit with a crisis. They didn't plan out a regimen for health, for example, until they got sick.

In a sense, the nun study told us, "Don't do that. Don't wait for a crisis to happen before you figure out your goals." Don't wait for your spouse to leave before you realize the importance of your marriage. Don't goof off on the job and then lose your job before you figure out how important your job is. Affirmations will force you to focus.

> Affirmations will force you to focus.

On one level, you already know the importance

of focus. If you're a businessperson, you would never think of creating a business without a plan. And the really smart businesspeople would create an organized plan for the next six, twelve, and eighteen months as well as a long-term plan. They would establish some benchmarks and bring in some consultants to show them the best way to reach their goals.

On another level, when you're decorating your house, you also understand the importance of focus. You don't throw a bunch of furniture into a room and hope it looks good. No, you think about where people will sit, where the best lighting is, and where the most convenient place for the TV is.

When you have thoughtfully considered and clearly written affirmations, you get the focus payoff. And that will bring you more of the results you want.

Three boys had to learn that lesson. As they were playing in the deep snow, a neighbor asked them if they wanted to have a race. He said he would give a prize to the winner. It sounded good to the boys, so they gathered around the man to learn more. He told them the winner would not be the one who ran the fastest but the one who ran the straightest line. He said he would go to the other end of the field, give a signal, and have them race to him.

The boys took off. The first one looked at his feet as he ran to make sure they were pointing straight ahead. The second boy wondered how straight the boys on either side of him were running and tried to line himself up with them. The third boy just kept his eyes fixed on the man at the end of the field. He kept his eyes fixed on the goal. And, of course, he won the race. His line was by far the straightest.

The two losers lost their focus. In fact, they made the two most common mistakes people make when trying to achieve their goals. The first boy became self-conscious. He spent too much time worrying about the possible mistakes he was making. The second boy spent too much time wondering how his competitors were doing. With clear affirmations to give you focus, you won't make those mistakes.

Affirmation Payoff #2: Motivation

If you're somewhat lacking in the energy, passion, attitude, and motivation departments . . . I know you're also lacking in the area of goal setting. There's no reason to be pumped up if you're not going anywhere in particular.

> There's no reason to be pumped up if you're not going anywhere in particular.

However, when you have exciting goals and affirmations, all sorts of powers are released within you. Inertia and procrastination are thrown out the window.

Perhaps you can relate. You may have a tough time getting out of bed in the morning. You push the snooze button on your alarm clock two or three times, and you slowly, reluctantly get yourself ready and off to work. After all, you figure, yesterday wasn't too exciting at work and today doesn't promise to be any better.

But let's say, instead, you get an early morning phone call. You're told by a reputable source that you've just won a trip to Hawaii and a half million dollars—provided you can be on the plane in three hours.

I suspect that new exciting goal would motivate you to achieve more that morning than you've achieved in the past thirty mornings put together. You would find places to send the kids and take the dog, and you would find people to fill in for you at work. You would be flying high instead of griping about your busy schedule or the drudgery of "another day, another dollar."

The Right Goals and the Right Affirmations Give You Energy

They excite you, and they release your pent-up, untapped enthusiasm. It's like the little boy who kept affirming, "I'm going to Disney. I'm going to Disney. I'm going to Disney." He was so excited about it that his grandmother tried to talk some sense into him. She said, "Darling, I don't want you to be disappointed, but we're not going to Disney until your Grandpa croaks." No problem. The little boy immediately ran over to his grandfather and asked, "Grandpa, can you make the sound of a frog?" That little boy had a clear goal. He knew where he wanted to go, and his goal energized him.

Affirmation Payoff #3: Victory

Better yet, with the right goals and affirmations, you will achieve more! I've seen it firsthand hundreds of times as I speak to audiences around the world. I know that goal setters who use the process of affirming achievement accomplish a great deal more than non-goal setters. They make more money, have better jobs, and build stronger families.

James Cash Penney Jr. (1875–1971), the legendary founder of the J. C. Penney department store chain, apparently saw it firsthand himself. He said, "Give me a stock clerk with a goal, and I'll give you someone who will make history. Give me someone without a goal, and I will give you a stock clerk."[10] How true! Few things in life push you to achieve more than having goals and affirmations.

This is even true on a national level. Look at the Japanese people. After a devastating defeat in World War II, the Japanese leaders in government, business, and industry said, "Let's set a goal. Let's become the number one nation in the production of textiles. And let's accomplish this in a decade." That was their affirmation, and they did it.

In 1960, the Japanese set the impossible goal of becoming the number one nation in the production of steel. An impossible goal you might think, because Japan had no iron, coal, or oil. But they did it again.

In 1970, they set another ten-year goal—to become the number one nation in the production of automobiles. They did it again.

Then in 1980, they established the goal of becoming the leader in the production of electronics and computers. You know what happened there.

With goals and affirmations, you're going to experience some incredible payoffs. Without goals and affirmations, you're going to miss out on a lot of things you want for yourself, your life, your family, and your career.

Affirmations Bridge the Gap Between Where You Are and Where You Want to Be

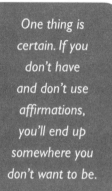

One thing is certain. If you don't have and don't use affirmations, you'll end up somewhere you don't want to be.

One thing is certain. If you don't have and don't use affirmations, you'll end up somewhere you don't want to be.

Are you willing to do that? Are you willing to let your future be determined by chance or circumstance? Or do you want the ability to shape your future and make your dreams come true?

Everyone will choose the latter. The great news is, it doesn't matter where you came from, or how difficult your past may have been, or how unfair your present situation might be. With the process of affirming achievement, you can reprogram yourself for the payoffs you want. You can reset your autopilot to the setting you would like.

Harriet Tubman should know. She escaped slavery herself and led other enslaved people to freedom along the route of the Underground Railroad. As she declared, "Every great dream begins with a dreamer. Always remember, you have within you the strength, the patience, and the passion to reach for the stars to change the world."[11] With affirmations you can and will turn your dream world into your new reality.

CHAPTER 11

The Process of Continuing Education

The Grand Mistake

Because he was getting older, the elderly carpenter told his employer that he planned to leave the house building business and live a more leisurely life. He would miss the paycheck to be sure, but he wanted to take it easy.

His boss, the contractor, was sorry to see his good worker go after nearly thirty years and asked if he could build just one more house as a personal favor. The carpenter reluctantly agreed, but it was easy to see that his heart wasn't in his work. He resorted to shoddy workmanship and began using inferior materials. It was an unfortunate way to end his career.

Finally, the carpenter finished the job, and his boss came to inspect the house. As the contractor and carpenter approached the completed house, the contractor handed the front door key to the carpenter.

"This is your house," he said. "It's my gift to you for your years of service."

What a shock! What a shame! If he had only known he was building his own house, he would have done it so differently. Now he had to live in the house he had built.

The same is true for all of us. We may build our lives in a haphazard way, putting in less than what might be required. And then with a shock, we look at the situation we have created and the life we are living. We're living in the subpar house we have built.

You need to think of yourself as a carpenter and consider the life you are building. Are you building a mansion? Or are you making the grand mistake and, unwittingly and unconsciously, building a shack?

Producers purposely and conscientiously build themselves, their lives, their careers, and their relationships through everything they do and don't do . . . just like the carpenter. They understand, as leadership expert Dr. John Maxwell puts it, "Their number one responsibility is cultivating their own discipline and personal growth."

> Producers purposely and conscientiously build themselves, their lives, their careers, and their relationships through everything they do and don't do . . . just like the carpenter.

What about you? Have you accepted responsibility for your own continuing education? Or are you waiting for someone else to take care of that for you? Let's check it out.

Four Ways to Check Your Commitment to Continuing Education

I find that almost everyone is good at talking the talk. Almost everyone says, "Yeah, I believe in education, in continual learning, in getting better and better." Almost no one says, "No, I don't believe in education because I already know everything." Almost no one *says* that, although those people's lives might tell a different story.

If you're truly committed to the **process of continuing education**, you will see four pieces of evidence in your behavior.

1. You're Humble Enough to Admit You Don't Know It All

You know that you don't know everything, and you don't pretend to know everything. You know there is always more to learn. And like all producers, you know there are certain skills and strategies you have to keep on learning to achieve the maximum payoffs at home or on the job.

You're in the continual learning mode, because you know it's easier to keep up than catch up.

Does that sound like you? If so, great! If not, this chapter will get you into the process of continuing education.

2. You Are Open to Change

The whole world is changing, and if you're not out there learning new things, you're in trouble. Big trouble. Take your job, for example. Whatever skills got you into your current job may no longer be enough to keep you in that job. Indeed, if you haven't been to several training seminars, read several books, or listened to several audio recordings on professional development lately, you may be in danger of extinction.

And how do you know if you're open to change? Ask yourself one question. Have you ever thought, "If I can just hang on a few more weeks and get through this change, I can get back to normal?" If so, you're in trouble. You've got to accept reality— that change won't go away. The change will never be over.

> It's easier to keep up than catch up.

Producers realize that life is not a movie with a neat ending. Today, change is more like a serial. It's never over. You've got to be ready to battle formidable competitors, every day, forever, without a break. And that takes continuing education.

3. You Take Ownership for the Educational Improvements You Need to Make

Despite the fact that these are challenging times, some people are still not committed to their ongoing development. I know; it's just plain crazy. But that does explain why so many non-producers and left-behinders are stuck. They look to someone else to bail them out.

That became very clear to me on a recent TV news program where people were being interviewed about company downsizings and possible company layoffs. One employee said, "I want to know what my union is going to do to save my job." Another individual asked, "How is the government going to make sure I don't lose my job?" And so went the interview.

No one asked the employees the *key* question "What are *you* going to do?" Everyone shifted the responsibility for job preservation or career enhancement to somebody else . . . which is a 100 percent indication that they were *not* committed to making the changes they needed to make or to learn the things they needed to learn.

And that, my friends, is a dangerous position to take. As Bettye Jean Triplett, the mother of entrepreneur Chris Gardner, notes, "You can only depend on yourself. The cavalry ain't coming."[1] You've got to stop blaming external people and forces in your life and start choosing the more appropriate response of continuing your education.

> Are you taking ownership for the educational changes you need to make? Or are you simply sitting around and hoping things will work out?

So I ask you, are you taking ownership for the educational changes you need to make? Or are you simply sitting on the sidelines, waiting for a light to appear at the end of the tunnel, and hoping things work out? If so, listen to writer Australian Sara Henderson's advice: "Don't wait for a light to appear at the end of the tunnel. Stride down there . . . and light the bloody thing yourself."[2]

4. You Refuse to Settle for "Good Enough"

Producers are never satisfied with getting by or squeaking through. As Debbi Fields, the founder of Mrs. Fields Cookies, would say, great leaders know that "good enough never is."

In his *Telephone Prospecting and Selling Report* newsletter, Art Sobczak says, "Good enough does not win championships or make people excellent, wealthy, or healthy." Champions know that good enough is seldom, if ever, actually good enough.

However, when I'm about to offer training in a company, some sourpuss will always say, "I don't need to go to those classes." "I've taken plenty of training in the past." "I've already heard all that stuff." And "I've been here a long time and I'm doing good enough as it is."

On the surface, the sourpuss might think he has a good point, but put his comment in another context. You wouldn't want to hear your cardiac surgeon say, "I had a class on heart surgery once back in medical school. That's good enough." Likewise, you would have your doubts about the professional baseball player who says, "I don't need to go to spring training. I've been playing the game for years. I'm good enough."

Of course, this commitment to ongoing development applies to organizations as well as people. Take Tastefully Simple, for example, a direct sales company that offers unique, easy-to-prepare foods. They refuse to settle for good enough and declare "personal development" as one of their core values. As a result, they offer a host of classes and conferences based on their TRIM model. They're constantly looking for ways to Train, Recognize, Inform, and Model to their thousands of consultants around the country.

If that sounds too touchy-feely for you or your company, if you think their emphasis on personal development would be a waste of time, money, and energy, you should tour through this company, watch the employees work, and notice their overwhelming enthusiasm. As I walked through the company, I heard singing and cheering. I saw motivational prints and slogans everywhere. And I came across employee after employee who said, "I love my job. I love it here." Tastefully Simple has turned their emphasis on education into an employee productivity factor and a healthy bottom-line result.

To achieve the maximum payoffs at work or at home, you must adopt and adhere to the process of continuing education. Try these strategies.

Continuing Education Strategy #1: Increase Your Replacement Value

During changing and challenging times, which seem to be happening more often than not these days, you need to forget about your old safety nets. What saved you in the past will not save you in the future. In the past, your longevity or seniority might have saved you. And some poor mistaken souls still think, "I've worked for this company for twenty-six years, and they owe me." No they don't. When you got your last paycheck, the company was all caught up. They don't owe you anymore. Traditional definitions of longevity and loyalty no longer apply.

> *Your knowledge and skills can become outdated so rapidly that your good performance may soon become irrelevant performance—if you're not in a mode of continuing education.*

Likewise, in the past, your good performance may have guaranteed a job, and that worked as long as the world stayed pretty much the same. These days, your knowledge and skills can become outdated so rapidly that your good performance may soon become irrelevant performance—if you're not in a mode of continuing education.

In today's world it's all about replacement value. In his book, *Earl Nightingale's Greatest Discovery* (Dodd Mead, 1987), Nightingale observed that, for the most part, the size of a person's paycheck is determined by how difficult he or she is to replace. The more difficult people are to replace, the more money they tend to make. And the more job security they tend to enjoy.

That being the case, I strongly urge you to ponder your answer to four questions. If you're ever going to have any semblance of control over your career, you must have an answer to each question. They are as follows:

• What are you doing to increase your value in the marketplace?

- What are doing to demonstrably increase your value to your current employer? Or to your clients and customers?

- What are doing to increase your value to prospective future employers?

- What are you doing to make yourself so valuable that you're the least likely to be cut or the last to be cut?

If you have a clear answer and a step-by-step plan for each question, I congratulate you. You just became a great deal more irreplaceable. If not, you will immediately have some ideas as to what kind of continuing education you need to pursue . . . now.

Continuing Education Strategy #2: Stop the Excuses

Stop finding excuses for *not* upgrading yourself, *not* learning more, or *not* getting better. Stop sounding like the pathetic souls who say, "That's just the way I am . . ." "I could never do such and such . . ." "I don't have time . . ." or "I don't have the money to take all those classes." You've got to keep on reading if you want to keep on growing. (Don't tell me you can't afford to buy all the books you should be reading. It isn't what the books cost; it's what they'll cost if you don't read them.)

Stop sounding like the crybabies who say, "Take evening classes and spend my own money? Hey, I already work hard all day. Besides, it's my employer's job to train me, or it's the government's job to look after my future."

Stop sounding like the whiners who say, "If these classes are going to give me skills I'll use on the job, my employer had better pay for them. And my company had better offer the classes during regular work hours. And if I have to go to classes on my time, I should get time-and-a-half."

In response to all those people, philosopher Eric Hoffer (1902–1983) said, "There are many who find a good alibi far more attractive than achievement."[3] And these alibi-makers, dare I say, will never find the payoffs they want. Purpose-driven producers don't make excuses. And they don't wait for somebody else to develop their careers.

Continuing Education Strategy #3: Aggressively Pursue Ongoing Personal and Professional Development

No matter how clear your purpose might be and no matter how much passion you might have, you'll always lack some skills for turning all of that into the payoffs you seek. Indeed, no one who becomes rich in any particular business or field starts with *all* the skills he or she needs.

If, for example, your purpose is to turn your kids into financially independent, self-sufficient adults, you may need to take some courses on a variety of financial topics yourself. How else could you possibly expect to model the right behavior or teach your kids the proper financial skills if you don't have them yourself? If you have the goal of winning over your competitor's customers without using price as a weapon, you may need to get some training on customer attraction and retention.

So what can you do to aggressively pursue ongoing personal and professional development?

Read Targeted Materials

Over the years, I've also noticed that leaders are readers. In fact, you can often judge a person's success by the size of his or her hardcopy or digital library.

Read materials that apply to the payoffs you want to achieve. Your time is your most valuable but most limited commodity. You don't have to read everything, so make sure a good portion of your reading time is focused on material that is likely to help you—in your life, career, relationships, or anything else that is important to you.

This literally became life saving for me when my doctors diagnosed me with rheumatoid arthritis. And their prognosis was not encouraging. They told me it was getting worse and worse. They had no cure, and I should get ready for a wheelchair. After all, the pain and stiffness had started out in one knee, and then moved on to include knees, hands, feet, neck, and shoulders. Walking became painful and then impossible without crutches. I could no longer drive my car, and my mother had to drive me to the university and help me up the stairs to my classrooms. Talk about a blow to my self-esteem.

Fortunately, I was smart enough to do some targeted reading, lots of it. I read everything I could find on rheumatoid arthritis from the worlds of medicine, natural cures, and overall wellness. And based on what I learned, I put together a program of affirmations, prayer, and dietary changes, and I was healed.

Certainly, it took some time to do all the reading and the research, and it took some time to implement what I learned—about three years. But the payoff has been an unrestricted, pain-free life ever since.

Of course, I can already hear some of you saying you don't have time to read all the latest and greatest business books, read every article written about your industry, or even skim every newsletter that arrives in your email inbox. I get that. But you do have time to read some of the best material if you adjust your priorities.

For example, the average American spends twenty-eight hours a week watching television. Just imagine what could happen if you spent some of that time on targeted reading. As basketball executive Pat Williams says, most people can finish an average-sized book in a week by reading an hour a day. That's fifty-two books in a year. And as Williams notes, "You can become quite knowledgeable about *any* subject if you read the right five books on *that* subject."

Read selectively. Read the best stuff. Read the stuff that will get your mind thinking and your motivational juices flowing. And make sure you read this entire book.

Attend Every Good Seminar You Can

Even though I've been speaking at various conferences and leading seminars in countless organizations over the past three decades, I never stop going to seminars and webinars myself . . . or listening to various recorded educational programs. I need to keep on learning so I can be at my best and give the best to my clients.

There are a lot of bad, fluffy, waste-your-time programs out there. I'm not suggesting you spend your time or money on those. Life is too short for that. You've got to choose carefully. So ask around and see which programs and what speakers are the very best. Ask successful people—that you trust—which seminars they would recommend.

If you don't have time to physically attend a program, turn your daily commute into a learning laboratory. Chances are, many of you spend one to three hours every day engaged in some sort of commuting activity. On the one hand, that could look like a colossal waste of time, and it probably is if you spend all that time listening to the radio, the news, or some talk show because none of those activities will add a nickel to your bottom line or add extra effectiveness to your daily life.

On the other hand, those one to three hours of commuting time could be a tremendous source of education and inspiration if you turn your car, bus, or train seat into a classroom. Bring some educational and inspirational recordings with you, and listen to them as you commute back and forth each day. You'll be amazed at the focus, energy, and insights they give you, not to mention the way your commute time flies by.

Just remember: formal education will help you make a living, but self-education will help you make a fortune.

To be a producer, you must be a proactive learner, continually taking the classes you need to take. You need to be a "doer" and not a "used to doer." As the eminently respected management consultant Peter

Drucker (1909–2005) asks, "What do you have to do . . . and . . . What do you have to learn . . . and . . . What do you have to change . . . to make yourself capable of living up to your expectations of life?"[4] You have to be in the process of continuing education.

> You must be a proactive learner, continually taking the classes you need to take. You need to be a "doer" and not a "used to doer."

Continuing Education Strategy #4: Use Proven Learning and Retention Devices

Time and again, when I've spoken at various conferences, I'll ask some of the audience members to tell me who spoke at last year's conference. And they don't remember. So I'll ask them what the topic was, and they'll say, "Um, topic, topic, now let me think." They recalled almost nothing.

In fact, research says that if a person just sits in a seminar without getting involved, three hours after the seminar he or she will only recall 50 percent of what was said. And one month after the seminar, his or her retention rate will be less than 5 percent.

As an educator as well as a motivational speaker, I find that intolerable. So I began to teach people how to learn, remember what they learn, and apply what they learn. Without that, a person is nothing more than a professional attendee. He or she is a seminar *goer* instead of a seminar *doer*. And in today's highly competitive business world, we can no longer afford that luxury.

To become a truly effective learner, use the following system. I've found that it works wonderfully well. If you're an adult using this system in an organization, it will help you excel. And if you're a student using this system at school, you will make the dean's list.

Take Notes

Don't fool yourself into thinking you will remember what was said. You won't. Passive learning equals minimal learning. You've got to *do* something while knowledge is being disseminated, and the best thing you can do is take notes.

Note taking decreases your daydreaming and increases your retention. In fact, Dr. Manny Steil, the world's foremost authority on listening, says you'll get 20 percent more from a meeting if you take notes. And you'll get 35 percent more if you put your notes into a report—saying what you learned and how you'll use what you learned.

Personally, I recommend a two-part note-taking system. Part one is the "capture" phase. When the seminar leader or speaker is talking, write as much as you can as fast as you can. Focusing on the most important things she is saying, of course. Don't worry about neatness.

Part two is the "take-home" phase. Within twenty-four hours, reread all your notes. And then rewrite them, summarizing all the key points you picked up. Write down those things that inspired you and seemed most important.

The most successful people always do that. I know. When I'm speaking at a sales conference, for example, I've noticed that the top salespeople typically sit right up front, taking lots of notes. However, many of the struggling salespeople will skip a few sessions, check their email, or doodle on their paper instead of taking notes.

I wonder. Could there be some correlation between attending seminars, really listening during the seminars, taking notes, and moving ahead? Why of course there is!

Turn Your Notes into Keepers

Turn your key points into "learning" statements. Write out several statements starting with such words as "I learned . . ." "I relearned . . ." "I now know . . ." "I need to stop . . ." "I need to start . . ." and "I need to continue . . . " By doing this, you take someone else's information and make it yours.

Review Your Keepers

Too many people pile or file their notes, and that can be deadly. In fact, 85 percent to 95 percent of what you put in your files will never be seen again. And if you don't review your notes, you will forget 70 percent of what you heard within four days of any learning event.

The good news is, when you review your notes, you reverse those figures. You retain 70 percent or more of what you heard.

Personally, I like the way psychologist Dr. Terry Paulson reviews his keepers. He puts all his keepers from various programs on sheets of paper or in various computer files, and he reviews them whenever he's put on one of those thirty-minute holds you get when you call a service hotline. He even records his keepers so he can listen to them when he's driving. As his grandmother taught him, "When you read something often enough, no one can take it away from you."

Continuing Education Strategy #5: Use the Ripple Effect to Your Advantage

Every choice you make today has a ripple effect on tomorrow. There is no such thing as making a decision or taking an action that does not affect you.

For example, if you eat two bowls of ice cream every night, chances are you'll get the ripple effect of obesity in your future. If you drink a quart of vodka every day, you'll probably reap the ripple effect of liver disease and premature death.

That being the case, what kind of decisions are you making today, especially when it comes to your continuing education? Are you making decisions that will build a mansion or a shack of your life? You're doing one or the other.

Are you learning material that will improve your relationships, your career, and your bank account? Are you learning material that will not only teach you how to *have* more but also *be* more?

I know the ripple effect has had a huge and positive impact on my life. Some years ago, I decided I would read something educational or listen to something motivational for ten minutes a day every day. That little bit of effort and commitment turns into sixty hours of extra personal and professional development per year. Sixty hours! That's huge! And those sixty hours of education have rippled over into my business being more successful, my marriage being stronger, my health staying excellent, and my desired payoffs becoming reality that much quicker.

Continuing Education Strategy #6: Learn from Champions

Another great source of continuing education is other people. You can learn a great deal from observing champions and following their lead. Interview them, and soak up their wisdom. It's what I do with one of my mentors, eighty-seven-years-young Dr. Sidney Simon, best-selling author and creator of some of the most innovative experiential approaches to education of all time. For the past ten years, we've been meeting at 6:30 in the morning, once a month, to walk the beach, watch the sun come up, ask Brave Questions (see chapter 13), and learn, learn, learn.

It's what I did when I was struggling with the definition of a "winner" versus a "champion." As you recall, I consulted with "Mr. Universe" Lee Labrada who clarified the difference.

> Surround yourself with champions and learn from them, individually or in a group setting.

Surround yourself with champions and learn from them, individually or in a group setting. Indeed, I would even recommend you find a number of people who perform with consistent excellence in the areas you want to master. Get together with them on a regular basis.

As I briefly mentioned earlier, I've been doing

that for more than twenty years, meeting with six world-class speakers, someplace in the world, four times each year, for two days at a stretch. Sure it's a huge commitment, because we are committed to be at every meeting, with the only excused absence being a family emergency. We bring every personal and professional issue out into the open, and get and give some gut-honest feedback, advice, direction, and encouragement to one another. What I've learned from those gatherings has been huge, so huge that I would place this experience of my mastermind group (Master Speakers International) in the top five learning experiences of my entire life.

Continuing Education Strategy #7: Learn from Losers

But you can also learn from losers. Just find out what they do . . . and then don't do that! As business philosopher Jim Rohn says, "It's too bad losers or failures don't give seminars. Wouldn't that be valuable? We could sit back and say, 'Pete . . . Henry . . . Mary . . . Jessica, you've screwed up your life for forty years. If I bring a notepad, and promise to take good notes, would you spend a day with me? Would you teach me all the things *not* to do?'"

That might sound kind of silly, but it's brilliant. Get in the habit of continuing your education by learning something from every person you meet.

> *Get in the habit of continuing your education by learning something from every person you meet.*

Continuing Education Strategy #8: Apply Your Learning

Even though these first seven strategies will get you on the path of continuing education, that's not enough. German author Johann Wolfgang von Goethe (1749–1832) acknowledged this when he wrote, "Knowing is not enough; we must apply. Willing is not enough; we must do."[5]

> Knowledge isn't power; the application of knowledge is.

You must also *apply* what you learn. You've heard people say, "Knowledge is power," but that's a myth. Knowledge isn't power; the application of knowledge is.

There's nothing more pathetic than a knowledgeable, educated person, sitting on his butt, refusing to use the knowledge he has gained. Indeed, if you take that approach, you might as well skip the learning. As spiritual business consultant Swami Sukhabodhananda puts it, "To know and not act on what we know is equal to not knowing."

To apply your learning, I suggest three strategies.

I. Keep an Action Log

Go beyond the process of continuing education. Go beyond recording your keepers as we discussed earlier. Turn your keepers into "action" statements. Write down *what* you're going to do with what you learned and *when* you're going to do it.

As you write out your action statements, be very specific. Instead of saying, "I'm going to be a better communicator," write something like "I am taking time to listen fully and completely to what others say before I respond to their comments."

Take the time to glance at your action log for a few seconds every day. It will keep your goals in the forefront of your mind and increase your chances of actually achieving them.

Then glance at your action log every week to review your progress. Take note of what's working for you, and write down any corrections you need to make so you become even more effective in the future. Better yet, when you look back, you'll be amazed at what you wrote two or three months ago, and you'll be amazed at how far you've come, even though you may still have a ways to go. It's highly motivating.

2. Teach Your Keepers

Take some time to go through all the things you've been learning, the notes you've been taking, and the keepers you've recorded. And then select a few insights that were especially important to you and would be valuable for someone else to know. The process could be as simple as sharing one or two items with your partner over dinner, or it could be as structured as an hour-long staff meeting with your fellow seminar attendees where each person shares all the lessons he or she learned at the training program.

Quite simply, when you tell somebody else what you learned, two things happen. Your *clarity* increases as you review what you learned, what it means to you, and how you can convey that information to others as easily as possible. Your *retention* increases. The more you review what you learned, the longer you will remember what you learned.

3. Ask Others to Hold You Accountable for Your Keepers

Privately held goals are easy to forget. You're busy. I understand that. If you share your keepers and goals with one or more people, however, they can remind you and encourage you to stay on track and follow through.

So ask your manager, spouse, or friend to watch you, observe you, and tell you how well you're applying your keepers to your job or home situation. Ask them to hold you accountable, and watch your follow-through increase dramatically. It's highly embarrassing to tell someone what you learned if you don't do anything with that learning.

What Got You Here Won't Get You There

Producers are learners. They know what got them to their present point at work, in life, and in relationships won't take them to their next desired point. Knowledge changes very rapidly. So they don't expect yesterday's knowledge to be enough to win tomorrow's victories.

Producers know that knowledge can become outdated rather quickly. If you don't believe it, go back and read one of your old textbooks. Compare the version you studied in school to the most recent edition currently in use—no matter how recently you graduated—and you'd find your version sadly outdated. You shouldn't be surprised that facts are changing all around us.

Whether it's the nutritional value of certain foods, the status of Pluto as a planet, the number of chromosomes in a single human cell, what motivates employees in the workplace, or what it takes to build a lasting and healthy relationship, our knowledge is in constant flux. Samuel Arbesman, a senior scholar at the Institute for Quantitative Social Science at Harvard University, says this can be dangerous, because "people make all kinds of decisions based on outdated facts all the time."[6]

It may be no big deal when you quote some half-remembered facts you read in a magazine years ago at a party, but using those facts as a basis for a decision can have profound consequences. That's why Arbesman declares, "We need to incorporate an *informational humility* into our lives."[7]

You must admit there's more that you need to learn. As Professor Hugh Nibley (1910–2005) says, "Your search for knowledge should be ceaseless . . . never resting on laurels, degrees, or past achievements." And conflict resolution consultant Paul F. Davis adds, "The greatest minds and highest achievers are committed to continual personal growth and inward expansion."

> *Your computer needs to be upgraded on a regular basis, and so do you.*

Your computer needs to be upgraded on a regular basis, and so do you. Adopt the process of continuing education and you can go from where you are to where you want to be. You can build a mansion of your life instead of a shack.

CHAPTER 12

The Process of Connective Communication

"What We Have Here Is a Failure to Communicate."

It was the most memorable line in the 1967 movie *Cool Hand Luke*. When the prisoners wouldn't listen, the prison guard uttered that ominous line: "What we have here is a failure to communicate."

That same sentence could be applied to many—if not most—organizations, teams, and relationships. Almost everywhere I go to speak or consult, the employee surveys say the same thing. The employees say there is a "lack of communication."

In his book, *The Practice of Empowerment* (Brookfield, VT: Gower, 1995), Dennis C. Kinlaw documents this. He asked one thousand people, "If you knew that a supervisor in your organization was doing something that was hurting the performance of the organization, would you confront that person about what he or she was doing?" Less than 50 percent of respondents said they would talk to or communicate with their bosses about the situation.

Kinlaw then asked another six thousand people two additional questions. He asked, "Do you know of some way that your organization could make a substantial gain in cutting costs or improving the quality of its goods and services?"[1] Almost 100 percent of the people answered "yes." And then he asked, "Will you do anything about it?" Fewer than

10 percent said they would bring up their idea and talk about it. Obviously, there is a failure to communicate in lots of places.

Perhaps you work or live in one of those places. You may even be discouraged or depressed about the lack of communication or the ineffectiveness of that communication. I've got some good news for you: communication works for those who work at it... intelligently. Producers have mastered this process, and so can you.

> Communication works for those who work at it... intelligently.

The **process of connective communication** comes down to avoiding three critical communication breakups and using two communication makeups instead.

In essence, a *communication breakup* is anything you say or do that pushes people away from you emotionally. It sends the message that I don't respect you, understand you, and/or care about you. As a result, people are less open with you, trusting you less and liking you less. And these breakups will absolutely kill off your effectiveness with people.

A *communication makeup* sends a different message. It's anything you say or do with other people—in person, over the phone, in writing, or electronically—that says, "You count. You matter. You're worthy of my time and attention. And I will do my best to make sure we understand each other." You may send that message directly or imply it indirectly, but the message is there nonetheless.

Breakup #1: Sharing Too Little of Yourself

Deeper relationships require deeper communication. Sticking to the superficial won't cut it. Humorist Robert Orben learned that when his son came home from college for the holidays. He asked his son, "How are things going?" His son said, "Good." Robert said, "How's the food?" He said, "Good." Robert asked, "And the dormitory?" Again he said, "Good."

Robert commented, "They've always had a strong basketball team.

How do you think they'll do this year?" His son said, "Good." Robert asked, "How are your studies going?" He said, "Good." Robert said, "Have you decided on a major yet?" He said, "Yes." Robert said, "What is it?" He said, "Communications."

We can chuckle about that, but when you share too little of yourself, your personal relationships are in jeopardy. According to research by marriage expert Dr. Gary D. Chapman, 85 percent of failed relationships show a lack of communication.[2] The people kept too much inside, and so they grew apart.

> *85 percent of failed relationships show a lack of communication.*

Healthy relationships have lots of communication, and most everything is out in the open. Sick relationships have people who keep too many secrets. As poet John Barrymore said, "We are as sick as we are secret."[3]

The Andersons discovered that. One day Mrs. Anderson came up behind her husband and slapped the back of his head. She said, "I found a piece of paper in your pants' pocket with the name 'Mary Lou' written on it. You'd better have an explanation."

Mr. Anderson replied, "Calm down, honey. Remember last week when I was at the horse track? That was the name of the horse I bet on."

The next morning Mrs. Anderson sneaked up behind her husband and whacked him again. The husband immediately complained, "What was that for?" She said, "Your horse called last night."

The same thing could be said of professional relationships. They're healthy when there is *plenty of appropriate self-disclosure*, and they're ineffective when information is hoarded. Of course, you're already wondering what constitutes "plenty of appropriate self-disclosure." We'll get to that when I discuss SATS communication a little later in this chapter.

Remember, when you withhold too much information or share too little of yourself, it seldom works with your coworkers on the job or your family at home. To grow or strengthen a relationship, to get the best ideas and make the best decisions, everyone needs to share what he or she knows, thinks, and feels.

Breakup #2: Talking Too Much

Sharing too little is a type of communication breakup, but talking too much is also a breakup. Talking too much comes in two varieties.

Communication breaks up when a person talks too much in general. I'm sure you know people who just talk on, and on, and on. I don't know what's driving their behavior. Maybe they love the sound of their own voice. Or they *need* to be the center of attention. But I do know they're usually driving other people nuts.

This was the main reason I stopped my relationship with one of my girlfriends during my teenage years. She was intelligent and attractive, but she never stopped talking, about anything and everything. And even though it may not have been her intention, her incessant talking sent the message that she was more interested in hearing herself talk than in connecting with me.

Communication also breaks up when a person talks too much about him- or herself in particular. I'm sure you know people like that. They bring every point made at a staff meeting back to them. And they turn every story shared at a party into an opportunity to say, "that reminds me of," which sends them into a lengthy monologue. In essence, they're sending the message, "I'm so important and I'm so interesting that you simply must know this about me." As David L. Levin points out in his book, *Don't Just Talk, Be Heard!* (Minneapolis, MN: Minneapolis Press, 2009), "Anything that says me, me, me is a disconnect."[4] It breaks up communication.

Author Les Giblin writes, "When you talk to people about yourself, you are rubbing people the wrong way and working against human nature. Take these four words out of your vocabulary—I, me, my, mine. Substitute for those four words, one word, the most powerful word spoken by the human tongue—you."[5]

Of course, Giblin is exaggerating a bit to make his point, but his point is well taken. If *you* will give up the satisfaction *you* get from talking about *yourself* too much, if *you* relinquish some of the attention *you* get from the use of the words "I, me, my, and mine," *your* personality, influence, and communication will be greatly enhanced.

Breakup #3: Discounting Others

Most people aren't consciously rude or deliberately hurtful, but they may do it anyway. They say something or do something that discounts another person. And their communication devalues or cheapens the people around them, saying in effect, "You don't count."

Of course, you may think this breakup does not apply to you. You don't discount others. I hope that's the case. But you may discount others without even knowing it. You may use some communication behaviors that seem natural or inconsequential to you, but they may have a huge negative impact on other people and your relationships with them.

Failing to Acknowledge Others

You discount others when you fail to acknowledge them. It happens all too often. You're in a store, waiting to be waited on, while the clerk keeps talking to her friend on the phone. And even though she sees you, she refuses to stop her conversation or even nod in your direction. It's a communication breakup. Whether she means to or not, she is communicating "I don't respect you enough to even acknowledge your existence."

> *Whether you mean it or not, when you fail to acknowledge someone, you are communicating "I don't respect you enough to even acknowledge your existence."*

In one supermarket, I was watching a cashier do that while her checkout line got longer and longer. Finally, the elderly lady in front of me had had enough. In a rather firm and loud voice, she said, "Just a minute young lady. I think you have things badly mistaken here. You are overhead, and I am profit." She was saying, "I'm your customer. I'm the one that creates profit for your company and pays your wages. I deserve some respect, and I want to be acknowledged."

The same principle applies to your internal customers. I'm sure you've seen managers and VPs chatting among themselves, while the underlings wait to be acknowledged or included. It's not cool. It's a communication breakup. You're discounting others.

So make sure you acknowledge people when they come into sight, whether it's nodding in their direction, saying "Hi" to a coworker who passes by in the hallway, or asking a question. It communicates some caring and some respect.

Interrupting Others

You discount others when you interrupt them. Most people know that interrupting others is not a good way to communicate. And as David L. Levin goes on to say, consider the message it sends. When you interrupt others, you're saying, in effect, "I'm much more interested in what I'm going to say next than in what you're saying to me right now."[6] It's a biggie in the world of discounting others. So for heaven's sake, watch yourself; catch yourself, and stop interrupting people.

Gossiping About Others

You discount others when you gossip about them. It's not always easy to do this. There's something very alluring, and maybe even a little satisfying, about sharing a negative tidbit. It may make you feel a bit superior, but you've got to fight the urge to bash others or add to the gossip that other people are sharing. You just can't do it, if you ever want to build trust with the person you are discussing. The real art of communication and trust is not only saying the right thing at the right time, it's also stopping yourself from saying the wrong thing at the most tempting moment.

I had to learn that the hard way when I was working my way through college as a shoe salesman. One day, two very attractive young women entered the store, and I immediately rushed over to be the one who waited on them. As we chatted and flirted, one of the young women picked up a pair of women's black, old-fashioned, high-top, lace-up shoes that looked a bit like army combat boots. She said, "I wouldn't be caught dead in a pair of shoes like this. Does anyone actually wear such ugly monstrosities?"

To be cute, I replied, "The only person I know who wears shoes like that is old lady Sampson, and I'm not even sure she's alive." The young women laughed a bit, and I thought, "Great! I've charmed them a bit. I'm making progress."

At that same moment, I turned and there stood Dr. Sampson, my English literature teacher, a dear sweet soul, about seventy-five years old. She had just watched and heard my utterly disrespectful gossip. She smiled and said, "Good morning, Alan. I look forward to seeing you in class tomorrow." I had to learn once again—and maybe you have too—that gossip is a discount you can't afford to take.

Makeups: Two Transformational Communication Techniques

Breakups happen. We all know that. So what can you do to remedy the communication breakups? What can you do to build your relationships on and off the job? Use two powerful communication *makeups* that will transform your personal and professional communication and relationships almost immediately.

The two techniques came out of my conversations with thousands of people I've met before, during, and after my training programs. During the breaks, people often come up to me, share a problem, and ask for my advice. They may tell me about their marital problems, the challenges they're having with one of their kids, a difficult coworker, or a disrespectful boss. Of course, their issues vary a great deal, but it usually comes back to the *quantity* or *quality* of their communication.

Makeup #1: Increasing the Quantity of Your Communication Through the DNDT

Some people just don't take enough time to talk to the other people in their lives. As clinical psychologist Dr. Dana Fillmore says, "The average couple can spend as little as one hour alone together per week; the average couple with kids—sometimes none." There is very little communication going on.

In a survey of two thousand parents by Virgin Holidays and Universal Orlando Resort that was reported in the *Daily Mail*, the average family spends less than thirty minutes of meaningful time together each day as work schedules, chores, and school routines divert their attention. Even when they are together, seven in ten parents say the time is spent sitting in silence in front of the television, reading, or playing computer games instead of talking to one another.[7]

Without even realizing it, many people take their personal relationships for granted and then wonder why there is a problem. I tell those people, "Don't fool yourself. Don't sacrifice your family for the sake of your job, because no success in business will ever make up for a failure at home." I know. I made that mistake one time, and it took me years to rectify the damage.

> The Big Truck Theory says, "If you get killed by a big truck today, someone else will be doing your job tomorrow. But you will never be replaced at home. You will be missed forever."

I teach them the Big Truck theory. The Big Truck theory says, "If you get hit and killed by a big truck today, someone else will be doing your job tomorrow. But if you get hit and killed today, you will never be replaced at home. You will be missed forever."

Now that might sound soft and sappy coming from me—a person whose entire career is focused on leadership, motivation, and teamwork programs for business, government, education, and health-care groups. But I've learned that it's very difficult for me or anyone else to exert inspirational leadership, disperse meaningful motivation, and build effective teamwork if your home life is a mess.

For people who lack communication *quantity*, I recommend Do Not Disturb Time (DNDT). Sid Slatter, a thirty-five-year-old general contractor who described himself as the "epitome of the husband who did not communicate with his wife," found DNDT transformational. He says, "If you were to see me and my wife now, you might think we were on our first or second date. This DNDT process has also helped me to build better relationships with my customers and employees."

And the world of work is just as challenging when it comes to communication time. One of the most frequent complaints I hear from my clients is "We're so busy we don't even have time to talk to each other. We're so focused on our own individual silos that we don't really know the other people in our company or understand what they're doing."

> Some people say, "We don't have much time for each other, but we make up for it in quality." Nice thought, but it seldom works that way. It takes time to build your relationships.

If that sounds anything like you, then I urge you to start using the DNDT technique. Here are some guidelines you need to follow.

Schedule and Hold DNDT Sessions on a Regular Basis

Of course, this takes time. And some people will try to beg off by saying, "We don't have much time for each other, but we make up for it in quality." Nice thought, but it seldom works that way. It takes time to build your relationships.

So schedule your twenty-, forty-, or sixty-minute get-togethers. Don't leave it to chance. Don't wait until you're free from other obligations. It will never happen. That's why my wife actually put a time on our calendar to talk about our marriage, our feelings, hopes, dreams, goals, and frustrations.

You've got to put it on your calendar. And nothing short of a real emergency should change that schedule. Skipping your DNDT sends the message that you don't care that much. Keeping your DNDT affirms the value of your relationship and affirms each person in the relationship, because you're taking time to connect with one another.

You've also got to meet with some degree of frequency. For people at work, it might be once a month. For people at home, it might be every week. Do not save DNDTs until they are needed. If you wait until you've got some serious issues to discuss, if you wait until the stress and pressures are at the boiling point, you'll be getting off on the wrong foot.

If you hold regular DNDT sessions, you can avoid the four scariest words known to man: "We need to talk!" And you can avoid the superficiality of asking, "How are you?" and always hearing "Fine." Hold DNDT sessions when things are going well. And hold DNDT sessions when things can be improved.

Establish Some Rules of Engagement That Create Safety

Each person needs to enter the discussion with a sense of ease instead of fear. And people need to feel they're entering a discussion that will be somewhat friendly instead of totally hostile.

Creating rules of engagement, in advance, will do that for you. You may decide, for example, that during your discussions there will be no put-downs or name-calling, ever. You may establish a rule of confidentiality—that after the discussion there will be no sharing of the discussion with other team members or no telling your mother. Draw up and write down your rules of engagement.

You may also agree on some mutually safe places to meet. You may want to avoid places that are the obvious turf of one party or the other. And you may want to choose a location that offers a degree of privacy, where no one else is observing you or listening in. The very fact that you will be sharing your thoughts and feelings and that you will be giving feedback to one another suggests some degree of privacy.

Make Understanding Your Primary Focus

That's the primary reason you even have DNDT sessions—not to clear the air, solve problems, or confront the other person. You're there to understand each other.

In any relationship, the people in that relationship see it from different points of view. The househusband thinks it's important that his wife actually tells him that she loves him, and the wife thinks, "I bring home the paycheck. That should tell him that I care." One teammate thinks the boss should praise her when she does her job exceedingly well, and the boss thinks, "I don't have to praise my employees for doing their jobs. That's what they're paid to do." In each case, the parties are in the same relationship but each person perceives it quite differently. That can be troublesome.

In DNDT, you get the opportunity to share your perceptions and build understanding. You get to share how you see the other person, and he or she gets to share how they see you and the relationship. And this is critical: you're sharing perceptions, not truths. You do not debate who is right and who is wrong. As family therapist Virginia Satir (1916–1988) wrote, "Who is right is a path leading nowhere."

To increase your chances of achieving true understanding, take your time. Don't try to rush through your discussion.

Maintain your focus. As the DNDT phraseology suggests, Do Not Disturb Time means no interruptions are allowed. No phone calls are taken, no doors are answered, and no email is checked. You just focus on each other.

Check out what the other person is saying. Instead of assuming you understand the other person, use such phrases as "If I'm hearing you correctly, you're saying . . ." And ask things like "Do you mean . . ." You can't get by just nodding your head, saying "uh-huh," and taking turns in talking.

And listen for the "buts." Years ago, when I would counsel someone, I often noticed the other person would talk on and on but never seem to get anywhere. Then suddenly, the other person would say "but." That's when my very best listening kicked in. That's when I would take lots of notes, because I knew that's where the real important stuff was about to be said. Everything before that was just a warm-up.

Look for the Good and Comment on the Good

According to marriage relationship researcher Dr. John Gottman, this is extremely important. After thirty years of research, Gottman concluded that when a couple's comments approach five positives for every negative, they *will* have a successful relationship. As your ratio approaches one positive for every negative, however, your chances of the relationship ending are fairly certain.[8]

As mentioned in chapter 6, Dr. Ken Blanchard, the author of *The One Minute Manager*, reported similar results in the world of work. In the corporate study where positive and negative comments were actually tabulated and the reactions measured, where there was one criticism for each praising, the employees felt as though they had a totally negative relationship with the boss. When the ratio was changed to two praisings for each reprimand, people still thought their boss was all over them. It wasn't until they got to four praisings for each criticism that people began to feel as though they had good relationship with their boss.[9]

> It takes a ratio of four praisings for each criticism from the boss before the employees feel as though they have a good relationship with their boss.

Start each DNDT session with a positive comment. Share a word of genuine praise, sincere appreciation, or humble thanks. Insert other positive observations throughout your discussion. And end each session on a positive note that refers to a good quality in the other person or a good feeling you have about the relationship.

Go Beyond the Superficial

In many relationships, communication is superficial at best. Conversation is reduced to the road conditions on the way to work, the time for dinner, and how your football team is doing.

To get beyond the superficial, *make sure you have something worthwhile to say before you say it*. Before you speak, ask yourself a few questions: "Do others want to hear what I have to say? Are my comments worth saying?"

As the great philosopher Plato said thousands of years ago, "Wise men talk because they have something to say; fools, because they have to say something." Good advice for all of us. Let's make sure we take it.

To get beyond the superficial, *remember the privilege of the platform*. Every time you speak, you are using up someone else's time. And considering the precious nature of time, it's quite an honor when people tune into you. So don't waste too much of the DNDT on the superficial.

As professional speaker Naomi Rhode says, "Don't ever take the act of talking or speaking for granted. Don't ever forget the privilege of the platform."[10]

The great actor Charlton Heston took that privilege seriously. One of my colleagues learned that when he was seated next to Charlton Heston on a plane. As they talked, Heston mentioned he was coming from a conference where he had addressed 112 people. Of course, my colleague thought how disappointing that must have been for Heston, being a world-famous actor, when only a few people came to his presentation. Nonetheless, my colleague knew Heston was also a world-class communicator, so he asked him what the secret to his powerful communication ability was.

Heston replied, "I have never gotten over the miracle that someone will come to listen to me speak." He held the communication process in such high regard that he made sure he never abused the process.

To get beyond the superficial, *share your joys and concerns*. In the busyness of life, the deeper joys and more troubling concerns can get pushed aside. There just doesn't seem to be any time to discuss them. Not smart! As the Swedish proverb reminds us, "Shared joy is a double joy. Shared sorrow is half a sorrow."

That's it, five essential guidelines for making your DNDT effective. I know you're busy. Who isn't these days? You've got a hundred things to do at work and a hundred things to do at home. That's why the *quantity* of communication can be such an issue. Just don't forget the reason you're here on earth. You're here for the people, not the things. And DNDT is a great way to get there.

Makeup #2: Increasing the Quality of Your Communication Through the SATS

Throughout my career, I've come across many managers and leaders who say, "My people just don't speak up. I ask them for their input, but they don't say much at our meetings. So I suppose we're all pretty much in sync."

Not necessarily. When an individual contributor refuses to tell his boss the complete truth about the costly inefficiency of a new policy or procedure, there's a problem in the quality of the communication. When kids tell their parents what they want to hear instead of sharing what's really in their hearts, there's a problem in the quality of the communication. Do not mistake silence or a lack of dissent for agreement.

> Do not mistake silence or a lack of dissent for agreement.

To put more *quality* into your communication, I recommend Sharing and Truth Sessions (SATS). This is a communication makeup that tells the other person or other people, "You count. You matter. You're worthy of my time and attention. And I will do my best to make sure we understand each other."

Debra Boggan, coauthor of *Confessions of an Unmanager*, said it made a huge and positive difference in her organization. She found that the supervisors were giving lip service to the new empowerment program, but they weren't really using it.

When she asked them about their commitment to the program, they all said they were behind it 100 percent. When she asked them how honest they'd just been in answering her question, they all avoided the question. She concluded that her team had a trust and communication problem.

So she asked her team members, "Do you trust everybody else in this room?" She asked them to anonymously write out their answers on a slip of paper. Everyone wrote, "No."

Fortunately, Boggan was emotionally intelligent, and she was a risk-taker. She knew her team couldn't make any progress as long as they had a failure to communicate. So she offered to put herself on the chopping block. She said, "Let's start with me. Why don't you trust me? And how exactly can I be better at my job?"

For the next couple of hours, her staff gave feedback. One said she wasn't a good listener, that she seemed so preoccupied with her own ideas that she shut out the ideas of others. Another one pointed out that when they were talking one to one, she would take phone calls or speed-read her mail. Still others said she gave mixed signals—that sometimes she wanted the team members to take initiative and other times she wanted to run everything.

As the session progressed, an important shift came when a supervisor said, "I give mixed signals too." Then others looked at how they could improve.[11]

Boggan knew that one of the traits of a good leader is the extent to which his or her teammates speak up, share their ideas, and question that leader's point of view. She had taken the first step in making sure that would happen. She was overcoming a failure to communicate.

So how can you put the SATS technique into practice and hold effective Sharing and Truth Sessions?

Adopt a Mindset That Values Input

Good communicators know they can't think of everything. And they know they are much more apt to find the right answer to a problem if they have several possible solutions in front of them.

It's one of the characteristics of effective leadership. President John F. Kennedy certainly knew that. One of his close advisers said Kennedy tried to "surround himself with people who raised questions ... and was wary of those who adapted their opinions to what they thought the president wanted to hear."

The honest input of other people is tremendously valuable. Adopt that mindset. When Scott Brunswick, a school principal in Wisconsin, did that, he used the SATS technique to change the culture in his school and improve his leadership abilities. Like in many schools, Brunswick knew that his teachers and staff did not really know each other very well. Most of the people stuck with their own little cliques in their own grade level or their own area of service. To change that, he put time aside for some Sharing and Truth Sessions where the people were put in groups with people they did not know as well and given some of my "Brave Questions" (discussed at length in my book *Brave Questions: Building Stronger Relationships by Asking All the Right Questions* [Peak Performance Publications, 2012]) to ask one another.

As Brunswick said, even though a number of the staff were quite reluctant at first, the results were extremely positive. "We built new levels of friendship and understanding among one another, and I learned what made my staff tick."

Encourage Open Communication

This is a biggie. It's one of the most important characteristics of quality communication. Everyone in an organization, on a team, or in a family is encouraged to share what he or she really thinks, feels, knows, and wants—which may or may not be politically correct or what the other person wants to hear.

You encourage open communication when you create a welcoming climate. Producers, successful leaders, and even effective parents do five things:

- They encourage other people to speak up by emphasizing the importance of doing so.

- They ask for the opinions of others before they have totally formulated their own.

- They hear people out by giving their full and undivided attention.

- They refrain from immediately arguing or taking offense at ideas that are different from their own.

- They show in their attitude and their actions that they value a person who speaks his or her mind.

Get Everyone to Participate

Some people will quickly and easily share their input. Others need a little help to do that. Ask them specifically what they're thinking or how they're feeling. Some people wait for an invitation before they speak. It's just the way they're wired.

And when you ask for their input, refrain from superficial "yes" or "no" questions. Refrain from questions that ask something like "Are you okay with this?" The quiet people may give you a polite "Yes" or "Yeah, I'm okay." But that's a far cry from openness or sharing the whole truth.

Use behavioral descriptions followed by a question. For example, "I notice you haven't said anything for thirty minutes" or "I notice you looking down. What are you thinking about all of this?" You'll probably get a much more informative response.

Try the "one-word go-around." If you're having a team meeting or even a family discussion, go around the group and ask each person how he or she feels in one word. You'll often be surprised by their answers.

Finally, when someone shares a thought or an idea, make sure you respond to it. Say something like "Thanks for sharing" or "It's good to know where you stand." You're not saying you agree with what was said; you just appreciate the fact the other person contributed to the discussion. If you give no response, the other person feels overexposed or violated and will share even less in the future.

The same principle applies when someone shares a feeling. Make sure you honor that feeling. Respond with something like "Of course you're feeling confused. Who wouldn't be in this situation?" Or "Your frustration certainly makes sense." Again, you're not saying her feeling is right or wrong; you are simply acknowledging the feeling.

Ask Questions

Ask lots of questions. If you have a family meeting and one person— typically a parent—does almost all the talking, that's a lecture, not a Sharing and Truth Session. If you attend a team meeting where one person—usually the supervisor or manager—makes a number of announcements or gives a straight presentation, if there's no interaction from the other attendees, that is not a team meeting. That's what copy machines are for—to deliver one-way messages.

In a Sharing and Truth Session, there's give-and-take from everyone. For example, if you're trying to solve a problem using everyone's input, I find seven questions especially helpful:

- What are the *facts* about this issue?

- What are your *feelings* about this issue?

- What are the *possible solutions* to this issue?

- What are the *advantages* of each possible solution?

- What are the *disadvantages* of each possible solution?

- What kind of *agreement* can we reach on a particular solution?

- How will we *implement* our chosen solution?

The more questions you ask the more sharing and truth you're likely to get. As I advise my clients, "If you want to G-E-T, you have to A-S-K."

It's Time to Get Past a Failure to Communicate

Miscommunication can be funny. In the women's fashion store where I worked as a salesman years ago, one of their window displays had a large sign that announced, "Bras half off." That got a lot of snickers from passersby on the street. And in one health-care organization where I was speaking, they showed me their new marketing slogan. It read, "If you're at death's door, let our doctors pull you through." I suggested they not use the ad.

Yes, miscommunication can be funny. It's the very essence of what most comedians and television sitcoms do. But in your world, on the job or at home, a failure to communicate wastes your time, money, and energy. At best, a failure to communicate is an inefficient use of your time; at worst, it destroys your relationships if not your business. Anything less than clear, open, honest, caring, and respectful communication will hurt you, not help you.

> *At best, a failure to communicate is an inefficient use of your time; at worst, it destroys your relationships if not your business.*

With the use of Do Not Disturb Time and Sharing and Truth Sessions, you have the tools to implement the process of connective communication and to work through your failure to communicate.

CHAPTER 13

The Process of Compassionate Listening

Talking Is Sharing But Listening Is Caring

I was invited to a wedding along with my eighty-three-year-old grand-mother. It was a two-hour drive that I wasn't looking forward to. None-theless, I decided to make the best of it. I had just learned about Brave Questions from Professor Emeritus Dr. Sidney Simon and decided I could at least practice the technique.

As Simon taught me, Brave Questions are deeper, more personal questions that get away from the superficiality of "How are you?" and "How about that football team?" They take guts to ask and guts to answer. Mixed with the process of compassionate listening, however, they can transform relationships.

Of course, it was a risk for me to initiate the process. Our entire rela-tionship of some thirty or forty years had consisted of nothing more than superficial conversation. We'd talk about the crafts she was making or what she was doing at the senior citizens' center, but we never talked about what she thought, how she felt, or what really counted in life.

So as nonchalantly as possible, I told Grandma we had a long drive ahead of us, and I asked if she would be open to a little discussion exer-cise I had learned. "You can ask me anything at all, and I can ask you anything. Would that be okay?" She said that would be fine.

I started the process with a relatively easy question. I asked, "Grandma, you've lived a long time. What was the happiest moment of your life?"

She responded, saying she didn't know the happiest moment but she could think of the most blessed moment. Would that be okay? "Absolutely," I replied.

She went on to tell me that when she was sixteen, she was single and got pregnant. It stunned me. While it's not acceptable to be sixteen, single, and pregnant today, I could only imagine how awful that must have been some eighty or ninety years before in a small, conservative Midwest farm town. I continued listening, using the best and most supportive listening skills I could muster.

Grandma continued, telling me that her parents had disowned her. She had nowhere to go. But a nearby farmer said she could stay in a room attached to his barn. The night she was giving birth, she was crying, feeling full of shame and remorse, and saying her whole life was ruined.

The midwife who came over to help her that night said, "I don't see it that way. You could have left town, tried to abort, or cover your tracks so no one could have put you down. But you did what you thought was right—to give birth to this child. And for that, I respect you."

I was stunned. I thought my first question for Grandma was an easy one that would bring a light answer. I was wrong. Our conversation went on and on as we continued our drive to the wedding.

A bit further into the drive, referring to her pregnancy, I simply said, "Grandma, help me understand." (You'll learn more about this powerful statement-question later in this chapter.) Grandma went on to explain that when she got pregnant, she wasn't doing anything wrong. In fact, she had never even had a date her entire life. Her only social event was a community dance when she turned sixteen.

Tragically, on the way home from that dance, she was raped. She tried to push the man away, but she couldn't do it. She had no recourse, because in those days, she said, people thought, "Boys will be boys," and if a woman got raped, "She was asking for it."

I was surprised and saddened. She had been carrying her secret burden for decades. But the **process of compassionate listening** made her feel safe enough to open up, and it put a depth into our relationship that we had never had before.

Let me tell you, there's power in this process. It dramatically improved my relationship with my Grandma and every one of my relationships since then.

So how can you get this same power working for you? Follow these guidelines and you'll soon be seeing the payoffs with the people in your life.

There *Is* a Problem in Listening

Accept the fact that there *is* a problem in listening. No question about it. The higher people go in management and the more authority they wield, the less they are "forced" to listen to others. Indeed, the less they listen at all. In a survey by the research firm Watson Wyatt Worldwide, they found that only 19 percent of managers say they listen to and take into account the comments of their employees before they make policies.

> The higher people go up in management and leadership, the less they tend to listen but the more they need to listen.

That's dangerous. As people go higher up in management, the *more* they should listen. After all, the farther they get from the front line, the *more* they have to depend on others for information.

The problem comes when people figure they don't have to listen all that well because they already understand what the other person is saying or about to say. They assume understanding. But more often than not, when you and another person automatically *assume* you understand one another, as the word spells . . . a-s-s-u-m-e . . . , you make an ass of you and me.

No matter how good your communication skills might be—no matter how clear you think you are—your message is seldom, if ever, perfectly understood by the other person. People simply see and hear things differently, all the time. So you need to accept the fact there is a problem in listening.

That would have been a wise course of action for one rich man to remember. One day, as he was sitting at home, a poor, shabby-looking fellow knocked on his door. Having nothing to eat and no place to sleep, the poor fellow said, "Sir, I'm hungry. Can you give me a meal?"

The rich man replied, "No, I won't do that, but I'll give you a chance to earn it. Wait here."

A few moments later, the rich man came back with a can of paint and a brush and said, "Here you are. You go around to the back of the house. You'll see a porch there. I want you to paint it. When it's finished, you come back here, ring the bell, give me the paint and brush, and I'll give you a meal."

A short time elapsed. The front doorbell rang. The rich man answered it. There was the poor man saying, "I finished the job. Can I now have my meal?"

The homeowner asked, "You painted the whole porch already?"

"Yes," replied the painter. "The only thing is, sir, it wasn't a Porsche, it was a Mercedes."

Each person heard what the other one had to say, and they both assumed they understood the agreement. Their talking skills were okay, but their listening skills failed.

For example, if you're in a position of leadership and find one of your employees is not performing to your expectation level, don't automatically conclude it's a performance or motivation problem. Often it's a listening problem. You should be asking, "Is the employee's job description crystal clear in my mind and his mind?" Stop assuming there's a meeting of the minds just because you said something in the past.

To become one of the greatest basketball coaches in history, Rick Pitino had to admit he had a problem listening. Like any other college basketball coach, he had the tough task of convincing the high school prospects to select his college over dozens of others.

He used to go to a recruit's home and make a dynamic presentation. He would talk about the strengths of the University of Kentucky, the team's academic support team, the weight training facilities, and the thrill of playing in front of 23,000 devoted fans in Rupp Arena. But then, when he returned home and called the recruit the next day, he'd learn Kentucky wasn't even on the recruit's list.

Pitino would be shocked and would ask himself what went wrong. Wasn't he enthusiastic enough or articulate enough? Eventually, he figured out his performance was fine but his approach needed changing.

On future recruiting visits, he would say very little. Essentially, he would listen. What did the recruit want in a college and a college basketball team? What did the family want? They did most of the talking.

When he followed up the next day, he would learn Kentucky was in the final two. Why? Because Pitino had listened. As he says, "By allowing other people to speak and by clearly valuing their thoughts, I started building a relationship with them instead of giving a performance." Pitino now recommends a ratio of 4 to 1.[1] Listen four times more than you speak if you're going to be an outstanding producer. To be specific, here are some skills I suggest you use to make that possible.

Listening Skill #1: Decide to Listen

One of the reasons for poor listening is our lack of training. Even though an adult spends 45 percent of his or her time listening to somebody or something, less than 5 percent of the world's population has been trained in listening. For most people, their only listening education was the parental injunction to "shut up and listen."

Nonetheless, when I ask my audience members, "How many of you can turn on your ability to listen if you need to or want to?" all the hands go up. Apparently, people have the ability to listen somewhat better; they're just not willing to do it. So it's obvious that good listening starts when you decide to listen.

Take Responsibility

And deciding to listen continues with your assumption of responsibility. You can't sit back and wait for the message to be dumped into your brain. You've got to take responsibility for getting the message. Ask yourself what you can do to get the most out of each and every listening experience. And then do it.

The Japanese have this down pat. In their culture, they believe it's the listener's job and it's the listener's responsibility to get the message. In fact, 90 percent of the responsibility *is* in the listener's lap. No matter how good or bad a speaker or teacher might be, they've got to get the message! No excuses allowed.

> Ask yourself what you can do to get the most out of each and every listening experience. And then do it.

Americans are a bit different. I've seen it. I've taught in American and Japanese universities, and I've noticed American students take a lazier approach. They expect the speaker to give them the message—and be entertaining as well. They figure if a speaker or teacher isn't that good at delivering the message, they don't have that much responsibility to listen.

If you're going to be an excellent listener, you've got to take responsibility for getting the message. And that means, in part, to put aside your preoccupation with your present circumstances.

Don't Focus on Your Present Circumstances

In the midst of a conversation, you or the other person may be guilty of focusing on something going on in your life instead of what is being said at that very moment. I know I'm guilty of that some of the time. We get preoccupied with our present circumstances.

In fact, one New York columnist believed that was the case with a certain socialite who was so preoccupied with making an outstanding impression that she was unable to hear anything her guests were saying. To test his theory, he came late to her next party, and when he was greeted effusively at the door by the hostess, he said, "I'm sorry to be late, but I murdered my wife this evening and had the darndest time stuffing her body in the trunk of my car."

The super-charming hostess beamed and replied, "Well, darling, the important thing is that you have arrived, and now the party can really begin!"

Preoccupation with your present circumstances can be costly. We have millions of divorces each year, and many of them are related to the inability or unwillingness of óne or both of the partners to listen. And we have witnessed needless tragedies—where lives were lost: the *Titanic*, Pearl Harbor, the *Challenger*, and Katrina—because someone was too preoccupied to listen to the information being given to them. Equally as destructive is preoccupation with your past experiences.

Don't Focus on Your Past Circumstances

As soon as these pop into your mind, a listening devil is begging you to turn off the listening process in which you're presently engaged. If, for example, your weekly staff meetings have almost always been a waste of time, you may enter a meeting expecting to learn nothing. So you actually come to the meeting with something else to do or think about.

If you're not careful, you may even use your preoccupation with your past experiences to prejudge the communication that is about to take place. You prejudge it as either unworthy of your time or nothing more than what you've heard before. Of course, you could be right, but you might also miss some important things you need to know.

Or you may misinterpret the meaning of something—if you only rely on your past experience, and if you fail to ask the right questions. Kids do this all the time. One of my audience members, an in-home nursing assistant, talked about taking her four-year-old daughter with her as she visited her elderly shut-in patients. She said her daughter was especially intrigued with all the canes, walkers, wheelchairs, and other equipment used by the patients. But one day she found her daughter staring at a

> When you decide to listen, when you assume responsibility for understanding, you've taken the first giant step toward compassionate listening

pair of false teeth soaking in a glass. As she braced herself for a barrage of questions, her daughter merely turned and whispered, "The tooth fairy will never believe this!"

When you *decide* to listen, when you *assume* responsibility for understanding, you've taken the first giant step toward compassionate listening. And then to counteract the preoccupation devil, remind yourself, throughout the conversation or throughout the meeting, to "Focus. Focus. Focus." If you catch yourself being preoccupied, and if you're not sure what you might have missed in the other person's comments, just say, "Excuse me. Would you please go over that last point again?"

Listening Skill #2: Position Yourself to Listen

If you're about to have a one-on-one conversation with someone or gather together for a staff meeting, whether in person or via a video chat that includes folks from numerous countries, put yourself in a position to do nothing but listen. It will make all the difference in the world when it comes to your attention, comprehension, retention, and may even affect how much people like and trust you. Here are some ways to help you position yourself:

- **Remove or reduce physical barriers.** When there are things between you and the other person, listening can become more difficult. If you're on a job site, for example, and there's a piece of equipment between you and the other person, it will be harder to hear as well as pay attention. If there's a desk between you and somebody else, the desk may imply that one person is above the other, and that kind of discomfort will disrupt the listening process. For example, one researcher found that only 11 percent of patients are at ease when the doctor sits behind a desk, but 55 percent of the patients are at ease when the desk is removed.

- **Minimize distractions.** Put aside everything and anything that is not related to the listening process you're supposed to be engaged in. Don't try to read your email at the same time you're listening to your colleague. Don't try to watch the television at the same time your spouse is talking to you. These actions suggest you have more important things to do than listen to the other person. It will undoubtedly lower your listening effectiveness and damage your relationships—especially if you get caught.

- **Lean forward and face the person you are talking to.** When you do this, your nonverbal communication is saying, "I want to hear what you have to say. I don't want to miss a single word. Please go ahead." You're demonstrating your commitment to the communication process, and you encourage the speaker to share fully, openly, and honestly. However, if you lean back in your chair or get too relaxed, your attention will wander. Effective listening is active rather than passive, laid back, and taking it easy.

- **Use lots of eye contact.** Look at the other person when he or she is speaking to you, or look at each individual in your meeting as he or she speaks. Don't fool yourself into thinking you can "sorta" listen and at the same time sneak in a few glances at your incoming email, text messages, your watch, and your desk filled with work—and get away with it. You can't! No matter how good you are or think you are at multitasking, if you do anything other than look at and listen to the person who is speaking, you're communicating disrespect. The other person will always wonder if you care more about those things than you do about him and what he has to say. And that would be the exact opposite of compassionate listening.

Listening Skill #3: Listen with an Open Mind

The communication and listening processes are strange phenomena. A message can travel around the world in a matter of seconds. But it can take years to travel that last inch into your brain if you have preconceived ideas standing in your way.

Manage Your Tune-Out Buttons

As I've mentioned previously, you've got to tune into the other person's feelings when you're listening, whether he or she is explicitly expressing those feelings or not. But just as important, you've got to tune into your own feelings because they may be getting in the way of your listening.

For example, some words are so emotionally charged that as soon as you hear them, you shut down. Your tune-out button is up and working, and you stop listening. It could be the B word, the N word, and the F word that you find so utterly offensive. It could be sexist phrases used by a coworker, like "baby," "honey," "sweetie pie," or "beefcake." Or it could be cursing comments made by a spouse or a customer, all of which you find disrespectful and unprofessional.

Of course, using language like that is usually considered inappropriate and morally reprehensible. And you may have a host of words, phrases, and topics that are so emotional for you that once they're brought up, it's difficult for you to keep on talking with any degree of rationality or keep on listening with any degree of true understanding. These are tune-out buttons for you.

Just because you don't approve of the way someone says something does not mean you should stop listening to what he or she has to say. Sometimes you need to know what that person is saying. And yes, there may be a need and a time to confront people on their use of language, but you must understand their message—first. Don't go into emotional overdrive right then and there.

To manage your tune-out buttons, remind yourself to stay calm and in control. Remind yourself to thoughtfully respond to what is being said rather than emotionally react to what is being said. Don't let the other person's inappropriate remark or your own hypersensitivity steal your peace.

Refrain from Defensiveness

To refrain from defensiveness, check it out before you speak it out. Don't jump to conclusions. Don't respond too quickly. Check it out to see if you really understand what the other person is saying, rather than assuming you understand. Otherwise, you're bound to miss some things that are being said and imagine other things that were never said.

For example, a husband and wife may be out shopping for a new car for the woman's new job. The car salesman quotes a price and the wife says that sounds good. Immediately, the husband interjects, "Your price is too high." And the fight starts.

The husband says, "I was just trying to help you save some money." She responds, "Are you trying to tell me I'm incapable of negotiating my own deal?" Because of their quick jump into defensive positions, it's doubtful that either one of them truly understands the other person's intentions, thoughts, and feelings. Their urgently needed open minds have turned into closed minds . . . because they overlooked one critical point in compassionate listening. They need to withhold evaluation until comprehension is complete.

> *Remind yourself to thoughtfully respond to what is being said rather than emotionally react to what is being said.*

Keep Your Stereotypes in Check

It's so easy to take a few ambiguous bits of information about people and then jump to some huge generalizations about their entire character—and the character of everyone else like them. And if you hold any stereotypes, you can be sure of one thing. Whenever you are listening to someone who falls into your stereotyped category, you are not going to clearly and accurately hear what that person has to say.

I saw this happen repeatedly when I was a university professor. A conservatively dressed member of the faculty may hear a bearded, T-shirt wearing, jean-clad colleague say, "A bachelor's degree in general studies would serve some of our students better than a traditional major," and angrily dismiss the comment as an attempt to downgrade the standards of the university. Yet another conservatively dressed colleague might make the same proposal, and the first conservatively dressed faculty member would respond, "Yes, that may be exactly what we need."

To hold your stereotypes in check and to stop them from killing off your listening effectiveness, become aware of the kinds of people that turn you off. And when you're listening to them, remind yourself that you don't have to like them or even agree with everything they say. All you have to do is give their comments a fair hearing to see if you can learn anything you can use.

Beware of Charisma

The charisma of the message sender may affect how well you listen. You see this in politics all the time. Quite often, candidates are chosen and elected not so much for the brilliance of their thought as the brilliance of their delivery. A charismatic politician can make a tired, trivial, stupid, or just-plain-wrong message seem new, exciting, and right, fooling the listener into thinking that he or she doesn't even have to question or clarify the message.

Perhaps this has happened to you. You got so carried away by someone's charisma that you stopped listening to anyone else or any other message that did not agree with your charismatic speaker. You traded your open mind for a closed mind, shutting down your listening effectiveness and intellectual acuity in the process. Or you may have failed to listen to someone who had something important to say simply because that speaker's delivery was dull. If so, remind yourself that *what* a person says is ten times more important than *how* he or she says it.

Listening Skill #4: Ask More Questions

As my colleague Michael Atlshuler says, "What people say is unimportant; what people *mean* by what they say is everything." And the only way you're going to know what they mean is through the art of asking questions. Here are a few ideas about how to do that.

Get More Information

When you ask for more information, it replaces assumptions with realities. One of the easiest ways to do this is to use the word "and" with a pause and questioning tone to your voice. Perhaps a colleague is telling you about an incident at work. You listen carefully to his story, but want to learn more. Just ask, "And?" Pause for a moment and the other person will invariably go on and give you more information.

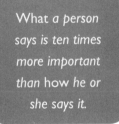

What a person says is ten times more important than how he or she says it.

Or you could use the three magical words, "Help me understand." When used with a non-threatening, inquisitive tone of voice and appropriate facial expressions, you encourage the other person to give you more details. You come across as someone who really cares about the other person rather than someone who is grilling the speaker.

Encourage More Depth

Ask open-ended questions that start with the five Ws and the one H: who, what, when, where, why, and how. Unlike questions that can be answered with a simple "yes" or "no," open-ended questions encourage a speaker to go beyond the superficial and go deeper. If you add a touch of risk or vulnerability to your questions, or ask Brave Questions that you typically do not discuss, you build the foundation for a stronger relationship, just like I did with my grandmother.

When you listen to someone's response to these questions, do more than listen *to* that someone; listen *for* something. If the other person is describing a situation, listen for the facts, the key points, or the main ideas she is giving. Behind every fact there is a feeling. Listen for those feelings, whether or not they are expressed. You'll get a lot more out of the conversation. You will also stay much more alert and engaged in the conversation than you would if you just sat back, did nothing, and merely waited for the other person to finish talking.

Clarify the Facts

As Alan Greenspan, the former chairman of the Federal Reserve Bank, put it, "I know you think you understand what you thought I said, but I'm not sure you realize that what you heard is not what I meant."[2]

You've got to clarify the facts. And the only way you can do that is to rephrase what you heard the other person say and ask him or her if that is correct. When you get into the habit of asking questions to clarify the facts, two very positive things take place in the process of compassionate listening. First, you tend to stay with the speaker instead of planning your next remark. Second, you're telling others that they and their message are so important that you want to make sure you got it right. And whether you initially understand or misunderstand the message the other person shares, you both win. If you get the speaker's message right, he'll feel good and affirm you. If you get the message wrong, he'll clarify.

> Behind every fact there is a feeling. Listen for those feelings, whether or not they are expressed.

Define the Slippery Words Being Used

Almost any word can be interpreted in more than one way, perhaps even many ways. That can easily cause communication breakups. But untrained listeners don't even think about that. They hear something and automatically think they've got it. More often than not, they don't.

Some words are much more likely to cause listening difficulties than others, and you have to be especially diligent when you hear someone use them. Sales trainer extraordinaire Jeff Thull calls them "fat words."[3] Words such as *almost, maybe, might, quality, soon, user friendly, easy,* and *improved* are fatter or much more slippery than others. There are dozens if not hundreds of different things each of those words could mean.

For example, if you are a salesperson and your prospect tells you, "I'm not sure your level of quality will meet our requirements," what would be your most likely response? To give a sales pitch about your product or service? It would be the exact wrong thing to do. As Thull states, "It's not appropriate to answer a statement as if it were a question"[4] because you don't even know what your prospect is saying.

The prospect's statement is filled with slippery words. You have no idea what he means by "not sure," "level of quality," and "meet our requirements." To eliminate this listening challenge, you have to clarify or define the slippery words before you respond to them.

Clarify Feelings

Whenever you're communicating with another person, you can be sure of one thing. The other person always has some feelings going on, whether it's about her current situation, your present topic of conversation, or a hundred other things. She may or may not be aware of those feelings, and she may or may not be expressing her feelings, but the feelings are there nonetheless. And sometimes it's critically important to understand those feelings before a problem can be resolved or the relationship improved.

If that seems to be the case, use a perception-check question. You could say something like "You seem rather concerned about that new product line" or "You sound somewhat disappointed by my remark. Is that right?" You're not judging the other person's feelings or telling the other person how to feel. You're simply extending the courtesy of telling the other person what you're picking up and giving that person the chance to set you straight about what she is feeling. It's polite, respectful, and most often relationship building.

Listening Skill #5: Refrain from Interrupting

As we discussed in chapter 12, this is a very difficult skill for some people to master. They're used to hearing someone say a few words and then jumping in with their own comments. In fact, they're so used to saying things like "that reminds me of . . ." "let me tell you about . . ." or "that's nothing compared to what I went through," that it almost seems natural and right.

Well, it may seem natural, but it's not right. When you interrupt someone, it's a sure sign that you're not using the process of compassionate listening, and you don't care that much about the other person's comments. And that's not a good place for any relationship to be.

Interruptions seem to be especially tempting when someone comes to you with a problem. You may want to jump right in and give advice. More often than not, however, the other person simply wants you to listen patiently.

Of course, this sounds good in theory, right? But what if you're pressed for time? You may be thinking if you don't interrupt the other person, if you don't stop the other person from talking, you'll be late for something else. That may be true. In that case, tell the other person that you'd like to give him or her your full attention, but that's not possible at the moment. Agree on a time the two of you can continue the conversation when you may give it your very best attention.

We're all busy these days. So it's very tempting to try to speed things up in a conversation by interrupting the other person. But that's usually a poor trade-off. Typically, it takes a lot less time to get the information right the first time than to straighten out all the misunderstandings later on.

Listening Skill #6: Slow Down Your Back-and-Forth Exchange

Too many people are guilty of jumping into a conversation with their response the very moment the other person stops talking. Some people even jump in before the other person stops talking. (Remember our discussion about interrupting?) The problem is, it seldom works. It almost always hurts the listening process and the people involved in the discussion.

Adopt the Acknowledgment Technique

Specifically, when someone is talking to you, instead of jumping in with your response as soon as the other person finishes, you must first acknowledge the fact that you heard what she had to say. It could be as simple as saying, "Interesting point . . ." "I know what you mean . . ." or "If I understand you correctly . . ." Comment on what the other person said before you give your response. It will force you to spend more time listening to what is being said than thinking about what you're going to say next.

Try the Three-Gulp Rule

Bob Parsons, a director at InsideOut Development, taught me this. When Bob hears someone share an important point, he does not give an immediate response, outside of a nonverbal acknowledgment such as a nod of the head or a verbal "hmm." He then ponders what he heard and how he's

> *Typically, it takes a lot less time to get the information right the first time than to straighten out all the misunderstandings later on.*

going to respond as he takes three gulps of water. It gives him time to think about his response, and it tells the other person he's going to get a thoughtful response rather than a flippant, off-the-cuff remark.

The technique works wonders. It offers respect to both people in the conversation. And it eliminates the fast and furious give-and-take communication that characterizes most of the political talk shows these days—and many business meetings and marital conflicts.

Listening Skill #7: Reinforce Your Retention

Of all the listening skills I've addressed thus far, this is the one I need the most. I'm all too guilty of hearing someone tell me something and then forgetting what they told me. Just ask my wife or kids. Perhaps you're in the same boat with me. So what can we do about it? I've found two things that work:

- **Listen for value.** When someone else is talking, ask yourself such questions as: "Why do I need to know this? How can I use this information? And how will this information help me, my life, my work, or my relationships?" The more value you consciously attach to someone's comment, the longer you will remember it.

- **Use mental reviews.** When you're listening to someone, periodically review what the other person is saying and has said. In a few seconds, you can mentally review everything a presenter has said in the past hour at a work seminar, or you can review everything your spouse was sharing about the challenges of her day. This little technique not only doubles your listening retention, but it also keeps your mind from wandering to other thoughts.

Perfecting the Art of Compassionate Listening

When someone tells me he loves his wife but never listens to her, I know he's either lying about his feelings or doesn't know how to listen. When a manager says she cares about her teammates, but her teammates say she never listens to them, I know that manager may have good intentions, but she's not the producer she could be. If you really care about the people in your life, you will care about listening to them, and you will use the seven skills of compassionate listening. If you do, you're going to get some significant payoffs. Indeed, I've noticed that when I use these skills my business improves, my relationships are strengthened, and my life goes better. I even get smarter. As American columnist Doug Larson writes, "Wisdom is the reward you get for a lifetime of listening when you would have preferred to talk."[5]

> When someone tells me he truly cares about his wife but never listens to her, I know he's either lying or doesn't know how to listen. The same principle applies to a manager and her team.

The same will be true for you. The better you get at listening, the more payoffs you will realize. After all, it takes time, and when you give your time to someone else through the process of compassionate listening, you're sending a powerful validation. You're telling the other person, "*You* are important to *me*."

Every person, friend, relative, coworker, or customer—on and off the job—is waiting to hear that message. And when they hear it, you form relationships, build teams, solve problems, and change the future for the better.

This process pays off in a thousand ways. So spend some time perfecting the process of compassionate listening. You'll be glad you did. You really will.

PART IV

PAYOFF

CHAPTER 14

The Payoff Principle Continues to Pay Off

Your Search for Happiness and Success Is Over

Imagine a plane full of passengers. The captain comes on the intercom and says, "Thank you for choosing our airline. I'm not exactly sure when we'll take off or when we'll arrive. As a matter of fact, I'm not even sure where we're going or how we're going to get there. Hopefully, our fuel tank has enough gas and we'll get to where you want to go at the right time. For now, just sit back and enjoy the ride."

You would probably think, "That's the scariest thing I've ever heard." Yet, that's very close to the way a lot of people live. They have no particular direction for their life or their career, and they lack the energy and skill to complete their journey. They're just putting in time and they hope it all works out. That's what life and work are like without the formula offered in this book.

Fortunately, your life and career don't have to go that way. In fact, your search for the two great eternal desires—more happiness and greater success in your life and career—is over.

You no longer have to wonder what would make you happier, worry about how you could possibly achieve greater success, or waste your time on useless approaches. You no longer have to study the flavor-of-the-month business fad or pop psychology filled with clever catchphrases that don't deliver everything they promise. You no longer have to toss aside your dreams of achieving greater success. You no longer have to settle for good enough and getting by when you can have the extraordinary. Even though life is challenging, work is tough, and relationships are demanding, there's a formula for success that addresses every one of those areas.

Purpose + Passion + Process = Payoff

The key is, you must *activate* all three elements of the formula, and most people overlook one or more of these key elements. Some people work hard, but without a clearly defined **purpose**, nothing is very fulfilling. Other people have great dreams, but without an enduring **passion**, they give up before they see the **payoffs**. And still other people have the best of intentions and positive attitudes, but they lack the **process** for turning it into reality. This book brings all three elements together and shows you how to get what you want professionally and personally.

> *You must* activate *all three elements of the formula and then* integrate *them into every aspect of your life and work.*

The other key to unlocking the powers of this formula is, you must *integrate* all three elements into every aspect of your life all at the same time. You can't focus on purpose for a while, and then turn your attention to passion or process for a while, if you want the really big payoffs. You can't focus on pumping up your passion at work and ignore your attitudes at home, if you want the really big payoffs. No, this formula is about a new way of thinking and behaving so you're always purpose-driven, passion-filled, and process-guided, on and off the job.

All you have to do now is implement the formula. And I can't emphasize those two words enough—*now* and *implement*. Don't fall into the "as soon as" trap that says "as soon as I get the time and energy . . ." or "as soon as certain things happen . . ." or "as soon as I get around to it, I'll give *The Payoff Principle* a try."

Author, track star, and cardiologist Dr. George Sheehan talked about people who are forever waiting—don't be like those people. As he said, "There are those of us who are always about to live. We are waiting until things change, until there is more time, until we are less tired, until we get a promotion, until we settle down—until, until, until. It always seems as if there is some major event that must occur in our lives before we begin living."[1]

Producers *implement now*. Producers know some moments are better than others for action, but there is never a perfect moment. So they do it now, if at all possible, and if at all sensible. And I urge you to do the same. Your search for greater happiness and success is over. It's all about what you do *now*.

> *Producers know some moments are better than others for action, but there is never a perfect moment. So they do it now, if at all possible, and if at all sensible.*

A Tried-and-True Formula for the New-and-Complete You

As a little reminder, *The Payoff Principle* says, "When you find **purpose** in what you do, exhibit **passion** for the outcome, and master the **process** to make it happen, you produce the **payoffs** you want, need, and deserve." In effect, you become a **producer**.

And hundreds of thousands of people have done exactly that . . . whether consciously and deliberately or accidently and luckily. The good news is you don't have to depend on luck anymore to get what you want. You have a formula for getting what you want—a formula that has stood the test of time. You have a practical set of strategies guaranteed to deliver greater happiness and success than you've ever experienced.

The formula (**Purpose + Passion + Process = Payoff**) puts you on the path for *the new-and-complete you*—both on and off the job. And amazingly enough, the formula brings the spiritual, psychological, and business worlds together. Virtually every spiritual belief or major religion emphasizes the critical importance of finding your purpose and living on purpose. The psychological research is filled with studies that document the power of passion or having the characteristics of attitude, persistence, and character working for you. And the business world continually focuses on the best practices, or the processes, that bring the best results.

I find it extremely satisfying to know that this formula is supported by years and years of belief, research, and everyday experience. And I find it extremely motivating that there isn't a part of your life or career that cannot be enhanced by this formula.

I've experienced the new-and-complete you because of this formula. The evidence can be seen in everything from my health and finances to my goals and relationships. The evidence can be seen in my business growth, from a kid walking the streets selling door-to-door to being inducted into the Speaker Hall of Fame.

I've seen the new-and-complete you take place in the lives and careers of hundreds of thousands of people. You've read a few of their stories in this book.

I'll never forget the first time I consciously noticed how this formula could and did change lives. I was in high school when Richard Chaput spoke at our high school assembly. He was rolled onto the stage, flat on his back, in his rolling hospital bed, encased in his iron lung. Even though there were several hundred students in the auditorium, you could have heard a pin drop when he uttered his opening line: "Every dream I've ever had I've been able to accomplish."

He began to share his story. When Richard was nine years old, he was diagnosed with polio. The disease left him completely paralyzed. His paralysis was so severe he had to breathe by physically gulping for air, somewhat like a frog. At night, he slept in an iron lung.

Initially, Richard did not handle it well. He gave into self-pity, until one day his parish priest helped him snap out of it by letting him know his life wasn't over. There was a *reason* he was alive and with the right *attitude* and *plan*, he had a life of achievement and satisfaction ahead of him. (It sounds a bit like *The Payoff Principle*, doesn't it?) From that moment on, Richard started living with purpose and passion, and he put a process in place where he would help others by speaking to any group that would listen to his story—including audiences at the White House with two different US presidents.

As a teenager sitting in his audience, I was stunned as Richard talked about writing books and speaking to thousands. I was inspired by what a person could accomplish with a driving sense of purpose, a healthy dose of passion, and a practical set of processes. Richard had become new and complete. That's why I'll never forget his closing line: "Life is a banquet, but most people are starving to death" because, as he implied, they don't have these three elements working for them.

If Richard Chaput could experience the new-and-complete you, then there's no reason you can't too. You have all the tools, techniques, skills, and strategies outlined in this book; you can expect to get the magnificent payoffs when you start applying them.

Your Future Filled with Payoffs—On and Off the Job

Of course, *The Payoff Principle* is not some get-rich-quick kind of scheme. It's not a recipe for overnight success with little or no effort. The old saying still applies: if anything seems too good to be true, watch out.

I'm not saying *The Payoff Principle* is quick and easy. But I am saying it works. Take a good close look at all the people you have deeply admired and respected in your life or throughout history. Look at all those people who have found great happiness and success at home, on the job, and in the world. Look at all those producers and you will see the three elements of purpose, passion, and process at work in their lives.

> I'm not saying The Payoff Principle *is* quick and easy. But I am saying it works.

The best news of all is *The Payoff Principle* is not reserved for famous people or a few gifted people. I see this principle working all the time in the personal lives and professional careers of my clients. And I know it will work in your career, your home, your life, and in the lives of others.

Payoffs in Your Work Life

You will spend a major portion of your life doing some kind of work; so I hope to God your work not only pays off financially but also pays off in productivity, teamwork, and emotional health. And I know *The Payoff Principle* ensures those kinds of positive results. Here are a few examples of people who found *The Payoff Principle* and how it changed their lives. You can use the formula to

- **Motivate the best in others.** Allan Hermson, accounting manager at Seedorff Masonry (a construction company), found out how powerful it was to frame things positively. Allan says, "Now that I'm doing that, people are responding so much better in our new positive team environment. I was able to turn a non-performer into a real performer."

- **Get more engagement from your coworkers.** Paul Faust, a project manager at Wells Fargo Financial, used to look at soft skills somewhat skeptically, while he focused on the technical aspects of his job and took the people stuff for granted. After learning the communication techniques of *The Payoff Principle*, Paul said, "I learned exactly what I had to do to elicit the full and willing cooperation of my coworkers. More importantly, I've noticed a huge increase in performance."

- **Improve your work relationships.** Ty Inglis, a partner at Eide Bailly LLP (an accounting firm), used to keep on working when staff members came into his office, leaving his coworkers with the impression that he wasn't interested in them or their concerns. Then Ty said, "I made a concerted effort to employ the amazing listening techniques you taught us, and this has dramatically improved the relations with my staff."

- **Move up in your career.** Cheryl Stevens was a hardworking and talented professional at Tyco Healthcare, but she wanted to go further in her career. After studying the purpose-clarifying questions and after she wrote out her purpose statement, she became more focused and purpose driven. Her vice president noticed the change and promoted her to the position of a regional sales manager. As Cheryl puts it, "I have to say that your program—*The Payoff Principle*—has been the most positive and influential aspect in my life these past five years."

- **Create a more positive work environment.** Colleen Kokenge, a team leader at Blue Cross Blue Shield, says her eyes were opened when she realized a person's autopilot can be stuck on the wrong setting. Colleen says, "I didn't realize how easily Killer Statements sneak into our comments at work, phrases like 'I'm too busy . . .' or 'We've always done it this way . . .' and 'That wouldn't work here.' I didn't realize that I was subtly, accidentally demotivating myself and my teammates. So I stopped using those Killer Statements, and the attitude, productivity, and overall success of my staff increased dramatically almost instantly."

- **Strengthen your team.** Terri Dammann from Delta Vacations (the airline company) wanted to do that, but being a very private person, she thought some of the techniques would be too far outside her comfort zone. But one day she decided to share some of her personal trials with her work team, ask them some Brave Questions, and listen to their responses. Terri said, "I can't believe the things people shared with me, and our team has become stronger as a result. It's amazing. Everyone back on the job is benefiting from my learning *The Payoff Principle*."

- **Build stronger ties to your customers.** Scott Jerabek, a small business owner in the dry pea and bean industry, was running into a series of barriers when trying to sell his products and services to his customers and prospects. By using just one of the techniques—the attitude of gratitude—Scott says, "I've broken through the barriers in my career as a professional salesperson. And I've been able to dramatically improve two of my tougher customer relationships."

From these examples, it's obvious that you can transform your work from something that may be overly stressful to something that is rewarding and inspiring. Indeed, those payoffs are not only possible but also very likely when you activate and integrate *The Payoff Principle* into your work.

Payoffs in Your Home Life

For many of you, the most significant payoffs—or the payoffs you desire the most—will be found at home. Use *The Payoff Principle* to

- **Strengthen your marriage or key relationship.** Dan Holka, an account representative from Thomson Reuters (a multinational media corporation), said he used to turn ordinary events—even raking the leaves in the front yard—into stressful ordeals between himself and his wife. "Then I literally decided to have a positive attitude, as you suggested." Dan says, "The result? Ruth and I had a wonderful experience raking, laughing, and enjoying each other. She has definitely seen the change in my behavior ever since."

- **Become a better parent.** Allen Wyatt, center director for the Social Security Administration, became a much better father once he learned the "apply patience" persistence technique. As he puts it, "I used to yell right off the bat, without talking or discussing anything first. Now, I find it a lot easier to talk and work out problems between myself and my children without blowing up. It is bringing us closer every day."

- **Get willing cooperation from your kids.** Without begging, bribing, or threatening, Joanne Kaczmarek, human resource manager at Worldwide Dispensers (a plastics manufacturing company), was able to get her teenage children to clean up the house after playing in the rain with their friends and leaving a muddy mess everywhere. Instead of yelling at them, she left a note the next morning that read, "I'll be home about noon. I had a good time with your friends last night. I hope you enjoyed it also. With the fun comes clean up. Clean up needs to be done today." When she came home, the house was vacuumed; the food and beverage items were put away; the garbage was taken out; and the recycling was done. As Joanne concluded, "If it wasn't for the positive techniques I learned in *The Payoff Principle*, I would have left my original negative message. I would have also returned home with nothing accomplished."

- **Bring out the best in your family members.** John Biggi, director of service operations at Northwest Pump (a distributor of industrial pumps), was able to apply the "reject defeat" technique with his twelve-year-old daughter Megan and her swimming. John said, "Needless to say, it has worked like a charm. She has continued to drop her times in all of her events. Yesterday, she dropped ten seconds off of her personal best in the hundred-meter Individual Medley."

- **Set a positive tone in your home.** Brad Stiemel, a manager at the nation's largest auto insurance company, used to walk around the house like the gloomy, pessimistic Eeyore from *Winnie-the-Pooh*, which wasn't really setting the tone he wanted. So he decided to try the "act as if" strategy instead. He started by walking around smiling, with his chin and eyes up. He continued by saying only positive things to his family members and encouraged them to speak more positive comments. Brad concluded, "Everyone is getting along so much better!! My daughters now walk around the house smiling instead of buried in the computer."

These payoffs were huge for the people involved. And every one of them is waiting for you when you apply *The Payoff Principle*. Remember, you are not the victim of your circumstances; you are the creator of your circumstances.

> *You are not the victim of your circumstances; you are the creator of your circumstances.*

Payoffs That Transform You

It's wonderful to achieve more payoffs at work and at home. But it's magnificent when the payoffs transform *you* as well. With *The Payoff Principle* you will

- **Have more energy.** That's the payoff Mark Matter, director of continuous improvement at Universal Strap (webbing and braiding manufacturer), was looking for. Mark wrote, "I used to be very sluggish and could easily spend nights on the recliner. Now it's nothing to be out in the garage working until 10:00 or 11:00 p.m. on projects. My coworkers tell me I'm more upbeat."

- **Have less stress.** Phil Lee, chief operations officer of the Britannia Building Society in the United Kingdom, says, "After learning and using the technique of 'start your day with a six-pack,' I lost fourteen pounds in weight. I am now swimming freestyle 50 percent faster. I'm much calmer and relaxed than previously. And the payoffs just keep coming and coming!"

- **Gain control of your life.** David Sleigh, account manager at Lloyds Bank in the United Kingdom, like so many other people, was feeling overwhelmed until he learned "the producer is disciplined" approach and the process of continuing education. As David writes,

"I was able to say 'no' to meetings that did not add value to my life and work, and I brought my workweek down to a more reasonable number of hours. I'm taking time to plan out my self-development rather than rush around unplanned all the time."

- **Become more assertive.** Missy Bailey, accounts merchandising liaison from the Target Corporation, wanted to be more effective at getting what she really wanted. A mere ninety minutes after learning about communication breakups and makeups, she had a chance to use her newly acquired skills. Missy says, "I asked for what I wanted and got it. Wow! These skills really, really work."

- **Achieve more of your goals.** As the country manager—Nigeria for UPS, Joseph Caulcrick certainly knew the importance of goal setting but wasn't sure about the best way to do that. After learning and applying the "affirming achievement process," Joseph said, "My self-confidence has grown enormously, and I'm achieving more goals more quickly than ever before." Indeed, he went on to create the Foundation for Value Transformation that is now sharing these techniques with future leaders throughout Africa.

- **Get a lifestyle makeover.** Teri Rokusek, first vice president of Lincoln Savings Bank, grabbed on to all the strategies outlined in this book. Teri says, "I credit *The Payoff Principle* for saving my marriage, enhancing my relationship with my son, getting me back to church, bringing exercise into my life on a regular basis, and getting me to a financial planner. It has even assisted with my latest promotion and salary raise as I've spread Dr. Z throughout our leadership trainings."

The transformations these people received were life changing. And you will have similar victories in every part of your life when you activate and integrate *The Payoff Principle* into your life.

Payoffs That Transform the World

Imagine a world where everyone is purpose driven, passion filled, and process oriented. As you learn and use *The Payoff Principle*, as you make big changes in *yourself* and *your* world, it inevitably affects others around you, changing them for the better—one person, one group, one team, one classroom, and one company at a time. Indeed, you will see payoffs:

- **One person at a time**: After Karen Harthorn, director of Purchasing Services at the University of St. Thomas, learned about giving your autopilot a permanent reset, she taught the technique to her ten-year-old son, Connor, who was afflicted with cerebral palsy. He liked to sing but was timid about singing in public. She encouraged him to enroll in voice lessons, and within three months he was singing songs for his class, singing for the school broadcast, and then singing in a concert. Well, that's what Karen wrote a few years ago, and then recently she wrote me another note. "I have continued to use these affirmation techniques with Connor, and I want you to know that he is now attending the University of Wisconsin where he was selected as the Freshman National Champion in wheelchair basketball."

- **One group at a time**: That's exactly what Doris Dean found out. As a supervisor for the FBI, Doris recognized the power of the passion techniques taught in *The Payoff Principle*, so much so that she began sharing them with her coworkers as well as her friends in business, education, and medicine and with youngsters throughout her county. She began speaking to various groups about these techniques and says, "I'm pleased to report that even the teens (a tough audience) are using your positive techniques!"

- **One team at a time**: As a manager at Iowa Lutheran Hospital, Beth Houts was particularly drawn to the DNDT and SATS communication techniques. Beth said, "Your techniques have contributed to our team building at work . . . which has shown up in much higher patient satisfaction scores. And we're celebrating."

- **One classroom at a time**: Middle school teacher Kevin Little says, "My teaching and my curriculum have improved dramatically, because I'm teaching my students with more purpose and more enthusiasm than ever before. And their grades and high interest levels reflect my efforts."

- **One company at a time**: As one of the principals of the Cool Beans! Coffee Company, Clay Anderson said he never knew about the power of positive and negative thoughts and how they affect business outcomes. He said, "I went back to work and taught *The Payoff Principle* to my employees, and now they realize that the thoughts they have of their customers are critical. Their positive thoughts turn into positive behaviors, and that turns into a more pleasant buying experience for the customer. BUT GET THIS: It's also creating a lot more generosity in the customers—which is showing up in the tips we receive."

If It Is to Be, It's Up to Me

I mentioned this short, quick, and witty phrase in chapter 2. It's motivating and inspiring. And in most cases, it's true. That's why I've also quoted it in many of my keynotes and seminars.

There's only one problem with the phrase: it leaves you hanging in midair. It doesn't tell you *where* you're going because it lacks purpose. It doesn't tell *what's* going to take you there because it lacks passion. And it doesn't tell you *how* you're going to get there because it lacks process.

That's the problem with so many positive-thinking books and self-help routines. They don't give you the *whole formula for success*. The old saying "a little knowledge is a dangerous thing" rings true. If you don't have all the information—or the whole formula for success—it will lead you into confusion and failure.

But those days of confusion, frustration, and dead ends are over because you now have the formula to achieve all the happiness and success you want—**Purpose + Passion + Process = Payoff.**

Use the formula. Apply *The Payoff Principle* and you'll see that the best is yet to come, at work, at home, and everywhere you go for the rest of your life.

Notes

Chapter 1: What Do You Really, Really, REALLY Want?

1. Jan Halper, *Quiet Desperation: The Truth About Successful Men* (New York: Warner Books, 1988).

2. "George Burns," *Wikipedia*, last modified June 28, 2014, http://en.wikipedia.org/wiki/George_burns.

3. Elisabeth Kübler-Ross and David Kessler, *Life Lessons: How Our Mortality Can Teach Us About Life and Living* (New York: Simon and Schuster, 2012).

4. Shamus Toomey, "Doorman Gets His Way Honorary Street Sign to Honor a Mag Mile 'Icon' of 40 Years," *Chicago Sun-Times*, December 2, 2004.

5. Aubrey Malphurs, *Ministry Nuts and Bolts: What They Don't Teach Pastors in Seminary* (Grand Rapids: Kregel Publications, 1997, 2009), 75.

6. Eleanor Roosevelt, foreword to *You Learn by Living* by Eleanor Roosevelt (Louisville: Westminster John Knox Press, 1960).

7. Ecclesiastes 2:11 (English Standard Version).

8. Ken Griffith, *From Ken's Desk* (Bloomington, IN: Xlibris, 2012).

9. Elizabeth Berg, *Range of Motion: A Novel* (New York: Random House, 2012), 193.

10. Richard Scott, *I Don't Have Time* (Croydon, UK: Filament, 2010), 40.

11. Zig Ziglar, *See You at the Top* (Gretna, LA: Pelican, 1975), 45.

Chapter 2: The Payoff Principle and the Producer

1. John Marks Templeton, *Riches for the Mind and Spirit* (West Conshohocken, PA: Templeton Foundation Press, 2013), 181.

2. Philip Humbert, "Nothing Will Change Until You Do!," *Trans4mind*, last modified July 2014, http://www.trans4mind.com/counterpoint/index-goals-life-coaching/humbert21.shtml.

3. Proverbs 29:18 (King James Version).

4. David DeFord, *1000 Brilliant Achievement Quotes: Advice from the World's Wisest* (Omaha: Ordinary People Can Win!, 2004), 4.

5. J. Matthew Becker, "Pick Yourself Up," on the *Authentic Excellence Blog*, February 2014, http://authentic-excellence.com/blog2/2014/02/pick-yourself-up.

6. Andrew DuBrin, *Essentials of Management* (Boston: Cengage Learning, 2011), 127.

7. Scott Stantis, "The Montana Christmas Menorahs," on the *Taking a Stantis Blog*, December 9, 2012, http://newsblogs.chicagotribune.com/taking-a-stantis/2012/12/the-montana-christmas-menorahs.html.

8. Clara Villarosa, *The Words of African-American Heroes* (New York: Newmarket Press, 2011), 27.

9. "Study Shows Achievers Share Certain Traits" *The Telegraph*, September 23, 1982, 37.

10. Forrest Beck, *Cultivating the Fine Art of Selfishness: Improving Community by Empowering Individuals* (Charleston, SC: Advantage Media Group, 2012), 9.

11. Dr. Purushothaman, ed., *Words of Wisdom (Volume 54): 1001 Quotes and Quotations* (Kollam, Kerala, India: Centre for Human Perfection, 2014), 46.

12. Ernest Hemingway and A.E. Hotchner, *The Good Life According to Hemingway*, (New York: HarperCollins, 2008), 30.

13. Susan Miller, *Oomph Power! How to Get Re-Energized for Outrageous Success* (Avinger, TX: Simpson-Wesley, 2003), 51.

14. Purushothaman, ed. *Words of Wisdom,* 144.

15. Daisy Saunders, *Big Eyes* (Charleston, SC: Advantage Media Group, 2007), 10.

16. Lynn Kidman, Rod Thorpe, and Robyn L. Jones, *Developing Decision Makers: An Empowerment Approach to Coaching* (Christchurch, New Zealand: IPC Print Resources, 2001), 60.

17. Susan J. Cucuzza, *Live Forward and Give Back: Weekly Coaching Moments for Leaders at All Levels* (Bloomington, IN: Balboa Press, 2013), 11.

18. Robert Biswas-Diener and Todd Kashdan, "What Happy People Do Differently," *Psychology Today*, July 2, 2013, http://www.psychologytoday.com/articles/201306/what-happy-people-do-differently.

PART I: PURPOSE

Chapter 3: The Power of Purpose

1. "Vincent van Gogh," *Wikipedia*, last modified July 20, 2014, en.wikipedia.org/wiki/Vincent_van_Gogh.

2. Richard R. Ellsworth, *Leading with Purpose: The New Corporate Realities* (Stanford: Stanford Univeristy Press, 2002), 94.

3. Charles McGuire and Diana Abitz, *The Best Advice Ever For Teachers* (Kansas City, MO: Andrews McMeel Publishing, 2001),145.

4. Bob Buford, *Halftime* (Grand Rapids, MI: Zondervan, 1994).

5. Bud Roth, *Be More Productive—Slow Down: Design the Life and Work You Want* (Bloomington, IN: iUniverse, 2011), 70.

6. Dan Buettner, "Find Purpose, Live Longer," *AARP* magazine, Nov/Dec 2008.

7. Friedrich Nietzsche, *Götzen-Dämmerung, oder, Wie man mit dem Hammer*

philosophiert [Twilight of the Idols, or, How to Philosophize with a Hammer] (Oxford University Press, 2009), 12.

8. Janet Kornblum, "For Kirk Douglas and Wife, the Playground's the Thing," *USA Today*, May 26, 2008, accessed July 28, 2014, http://usatoday30.usatoday.com/life/people/2008-05-26-kirk-douglas-playgrounds_N.htm.

9. Barbara Johnson, *Boomerang Joy: Joy that Goes Around, Comes Around* (Grand Rapids, MI: Zondervan, 2000), 228.

Chapter 4: The Practice of Purpose

1. Victor M. Parachin, "Being a Father Who Makes a Difference," *Scouting*, Mar–Apr 2001, 12.

2. Georgy, "How Temple Baptist Church, Philadelphia, Came into Being," on the *Turn Back to God Blog*, September 15, 2008, http://www.turnbacktogod.com/story-how-temple-baptist-church-philadelphia-came-into-being/.

3. Jerry I. Porras, Stewart Emery, and Mark Thompson, *Success Built to Last* (Upper Saddle River, NJ: Wharton School Publishing, 2007), 25.

4. Richard Leider, *The Power of Purpose* (San Francisco: Berrett-Koehler Publishers, 2010), 22.

5. Raymond Moody, *Life After Life* (New York: Harper Collins, 2014).

6. Mark R. Schwehn and Dorothy C. Bass, eds., *Leading Lives That Matter: What We Should Do and Who We Should Be* (Grand Rapids, MI: Wm. B. Eerdmans, 2006), 111.

7. Bob Buford, *Halftime* (Grand Rapids, MI: Zondervan, 2008), 121.

8. Mark Pendergrast, *For God, Country and Coca-Cola: The Definitive History of the Great American Soft Drink and the Company that Makes It* (New York: Basic Books, 1993), 195.

9. Andy, "Time Management Techniques: Tomorrows Top 6," on the *Time Management Blog*, 2009, http://www.time-management-techniques.com/time-management-techniques-tomorrows-top-6.html.

10. Skip Downing, *On Course* (Boston: Cengage Learning, 2011), 105.

11. A.R. Bernard, *Happiness Is: Simple Steps to a Life of Joy* (New York: Simon & Schuster, 2008), 71.

PART II: PASSION

Chapter 5: The Power of Passion

1. "Mahoney's Career Switch Pays Off," *New Straits Times*, February 10, 1994, 23.

2. Price Pritchett, *The Employee Handbook of New Work Habits for the Next Millennium* (Dallas: Pritchett Rummler-Brache, 1999), 10.

3. Proverbs 26:20 (The Living Bible).

4. Debbie Woodbury, "Casual Friday—Elizabeth Edwards Quote on Having a Positive Attitude" on the *Where We Go Now Blog*, http://www.wherewegonow.com/category/tags/elizabeth-edwards.

5. This quote is most often attributed to Coolidge. It was printed in a pamphlet in the 1930s by New York Life Insurance, Co., where Coolidge served as a director.

Chapter 6: The Attitude of Passion

1. Laura Lyesight, *1001 Life Changing Quotes 4 Teens* (Bloomington, IN: XLibris, 2010), E-71.

2. David DeFord, *1000 Brilliant Achievement Quotes* (Omaha: Ordinary People Can Win!, 2004), 12.

3. Jon Gordon, *The Positive Dog: A Story About the Power of Positivity* (New York: John Wiley & Sons, 2012), 6.

4. "Quotes by Earl Nightingale about Attitude," *Online Quotations Book*, n.d.," http://quotationsbook.com/quote/3493/.

5. Daniel Goleman, "Doctors Find Comfort Is a Potent Medicine," *New York Times*, November 26, 1991.

6. Ken Blanchard, "Praise v. Criticism," on the *How We Lead Blog* July 13, 2010, http://howwelead.org/2010/07/13/praise-v-criticism/.

7. Craig Jarrow, "7 Ways a Positive Attitude Can Make You More Productive," *Time Management Ninja,* Nov. 18, 2013, http://www.timemanagementninja.com.

8. Gyles Brandreth, ed., *Oxford Dictionary of Humorous Quotations* (New York: Oxford University Press, 2013), 85.

9. "Advice from an Old Man," *KindSpring*, last modified June 16, 2007, http://www.kindspring.org/story/view.php?sid=6915.

10. "Martha Dandridge Custis Washington," The White House, http://www.whitehouse.gov/about/martha-dandridge-custis-washington

11. Val Webb, *Florence Nightingale: The Making of a Radical Theologian* (Atlanta: Chalice Press, 2002), 80.

12. Philippians 4:8 (The Living Bible).

13. Roy B. Zuck., *The Speaker's Quote Book: Over 5,000 Illustrations and Quotations for All Occasions* (Grand Rapids, MI: Kregel Academic and Professional, 2009), 243.

14. Dale Anderson, *Act Now!: Successful Acting Techniques You Can Use Everyday to Dramatically Improve Health, Wealth and Relationships* (New York: John Wiley & Sons, 1995).

15. Barbara Bailey Reinhold, *Free to Succeed: Designing the Life You Want in the New Free Agent Economy* (New York: Plume, 2001), 131.

16. William Arthur Ward, *Fountains of Faith* (Anderson, SC: Droke House, 1970).

Chapter 7: The Persistence of Passion

1. Bridge Adams Eshun, *How to Start Your Business with or without Money: A Practical Approach to 'Small Beginnings'* (Victoria, BC: Trafford, 2013), 114.

2. Harvey Mackay, "Success Is a Marathon," *Inc.*, Last modified April 3, 2012, http://www.inc.com/harvey-mackay/success-is-a-marathon.html.

3. David G. Savage, "Interviews with 120 Top Artists, Athletes, and Scholars: The Key to Success? It's Drive, Not Talent, Study Finds," *Los Angeles Times*, February 17, 1985, http://articles.latimes.com/1985-02-17/news/mn-3575_1_top-artists.

4. Shelly Brady, *Ten Things I Learned from Bill Porter: The Inspiring True Story of a Door-to-Door Salesman Who Changed Lives* (Novato, CA: New World Library, 2002), 121.

5. Jim Bryant, *Life: Tips for the Journey* (Garland, TX: Hannibal Books, 2007), 41.

6. Joseph Demakis, *The Ultimate Book of Quotations* (Raleigh, NC: Lulu, 2012), 205.

7. Laurine Snelling, *100 Good Things that Happen as You Grow Older* (Hayward, CA: Bristol Publications, 1992), 45.

8. Ronald Calhoun, *Life in the Image of God* (Bloomington, IN: Westbow Press, 2013), 28.

9. Dennis Kimbro, *Daily Motivations for African-American Success* (New York: Random House, 2011), 57.

10. Armando Riverol, *Live from Atlantic City: The History of the Miss America Pageant* (Bowling Green, OH: Bowling Green State University Popular Press, 1992), 132.

11. James Buckley, *Muhammad Ali* (New York: Gareth Stevens, 2004), 1970.

12. Robert E. Lee Pettit and Bob Wolff, *The Drive Within Me* (New York: Prentice Hall, 1966), 10.

13. Douglas G. Long, *Learner Managed Learning: The Key to Lifelong Learning and Development* (Philadelphia: Kogan Page, 1990), 86.

14. Benjamin Franklin, *The Autobiography of Benjamin Franklin* (Mineola, NY: Dover, 1996), 123.

15. "Lucy Goes to the Hospital," *Wikipedia*, last modified March 18, 2014, http://en.wikipedia.org/wiki/Lucy_Goes_to_the_Hospital.

16. "I Love Lucy," *Wikipedia*, last modified July 28, 2014, http://en.wikipedia.org/wiki/I_Love_Lucy.

17. Bruce Lee and John Little, *Jeet Kune Do: Bruce Lee's Commentaries on the Martial Way* (North Clarendon, VT: Tuttle, 1997), 363.

18. Debra Warren, "M.I.H. in Your Business!," on the *Debra Warren Blog*, June 29, 2010, http://debrawarren.com/m-i-h-in-your-direct-sales-business.

Chapter 8: The Character of Passion

1. John Woolman, *The Journal of John Woolman* (Rockville, MD: Wildside Press, 2007), 201.

2. Donovan A. Shilling, *It's Showtime in Rochester* (Victor, NY: Pancoast, 2014), 47.

3. Cornelius D. Jones, *Inspirational Being* (Raleigh, NC: Lulu, 2012), 65.

4. Anne K. Chinoda, *Simply Significant: Leaving a Legacy of Hope* (New York: Morgan James, 2009), 121.

5. Roy B. Zuck, *The Speaker's Quote Book: Over 5,000 Illustrations and Quotations for All Occasions* (Grand Rapids: Kregel Academic, 2009), 58.

6. Louise Boone and David Kurtz, *Contemporary Marketing, Update 2015* (Boston: Cengage Learning, 2014), 84.

7. Carolyn B. Aiken and Scott P. Keller, "The CEO's Role in Leading Transformation," *Insights and Publications*, February 2007, http://www.mckinsey.com/insights/organization/the_ceos_role_in_leading_transformation.

8. Monty J. Sharp, "The Top Ten Ways to Change a Mediocre Employee into a High Performing One," *Articles Factory*, October 6, 2002, http://www.articlesfactory.com/articles/business/the-top-ten-ways-to-change-a-mediocre-employee-into-a-high-performing-one.html.

9. Rita Emmett, *Manage Your Time to Reduce Your Stress: A Handbook for the Overworked, Overscheduled, and Overwhelmed* (New York: Bloomsbury, 2009), 110.

10. Tanya Crouch, *Truth or Dare: Do You Have the Courage to Change Your Life?* (Springville, UT: Cedar Fort, 2003), 191.

11. J. Mark Fox, *Real Life Moments: A Dad's Devotional* (Indianapolis, IN: Dog Ear, 2008), 79.

12. Michael Josephson, "Commentaries, the Nature of Character," *What Will Matter*, October 22, 2012, http://whatwillmatter.com/2012/10/commentary-798-2-the-nature-of-character/

13. John Ortberg, *When the Game Is Over, It All Goes Back in the Box* (Grand Rapids, MI: Zondervan, 2007).

14. Friedrich Nietzsche, *Nietzsche: Beyond Good & Evil: Prelude to a Philosophy of the Future*, trans. Walter Kaufmann (New York: Cambridge University Press, 2002), 74.

15. Margaret A. Heffernan, *The Naked Truth: A Working Woman's Manifesto on Business and What Really Matters* (New York: John Wiley & Sons, 2004), 84.

16. Michael Hyatt, *Platform: Get Noticed in a Noisy World* (Nashville, TN: Thomas Nelson, 2012).

17. Diane Mary Gayeski, *Managing Learning and Communication Systems as Business Assets* (New York: Pearson/Prentice Hall, 2004), 8.

18. Dan Zadra and Bob Moawad, *Dare to be Different* (Mankato, MN: Creative Company, 1985), 47.

19. J. Gregory Dill, *Myth, Fact, and Navigators' Secrets: Incredible Tales of the Sea and Sailors* (Guilford, CT: Globe Pequot, 2006), 51.

PART III: PROCESS

Chapter 10: The Process of Affirming Achievement

1. John Baker, *Life's Healing Choices* (New York: Howard Books, 2013), 129.

2. John N. Williamson, *The Leader Manager* (New York: John Wiley & Sons, 1986), 87.

3. Ibid.

4. Jacqueline Whitmore, *Business Class: Etiquette Essentials for Success at Work* (New York: Macmillan, 2005), 48.

5. Jay D. Allen, *Humans in Training: Everything You Need, You Already Have* (Orange County, CA: HIT Pub., 2003), 133.

6. Tony Morgan, *Killing Cockroaches* (Nashville: B&H, 2009), 57.

7. Jim Anderson, *Principle-Based Leadership: Driving Your Success as a Leader* (Bloomington, IN: iUniverse, 2013), 167.

8. Chuck Palahniuk, *Fight Club: A Novel* (New York: W.W. Norton, 2005), 46.

9. Michael D. Lemonick and Alice Park Mankato, "Nun Study: How One Scientist and 678 Sisters Are Helping Unlock the Secrets of Alzheimer's," *Time*, May 14, 2001, http://content.time.com/time/world/article/0,8599,2047984,00.html.

10. Hirsch, *Stock Trader's Almanac 2011* (New York: John Wiley & Sons, 2010), 53.

11. Ibid.

Chapter 11: The Process of Continuing Education

1. "Chris Gardner," *Wikipedia*, last modified May 29, 2014, http://en.wikipedia.org/wiki/Chris_Gardner.

2. Bob Roth, *College Success: Advice for Parents of High School and College Students* (Bloomington, IN: AuthorHouse, 2010), 266.

3. Nancy Williams, *Conquer the Fear of Death* (Lancaster, CA: Epitome Books, 2009), 42.

4. Bob P. Buford, *Halftime: Changing Your Game Plan from Success to Significance* (Grand Rapids: Zondervan, 2011), 67.

5. Guerdon T. Ely, *Uncertainty Is a Certainty* (Maitland, FL: Xulon Press, 2009), 153.

6. Samuel Arbesman, *The Half-life of Facts: Why Everything We Know Has an Expiration Date* (New York: Current, 2013).

7. Ibid.

Chapter 12: The Process of Connective Communication

1. Dennis C. Kinlaw, *The Practice of Empowerment* (Brookfield, VT: Gower, 1995), 60.

2. Gary D. Chapman, *The Marriage You've Always Wanted* (Chicago, IL: Moody, 2009).

3. A 1982 book by the Hazeldon Foundation credits "We're only as sick as the secrets we keep" to Sue Atchley Ebaugh. And AA and other recovery orgs have also used this saying extensively.

4. David L. Levin, *Don't Just Talk, Be Heard* (Minneapolis, MN: Minneapolis Press, 2009).

5. Les Giblin, *Skill with People*, rev. ed. (2010), 13.

6. David L. Levin, *Don't Just Talk, Be Heard!* (Minneapolis, MN: Minneapolis Press, 2009).

7. S. Brinkman, "Survey: Families Spend Less Than 8 Hours Together Per Week," on the *The Women of Grace Blog,* July 16, 2013, http://www.women ofgrace.com/blog/?p=22778.

8. David and Claudia Arp, *The Second Half of Marriage* (Grand Rapids, MI: Zondervan, 2010).

9. Ken Blanchard, "Praise v. Criticism," July 13, 2010, http://howwelead .org/2010/07/13/praise-v-criticism/.

10. Dan Clark, *Privilege of the Platform: The Art and Science of Public Speaking* (Springville, UT: Cedar Fort, 2007), xi.

11. Debra Boggan and Anna VerSteeg, *Confessions of an UnManager* (Durham, NC: Dartnell, 1997), 64.

Chapter 13: The Process of Compassionate Listening

1. Rick Pitino, *Success Is a Choice: Ten Steps to Overachieving in Business* (New York: Broadway Books, 1998), 124.

2. "Alan Greenspan Quotes," *Goodreads*, n.d., http://www.goodreads.com/ quotes/204034-i-know-you-think-you-understand-what-you-thought.

3. Jeff Thull, *Mastering the Complex Sale: How to Compete and Win When the Stakes Are High!* (New York: John Wiley & Sons, 2010), 153.

4. Ibid.

5. Daniel Weis, *Everlasting Wisdom* (Trowbridge, Wiltshire, England: Paragon, 2010), 69.

PART IV: PAYOFF

Chapter 14: The Payoff Principle Continues to Pay Off

1. George Sheehan and Andrew Sheehan, *The Essential Sheehan: A Lifetime of Running Wisdom from the Legendary Dr. George Sheehan* (Emmaus, PA: Rodale, 2013), 44.

Acknowledgments

To any of you who have ever written a book or contemplated doing so, you know that a book doesn't just happen or magically appear on the pages of a computer document. Most of the time, it is the result of years and years of learning and time-tested experience, *and* the input of several significant people in the author's life.

In fact, without certain people in my life and work, this book may not have been written, or written quite as well. I want to thank a few of those people here.

To my father, mother, and stepmother: I have never known a day without your unconditional love and support. What a rare and awesome blessing! You believed in me before I believed in myself.

To the three teachers who carved a lasting legacy in my life—Virgelee LeDue, Sally Webb, and Sidney Simon: you did so much more than teach a class. You demonstrated professionalism, demanded excellence, cared deeply, and, even more incredibly, stayed in contact with me for decades after I left your classrooms.

To my office managers Mary Johnson, Vickie Perrier, Aaron Lynch, and Vibhas Gokhale: you took a thousand tasks off my plate so I could be free to focus on my strengths of researching, writing, training, speaking, and consulting. You always made a way where there seemed to be no way.

To my editor Chris Benguhe: you made my thoughts and ideas, my stories and experiences, and my tips and strategies come out more clearly and powerfully. My work is better because of you.

To the hundreds of thousands of people who have read and followed Dr. Zimmerman's *Tuesday Tips* for many years: your continual flow of encouraging handwritten notes and electronic emails made my day, day after day after day.

To my wife, Chris: you were the one who told me a thousand times . . . or was it ten thousand times . . . that I had to write this book . . . that people needed to hear what I had to say. And you were the one who sacrificed your time to make sure this book got finished and got in the hands of others. Your love and support mean the world to me.

About the Author

Alan Zimmerman has spoken to more than one million people across the United States and around the world, giving them the tools they need to achieve their goals on and off the job. As a prominent, sought-after author and speaker, Dr. Zimmerman works with a variety of organizations and professional associations from Fortune 500 companies to small and medium-sized businesses, from state and federal government to education and health-care groups. His clients universally characterize him as genuine, down-to-earth, practical, and powerful.

Alan has received numerous awards and honors for his contributions in the fields of attitude, communication, leadership, and speaking. Most recently, the National Speakers Association awarded him its highest honor, the Council of Peers Award of Excellence.

Born in Wisconsin, Alan received a bachelor's degree from the University of Wisconsin and his master's and PhD degrees from the University of Minnesota. He taught for several years at Emporia State University, the University of St. Thomas, the University of Minnesota, and Mankato State University. He continues to teach as one of the "Distinguished Faculty Members" for the Institute for Management Studies.

For more information, check out his website
www.DrZimmerman.com or send email to Alan@DrZimmerman.com.